Creative Ballet Teaching

How do teachers create a classroom environment that promotes collaborative and inquiry-based approaches to learning ballet? How do teachers impart the stylistic qualities of ballet while also supporting each dancer's artistic instincts and development of a personal style? How does ballet technique education develop the versatility and creativity needed in the contemporary dance environment?

Creative Ballet Teaching draws on the fields of Laban/Bartenieff Movement Analysis (L/BMA), dance pedagogy, and somatic education to explore these questions. Sample lesson plans, class exercises, movement explorations, and journal writing activities specifically designed for teachers bring these ideas into the studio and classroom. A complementary online manual, *Creative Ballet Learning*, provides students with tools for technical and artistic development, self-assessment, and reflection.

Offering a practical, exciting approach, *Creative Ballet Teaching* is a must-read for those teaching and learning ballet.

Cadence Joy Whittier (MFA, CLMA, RSMT) is Professor of Dance at Hobart and William Smith Colleges, New York, and Faculty and Co-Director of Laban Movement Analysis/Bartenieff Fundamentals Certification Programs at Integrated Movement Studies.

Creative Ballet Teaching

Technique and Artistry for the 21st Century Ballet Dancer

Cadence Joy Whittier

Illustrated by Kim Cooper Geigerich

Routledge
Taylor & Francis Group

LONDON AND NEW YORK

First published 2018
by Routledge
2 Park Square, Milton Park, Abingdon, Oxon OX14 4RN

and by Routledge
711 Third Avenue, New York, NY 10017

Routledge is an imprint of the Taylor & Francis Group, an informa business

British Library Cataloguing-in-Publication Data
A catalogue record for this book is available from the British Library

Library of Congress Cataloging-in-Publication Data
Names: Whittier, Cadence Joy, author. | Geigerich, Kim, illustrator.
Title: Creative ballet teaching : technique and artistry for the
    21st century ballet dancer / Cadence Joy Whittier ; illustrated by
    Kim Geigerich.
Description: New York, NY : Abingdon, Oxon : Routledge, [2017] |
    Includes bibliographical references and index.
Identifiers: LCCN 2016057006| ISBN 9781138669703 (hbk) |
    ISBN 9781138669710 (pbk) | ISBN 9781315618067 (ebk)
Subjects: LCSH: Ballet—Study and teaching.
Classification: LCC GV1788.5 .W49 2017 | DDC 792.8071—dc23
LC record available at https://lccn.loc.gov/2016057006

ISBN: 978-1-138-66970-3 (hbk)
ISBN: 978-1-138-66971-0 (pbk)
ISBN: 978-1-315-61806-7 (ebk)

Typeset in Bembo
by Apex CoVantage, LLC

Visit the companion website: www.routledge.com/cw/whittier

To Diane and Michael Whittier, my parents and my first educators.

Contents

Tables

Acknowledgments

My gratitude begins with my past and current students. I am deeply thankful for the many lessons I have learned from them over the years.

I enthusiastically acknowledge my first dance educators, Kathy and Dennis Landsman. I am deeply grateful for the dance community they created in Overland Park, Kansas. Their skillful instruction provided me with a rigorous and well-rounded education in dance. They served as my first examples of how I could pursue dance as a career and an academic area of study.

Although I did not know it at the time, the first drafts of this book project began in 2000 in the *Integrated Movement Studies* Laban/Bartenieff Certification Program. My final project at IMS—*Movement as Metaphor: Using L/BMA to Facilitate the Meaning Making Process in Ballet*—investigated the integration of L/BMA and ballet technique. Studying the L/BMA work with IMS faculty Janice Meaden, Peggy Hackney, and Ed Groff was a transformative experience. Their holistic instruction and mentorship nurtured my development as a performing artist and educator, and their examples as life-long learners continue to inspire me.

I am grateful to the dance faculty in both the Ballet and Modern Dance Departments at the University of Utah. My studies in Utah (1995–2000) gave me the opportunity to pursue my interests in teaching through pedagogy courses in ballet, modern dance, children's dance, and kinesiology. This, along with the focus on pedagogy at *Integrated Movement Studies*, provided me with the foundational knowledge to pursue this project.

It is important to also acknowledge my journey as a dance professor at Hobart and William Smith Colleges, which began in 2000. Colleagues both inside and outside of the Dance Department provided me with a supportive and enriching environment to develop and nurture the teaching perspectives presented in this book. They have served as mentors, writing buddies, editors, and friends. I am grateful for the academic freedom to pursue my interests and for the valuable feedback I've received over the years. Thank you also to my community of dance artists in the Finger Lakes Region of New York. Some of you served as first readers to early drafts of this book and others engaged me in lively discussions about teaching. I am glad I have spent my adult life performing, choreographing, and teaching with all of you.

Thank you to my wonderful illustrator Kim Geigerich. Your skillful drawings, knowledge of the body, and organizational skills made this an easeful process. I loved collaborating with you on this project! Thank you also to the entire Routledge staff, and specifically to Kate Edwards, Jenny Guildford, and Ben Piggot for seeing the potential of this book and for providing guidance as it came to fruition.

I'm appreciative of the many authors listed in my bibliography and to the many more whose work I've read over the years. I am indebted to their research and to the continued research of my contemporaries. Through our collective knowledge, research, and teaching practices, we continue to push the ever-evolving fields of ballet technique, dance education, and Laban/Bartenieff Movement Analysis in new directions.

Thank you to my parents for inspiring my journey into both dance and education. I am forever grateful for your encouragement and support as I pursued a career in dance. A special thanks to my mother for reading numerous drafts of this book, your keen eye and good questions guided me throughout this process. Thank you finally to my wonderful husband Dustin Cutler; your humor, kindness, and love—especially in the last year of this project—was invaluable.

Introduction

Creative Ballet Teaching is a textbook for teachers written by a teacher. For me, teaching is a complex mixture of creative wisdom, practiced pedagogy, and ongoing self-evaluation. Throughout my career I have been surrounded by colleagues who continue to evolve their teaching practices and pursue new pedagogical interests. I share in my colleagues' passions for continued learning, and it is in this spirit that I have written this book.

Creative Ballet Teaching and the accompanying online student manual—*Creative Ballet Learning*—focus on both the teacher's and the student's physical, intellectual, and artistic development. *Creative Ballet Teaching* includes numerous exploration activities designed for the dance educator: some focus on reflection through journaling; some on class planning and verbal cueing; and many explore technique concepts experientially through movement. *Creative Ballet Learning* parallels the information and concepts presented in *Creative Ballet Teaching*, and includes a number of activities to help students apply new technique concepts to their dancing.

Creative Ballet Teaching addresses the following questions:

- *How do teachers facilitate learning that enhances a ballet dancer's body knowledge and understanding of ballet technique?*
- *How do teachers create a classroom environment that promotes collaborative and inquiry-based approaches to learning ballet?*
- *How do teachers impart the stylistic qualities of ballet while also supporting each dancer's artistic instincts and development of a personal style?*
- *How does the education that occurs in the ballet technique classroom facilitate the versatility and creativity needed in the contemporary dance environment?*

My journey as a dance educator includes many spheres of influence, some direct and some indirect, but nonetheless influential. Some of the above questions originated many years ago in my undergraduate "Ballet Teaching Methods" course with Barbara Hamblin at the University of Utah. My final project explored how to develop a student's creative thinking skills concurrently with the development of their technical skills. This exploration deepened in gradu-ate school and during my certification training as Laban/Bartenieff Movement Analyst, and it has continued to be a primary focus in my professional life as a dance professor at a liberal arts college.

Reflection about one's spheres of influence seems paramount in a dance education textbook. Traditions and values are passed orally and physically from teachers to students. I consciously avoid some "lessons" I have learned in the past—those that are negative or contradictory to my values. But, many lessons, such as those discussed in the next section, I have consciously adopted. My students experience these spheres of influence in all of my classes: through my voice, my dancing, and my teaching methods.

Throughout *Creative Ballet Teaching*, I invite you—the dance educator—to reflect on your teaching practices and to confirm the theoretical and practical knowledge(s) you bring into the classroom. Your past experiences as a dance student are interwoven with your current identity and values as a dance educa-tor. So, as you read the next section, take time to also reflect on your spheres of influence.

Who are your mentors and teaching "ancestors?"
How have they influenced your teaching values and identity?

My spheres of influence

Growing up in a household with parents who were educators influenced my choice to pursue a career in dance education. In my youth during the sum-mer breaks from school, my parents designed learning activities for me that emphasized **problem solving and experiential learning**, two qualities that characterize my teaching of ballet technique and two qualities empha-sized throughout *Creative Ballet Teaching*. My father was a high school sci-ence teacher and my mother an elementary school visual arts teacher. It is no surprise I developed a love for the creative thinking processes involved in both scientific and artistic inquiry. Certifying in **Laban/Bartenieff Move-ment Analysis** with *Integrated Movement Studies* (*IMS*) was therefore an obvi-ous choice for me. It offered the perfect balance of objectivity and subjectivity, organized analysis and imaginative thinking. These early influences along with my experiences teaching at a liberal arts college affect how I perceive the dance discipline, and specifically how I view its role in **developing critical thinking and creativity.**

Although I did not know it at the time, my interest in contemporary approaches to ballet pedagogy also began in my youth with my first ballet educators, Kathy and Dennis Landsman. The Landsmans cultivated a **col-laborative teaching–learning environment**. They valued their students as thinkers, technicians, and artists. I was challenged to interpret choreography critically and personally and to make individual performance choices during technique classes. My understanding of and appreciation for the methodologies the Landsmans used has continued to deepen over the past two decades—they are my reference point for good ballet education.

Dennis Landsman choreographed humorous, well-crafted pantomime scenes for all of the story ballets our youth ballet company performed. I took many of his pantomime classes as a child, and I studied "Acting For Dancers" and "Choreographic Methods" with Bené Arnold at the University of Utah. Through these educational experiences I learned how to use movement to create expressive characters and "stories." My training with Janice Meaden, Peggy Hackney, and Ed Groff at *IMS* deepened these investigations. Through their mentorship, I developed a teaching project that explored methods for **developing a ballet dancer's expressive and technical skills and personal awareness**. For me, expressive and artistic development is as important to a dancer's training as technical development, a value that is embedded in every chapter of this book.

While a student in the Ballet Department at the University of Utah, I lead a dance education program called I CAN DO[1] with Peter Christie, Director of Educational Outreach programs at *Ballet West*. Peter and I offered Creative Dance classes as a part of the fifth-grade academic curriculum in the Salt Lake City School District. Our philosophy was simple: dance was an activity for all children. My work with I CAN DO taught me to view dance education broadly and to teach it inclusively. I have continued to teach dance to children and adults of varying physical and cognitive abilities since leaving Utah. This has influenced my approach to ballet education. All ballet students, regardless of their talent, abilities, or career aspirations, benefit from technique training that involves and stimulates the **whole person—the intellectual, the physical, and the emotional**. When taught well, **ballet, as a form of arts education**, lends itself to this type of holistic education.

Ballet as arts education

Throughout the previous section, I highlighted my teaching values in bold. These values are embedded in every chapter of *Creative Ballet Teaching* and

Table 1.1 Ballet as arts education

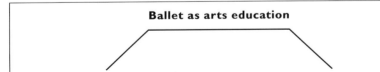

Ballet as arts education

Educate the whole person—the intellectual, physical, and emotional
Cultivate a collaborative teaching-learning environment
Strengthen a dancer's personal awareness, and expressive and technical skills
Develop critical thinking and creativity through dance
Emphasize problem solving and experiential learning

Creative Ballet Learning. The last one—ballet as a form of arts education—serves as an "umbrella" for many of the phrases highlighted above.

Sometimes when people learn that I am a dancer, they assume that I must be creative. *Does this happen to you too?* Creativity and the arts are often lumped together, but the arts do not have a monopoly on creativity. As you know, creativity comes in many forms and manifests itself in every discipline. Moreover, creativity is not an automatic outcome of one's training in dance. It is certainly possible for a dance student to participate in technique classes without engaging creatively in the class experiences. *Perhaps you have witnessed this first hand.*

For some of my students, reproducing balletic movement perfectly and accurately is more important than developing their creative and artistic skills. Technical mastery and creative development do not have to be at odds with one another, however. Experimenting with and interpreting the steps and vocabulary in personal and innovative ways illuminates different aspects of the technique and develops a student's physical skills. In support of this, Heli Kauppila's research argues:

> [I]t is possible to combine the development of specific, tightly codified dance skills and, at the same time, nurture the growing sense of one's self . . . paying attention to the latter will increase the mastery of the former . . . the growing sense of the self is connected to the birth of a personal relationship to the discipline studied and therefore in the dance context it is connected to the roots of artistic excellence.[2]

The teaching-learning methods instructors use in the classroom influence how dancers perceive themselves *and* the larger discipline of ballet. In *Creative Dance for all Ages*, Anne Green Gilbert emphasizes the important role Creative Movement classes play in developing a student's physical, cognitive, affective, and social skills.[3] This holistic development is equally important, and achievable, in ballet education. Collectively, the activities and teaching strategies in *Creative Ballet Teaching*:

- improve technique, physical coordination, and body awareness (physical skills);
- develop movement literacy, observation skills, and problem-solving abilities (cognitive skills);
- challenge dancers to integrate emotional and expressive nuance into their performance of balletic movement (affective skills);
- promote an interactive and collaborative classroom environment among teachers and students (social skills).

Creative Ballet Teaching promotes creative play, collaborative learning, and critical thinking in the ballet technique class. All ballet dancers can learn how to "play" with their art form: to experiment with artistic and technical choices, to imagine and investigate new movement possibilities, and to express newfound insights in creative ways.[4] When this happens, the learning in the ballet classroom becomes a springboard for a dancer's self-discovery as a person, as well as an artist and technician.

Watson, Nordin-Bates, and Chappell note that the degree "to which individuals are able to be creative will to a large extent be dependent on the encouragement and nurture they receive from the relationships and environment which surrounds them."[5] Certainly, the skills for creative play emerge in supportive learning communities where dancers are invited to collaborate with each other and to be reflective, imaginative, and decisive about their movement choices. Over time, this deepens a student's artistic and technical understanding of ballet.

A collaborative classroom environment: the subject-centered classroom

Creative Ballet Teaching applies the subject-centered teaching-learning model to ballet technique class. This model functions on the expectation that students engage in their learning as potential "experts" in the field. It is an ideal model for creating a collaborative and interactive classroom environment among students and teachers.

In his book *The Courage to Teach*, Parker Palmer proposes the subject-centered model as an alternative to teacher-centered and student-centered teaching-learning models.[6] According to Palmer, both the teacher and student-centered models create potential leadership imbalances in the learning environment.

In the teaching-centered model, the teacher is typically viewed as the expert who disseminates knowledge about the subject to the students. The students receive the information and meet the academic standards set by the teacher. Alternatively, in the student-centered model, "the student is regarded as a reservoir of knowledge to be tapped, students are encouraged to teach each other, the standards of accountability emerge from the group itself, and the teacher's role varies from facilitator to co-learner."[7] While this approach to education values the student learner as a source of knowledge, Palmer cautions that it may create a dynamic where the "students and the act of learning are more important than teachers and the act of teaching."[8] This, in turn, may cause teachers to "yield too much of their leadership,"[9] especially at points in the learning process when their leadership is needed.

Palmer's subject-centered model "de-centers" the educational environment from both the teacher and the students by placing the subject of study in the center of the educational learning environment. Like people, "a subject is available for relationship" and "as we try to understand the subject . . . we enter into complex patterns of communication."[10] Both teachers and students "must know how to observe and reflect and speak and listen, with passion and with discipline."[11] The subject-centered model does not focus on what is best for the students or the teachers in isolation, but instead what is best for the entire community engaging in the subject of study: *when is it important for teachers to direct the inquiry, and when is it important for students to do this?*

A subject-centered approach may sound useful in theory, but *how does it actually function in the ballet technique classroom?*

I researched methods for teaching ballet technique during my graduate studies in Ballet at the University of Utah. At that time, my teaching of technique classes was very teacher-centered: I designed all of the exercises, observed the students, provided most of the in-class instruction, and assessed the students' performance. Apart from the occasional student question, my voice—although positive and encouraging in demeanor—almost always dominated. As a result, the students relied on my corrections, praise, and instruction in order to initiate technical and artistic changes in their dancing.

Eventually, I felt their voices needed to be more prominent during class. I wanted to know how they were analyzing and assessing their dance technique. So, I began to integrate more student-directed learning into my classes: students engaged in peer feedback and shared their self-assessments verbally during classes. This deepened student comprehension and helped me assess the students' learning more effectively. However, student-directed learning took a lot of time to implement in class, which made it difficult to complete a full technique class (from *plié* to *grand allegro*) and to cover the curriculum needed to prepare the students for the next level of ballet.

As a result, I explored new pedagogical questions:

- *How could I effectively balance teacher and student-directed approaches in the classroom?*
- *How could I better balance student-directed activities that were simple and worked within the time structure of the technique class with those that were more complex?*
- *Was it possible to include both teacher and student-directed activities in every ballet class, and if so, what proportion worked?*

As I applied the subject-centered model to my ballet classes, I achieved greater balance in my teaching and I discovered (and still am discovering) pedagogical approaches for answering the above questions. Two such approaches are described below.

Curricular units

I design curricular units comprised of 5–12 classes that focus on specific technique concepts and skills.[12] I then assess how the curricular unit as a whole balances teacher-directed and student-directed learning. Sometimes I direct the majority of the in-class learning activities—when I need to teach new movement concepts and exercises and provide feedback to students—and sometimes the students do this. The proportion of teacher or student-directed activities therefore changes from class to class. For example, in a curricular unit with 12 classes:

- 5 classes might be 80 percent teacher-directed and 20 percent student-directed;
- 4 classes might be split 50/50 between teacher and student-directed learning;
- 3 classes might be 70 percent student-directed and 30 percent teacher-directed.

This organizational approach is used throughout *Creative Ballet Teaching*. Often, class activities are presented over 5–6 classes and progress from teaching-directed to student-directed.

Simple and complex student-directed activities

I vary the types of student-directed activities I use during a curricular unit. Some are simple and work within the timeframe of the ballet technique class and some are complex and require more time to implement. Additionally, many of the simple activities I use develop fundamental skills that students need for fulfilling the complex activities.

Table I.2 lists the types of student-directed activities used throughout this book. *As you read through both lists, reflect on some of the simple and complex student-directed activities you use in your classes. Perhaps you already use some of those mentioned in Table I.2.*

Subject-centered ballet classrooms challenge students and teachers alike to grow and develop in their art form as individuals and as members of a creative and dynamic community of learners. As I have applied a subject-centered model to my teaching practices, I have observed that it promotes collaborative education and individual responsibility toward one's education. Each person in the ballet classroom has the potential to contribute to the knowledge produced within the technique classroom. The teacher's wealth of knowledge influences how the dancers come to understand their experiences in ballet, and similarly, a ballet student's questions, curiosities, and physical knowledge pushes the subject of study in new directions.

Laban/Bartenieff Movement Analysis: a multifaceted teaching tool for developing technical and expressive skills

My MFA work at the University of Utah included coursework in both the Ballet and Modern Dance Departments. Studying modern dance instruction, performance, and composition simultaneously with my ballet studies in those same subjects broadened and clarified my knowledge as a dance artist and

Table I.2 Simple and complex student-directed activities

Simple student-directed activities	Complex student-directed activities
Students:	Students:
• Pose questions about technique concepts	• Discuss questions posed about movement concepts with peers
• Review exercises with peers	• Watch peers perform exercises and provide them with verbal affirmations and suggestions
• Observe a peer perform an exercise	• Embody images or rhythmical sounds other people generated
• Face a partner during a *barre* or *centre* exercise	• Teach a peer how to apply a technique concept in different parts of an exercise
• Generate personal images or rhythms for movements	• Explore with a peer different musical timings for an exercise
• Choose three places in an exercise to apply a technique concept	• Write individually about a technique concept in a movement journal or collectively on a dry erase board
• Improvise with a technique concept at the end of an exercise	• Create an exercise as an entire class
• Experiment with the musical timing of an exercise that is well rehearsed	• Create a short dance in pairs that utilizes new concepts or steps taught in class
• Create a personal story or narrative for an exercise	
• Create movement for small sections of an exercise (4–8 counts) that utilizes new concepts or steps taught in class	

instructor. During the first semester of graduate school, I began each day in ballet technique class with Sharee Lane, a fabulous educator whose classes were dynamic, rigorous, and grounded in a solid understanding of anatomical and kinesiological principles. Immediately after ballet technique class, I headed to modern dance technique class. It was during Donna White's modern dance technique classes when I was first introduced to Laban/Bartenieff Movement Analysis (L/BMA).

I recall exhaling deeply while standing in a *second position plié* with my arms extended wide when a soft tingling sensation coursed through my body—from arm to arm, feet to head, back to front. I felt simultaneously grounded and suspended, supported in my core yet able to expand my limbs with agility in space. It was an exhilarating sensation primarily because we were performing an *adagio*-based exercise, and I had always struggled with *adagio* in ballet technique classes. I was either too tense or loose, but in this moment, I was dynamically stable.

Soon after that class, I interviewed Donna about her teaching approach in the classroom. Like many educators, Donna cited various pedagogical influences, one of which was her Certification in L/BMA with *Integrated Movement*

Studies (*IMS*). When operating from a L/BMA perspective, there is a consistent focus on accessing whole body connectivity, a full range of motion in the body, and a large dynamic and spatial palette. Not surprisingly, Donna's classes challenged and stimulated my body physically, energetically, and spatially. Through Donna's encouragement, I enrolled in introductory workshops with *IMS*, and eventually in the full L/BMA Certification Program.

L/BMA is rooted in the work of Rudolf von Laban (1879–1958) and Irmgard Bartenieff (1900–1981). Laban and his many collaborators developed a comprehensive set of theories known generally as Laban Movement Analysis and Labanotation. Practitioners of these systems use the theories to analyze and notate the functional and expressive landscape of human movement.[13] Irmgard Bartenieff, a physical therapist and one of Laban's many collaborators, applied the LMA theories to somatic and rehabilitative practices, developing as a result the Bartenieff Fundamentals.[14] The Bartenieff Fundamentals are a body training practice that focuses on total body coordination, mind–body integration, and personal expression.

When I began studying L/BMA, I discovered a common language for movement regardless of what I was teaching: I used the theories to analyze movement in classical/contemporary ballet, modern/contemporary dance, and dance conditioning and exercise. After my Certification training, I expanded my use of L/BMA concepts to other applications: when designing inclusive dance classes, somatic therapy sessions with clients of different ages and backgrounds, and when working with athletes from different sports disciplines. For my dancers, the L/BMA concepts have served as a common language between different technique forms, and between their movement inside and outside of a dance context. Using L/BMA in the ballet technique classroom has changed the way they perceive and talk about their technique and their expressive capabilities as artists.

Parts II and III in *Creative Ballet Teaching* and *Creative Ballet Learning* apply theories from L/BMA to ballet technique and performance as a way to cultivate creativity, artistry, and technical versatility. A multifaceted tool for communication and self-understanding, L/BMA concepts provide dancers with numerous qualitative possibilities for embodying the balletic vocabulary. This deepens their movement literacy as they learn to make different artistic and technical choices from one class to the next. These skills are in line with the demands of the contemporary dance field. Increasingly, contemporary choreographers and artistic directors desire dancers who can work collaboratively, generate novel ideas during the dance-making process, and adapt to different movement styles.

Part II: Improving balance and motion uses L/BMA Shape, Space, and Body concepts to teach students how to move fully and three-dimensionally and to achieve stable and easeful balances. Part III: Deepening dynamism uses L/BMA Effort concepts to help teachers create dynamically rich and challenging classes and to facilitate a student's dynamic versatility.[15]

Even today, L/BMA practitioners are developing Laban's and Bartenieff's original theories. L/BMA is an evolving framework, one that continues to be refined and questioned as people apply the concepts to different disciplines and to a knowledge base reflective of living in the twenty-first century.[16] As you explore the L/BMA concepts in Parts II and III, know that you are joining a long legacy of inquiry, exploration, and research that has characterized the evolution of this work. *You are a part of that journey!*

Creative ballet teaching

Creative Ballet Teaching includes "Teacher exploration activities" in every chapter. The intent of these activities is on personal embodiment and continued investment in your own learning. The activities are best explored more than once, and throughout a lifetime of teaching. You will use new strategies and perspectives each time you repeat an activity. Over time, this deepens your embodiment and understanding of the concepts.

Class activities are also presented in every chapter. Developmentally, the activities target adolescent/young adult/adult learners. They are designed for pre-professional or upper-level technique students; however, many of the activities may also be adapted for beginning and intermediate level students in these age groups. Some of the activities are also fun to use with younger dancers, but when doing so, development differences in cognitive and psychomotor skills should be taken into account.

The methods presented in *Creative Ballet Teaching* are not intended to replace the methods you already use to teach ballet. Instead, this book is intended to serve as a resource for your continued explorations and research in ballet pedagogy. Each chapter includes activities for enhancing your students' creative abilities and artistic and technical development. Integrate these activities with those you already use with your students.

As you navigate the following chapters, keep the following suggestions in mind:

1   *Set small goals for yourself.* Explore one chapter for a few weeks before beginning a new chapter. Each chapter also presents more than one method or activity to use in class. It will be less overwhelming for both you and your students if you are selective about which activities and methods you want to explore first. You can always return to the chapter again when you want to explore something new.
2   *Repeat in-class activities.* Your students will achieve a deeper understanding of the concepts if they use them in class more than once. Additionally, when you repeat activities more than once, you discover new methods for teaching and presenting the activity to your students. This will help you alter the activities to parallel your teaching style and curricular goals.

3   *Move the material as you read.* Actively move the guided explorations and activities, learn the exercises presented throughout each chapter, and create your own exercises inspired by the movement concepts presented throughout the book.

4   *Keep a movement/teaching journal.* Write about your own embodiment as you explore the concepts and journal about your teaching practices.

Creative Ballet Learning: the student manual

Creative Ballet Learning is designed for the same student population as *Creative Ballet Teaching*. Collectively, the 16 chapters in *Creative Ballet Learning* focus on:

- *Developing greater body awareness and movement intention.* Students identify their movement capacities and challenges, learn about the body, and complete activities designed to strengthen their technical skills.
- *Moving with intent.* Students practice experimenting and improvising with different movement choices in technique class, and acquire new strategies for assessing and improving their technique.
- *Dancing expressively and fully.* Activities teach students to dance with dynamic variety, perform with feeling and emotion, interpret exercises in personal ways, and reflect on the expressive content of movement.
- *Deepening movement literacy.* Students learn how to apply movement concepts from Laban/Bartenieff Movement Analysis to ballet technique, and deepen their understanding of fundamental movement concepts relevant to all movement, including ballet.

The activities in *Creative Ballet Learning* invite students to explore technique concepts, engage in sensory-rich and imaginative movement investigations, and record their thoughts and discoveries in a dance technique journal. The active explorations and the journal assignments in *Creative Ballet Learning* provide students with structured ways to work on in-class material outside of class. The student manual parallels the activities and concepts in *Creative Ballet Teaching*. This makes it easier to coordinate the teaching-learning experiences, and it promotes comprehensive learning from your students.

Creative Ballet Learning and *Creative Ballet Teaching* share some of the same exploration activities and teaching tables. This is intentional, and is reflective of a subject-centered classroom environment where both teachers and students have access to the same information. In *Creative Ballet Teaching* you will, at times, adopt the role of student, and in *Creative Ballet Learning*, your students sometimes engage as teachers. I have always believed that students can and should engage in similar teaching-learning strategies as their teachers, and teachers are always learning from their students. *Creative Ballet Teaching* and *Creative Ballet*

Learning focus on this intelligent exchange between ballet teachers and ballet students.

Notes

1 Inspiring Children About Not Dropping Out.
2 Kauppila, H. (2007). Becoming an Active Agent in Dance and Through Dancing: A Teacher's Approach, in L. Rouhiainen (ed.), *Ways of Knowing in Dance and Art*. Helsinki: Theatre Academy, p. 135.
3 Gilbert, A.G. (1992). *Creative Dance for all Ages*. Reston, VA: The American Alliance for Health, Physical education, Recreation and Dance, pp. 6–7.
4 See also: Watson, D.E., Nordin-Bates, S.N., and Chappell, K.A. (2012). Facilitating and Nurturing Creativity in Pre-vocational Dancers: Findings from the UK Centres for Advanced Training. *Research in Dance Education*, 13(2): 153–173. This book assumes that creativity can be taught. In support of this the researchers state:

> The long-standing myth of the lone genius, where great creativity was viewed as a phenomenon arising solely from the abilities of a talented individual, continues to be eroded by many researchers who have looked behind the great innovations and artistry of individuals; uncovering instead a web of support, inspiration and knowledge exchange which underlies the emergence of creative genius" (p. 167).

In this quote, "many researchers" refers to the research of Csikszentmihalyi (1996), John-Steiner (2000), Sawyer (2007).
5 Ibid., p. 170.
6 Palmer. P. (2010). *The Courage to Teach: Exploring the Inner Landscape of a Teacher's Life*. 2nd edn. San Francisco, CA: John Wiley & Sons, Chapters 4–6.
7 Ibid., p. 116.
8 Ibid., p. 116.
9 Ibid., p. 119.
10 Ibid., p. 102.
11 Ibid., p. 104.
12 The number of classes is dependent on the complexity of the technique concept and technique exercises. Using movement concepts to teach ballet is the focus of Chapter 1.
13 For more information about Rudolf Laban, I recommend reading *Rudolf Laban: An Extraordinary Life* (1998) by Valerie Preston-Dunlop, or *Rudolf Laban* (2009) by Karen Bradley.
14 For more information about Irmgard Bartenieff and the Bartenieff Fundamentals, I recommend reading *Making Connections* (2000) by Peggy Hackney.
15 Chapter 5 introduces the L/BMA categories of Body, Effort, Shape, and Space.
16 The L/BMA theories have not developed in isolation; they are shaped and informed by other somatic disciplines and areas of study (i.e. neuroscience, behavioral psychology, phenomenology, human development, Body-Mind Centering, Feldenkrais Method, Alexander Technique, to name a few).

Part I

Rethinking creativity, community, and technique in the ballet classroom

Chapter 1

Drawing inspiration from creative movement

Teaching and planning from movement concepts

Creative Movement classes are offered in dance studios throughout the United States and in many countries. Many ballet dancers begin their training in these classes. My early dance experiences in Creative Movement classes sparked my interest in and love for dance. As a child, I remember moving with hula-hoops and scarves, dancing to varied music, making up stories, and pretending to be different creatures as I galloped and leapt through the space. Years later, when I began teaching Creative Movement classes, I learned how those early movement experiences helped me develop fundamental dance skills that underpinned my training in ballet.

Creative Movement teaching practices benefit students of varying skill levels, movement backgrounds, and ages, including those students studying classical ballet. In part, as dance educator Anne Green Gilbert notes, this is because "creative dance combines the mastery of movement with the artistry of expression," and she argues: "it is this combination, rather than a separation of the two, that makes creative dance so powerful."[1] When children "graduate" from Creative Movement classes, it is not uncommon for their dance training to become more codified and focused on learning specific steps and skills needed for studying a particular style of dance, such as ballet. Sometimes, as this happens, creativity and imaginative exploration become secondary goals. But these goals need not be in opposition to physical skill development. Integrating the two in dance training, even in pre-professional ballet training, establishes a well-rounded learning environment, one that supports the students' development as technically skilled performing artists.

Imagination, sensory-rich movement explorations, conceptual learning, and skill-development are the hallmarks of Creative Movement classrooms. If the "lessons" learned in Creative Movement classes benefit young dancers just starting their training in dance, incorporating those "lessons" into ballet education will likely have similar benefits. In my experience, integrating a Creative Movement approach in ballet education promotes the development of intelligent, skillful, and expressive dancers.

The intent of Chapters 1 and 2 is to remember and reflect on Creative Movement teaching practices in order to reexamine and broaden the teaching approaches (and therefore the learning outcomes) used in upper-level ballet training. These chapters explore the following questions:

> *What "lessons" do Creative Movement curricula teach us about good dance education?*

> *Which Creative Movement teaching approaches make sense in ballet curricula? What will best support a ballet dancer's technical and artistic development?*

Let's begin this exploration with the first lesson: Teaching from movement concepts.

Teaching from movement concepts

Hula-hoops are scattered along the floor like little circular islands in the space. Each island contains a dancer. The dancers are still, their bodies suspended in rounded and twisted shapes. I start the music: an urgent and boisterous song. The dancers explode from their stillness, leap from their islands, and move freely to the music through the space. Some run, some spin, many gallop and jump and skip. The music stops abruptly; dancers scatter to the hula-hoops, step inside them, and become rounded statues suspended in stillness. The music begins again; this time it is a slow and gentle song. The dancers glide softly into the space, leaving their circular islands behind. Some move through the space like floating feathers, others crawl quietly like sneaky kittens, and some delicately hop and tiptoe through the space. The music stops again; the dancers rush to their islands.

Creative Movement classes are exploratory landscapes designed to spark imagination, build movement literacy, and strengthen movement skills. In the above example, students learn how to stop and go, make rounded forms in their bodies, move with different movement dynamics, and travel through the space in different ways.

The Creative Movement curricula I grew up learning, and eventually teaching, was subdivided into larger movement categories—such as Body or Space or Energy—and our teachers taught us numerous movement concepts within these categories, such as rhythm, spatial pathways, and body actions. An exploration of these overarching movement categories and concepts developed our understanding of our bodies and of the basic elements of dance.

Table 1.1 presents a sample list of common movement categories, concepts, and skills I use when I teach Creative Movement classes. These are very similar to the categories and concepts I use when working with pre-professional ballet

(handwritten margin note: What they can learn)

dancers. The primary difference is that the skills explored and vocabulary used are more specific to ballet technique.

As you read through Table 1.1, which concepts and skills would be useful to explore in your ballet classroom?

Table 1.1 Categories and movement concepts explored in creative movement classes

Movement category	Movement concept	Skills explored
BODY	Movements of the body	• Discover singular body parts and movements • Move body regions (right, left, upper, lower)
	Relationships	• Explore how parts of the body coordinate
	Mobile and stable	• Practice locomotive movements through space • Learn about posture, balance, and stillness
SHAPE	Shapes	• Explore different body shapes (round, linear, twisted, flat, big, small)
	Forming	• Practice how shapes grow and shrink, open and close
SPACE	Spatial pathways	• Travel along curved, straight, zigzag, and meandering pathways
	Levels	• Move in different spatial levels: high, medium, low
	Directions	• Move in different directions: up, down, right, left, forward, back
ENERGY	Time	• Perform movements at different speeds: fast, slow, medium, acceleration, and deceleration
	Weight	• Explore movements that are forceful or gentle, or limp and floppy
	Flow	• Explore movements that are controlled or uncontrolled, smooth or choppy
MUSICALITY	Rhythm	• Explore the rhythms of different dance steps • Learn how to move to different rhythms and musical meters

Through studying basic movement concepts, such as those listed in Table 1.1, students in Creative Movement classes learn that their bodies change shape, energy, rhythm, and spatial directions all of the time, and dancing allows them to explore the many ways they make those changes. This develops foundational movement skills as they begin their training in specific dance styles and techniques. In this way, a student's dance skills develop in relationship to the movement concepts, and vice versa.[2]

Even though the skills and concepts listed in Table 1.1 reference those I often focus on in Creative Movement classes, all of them are applicable to ballet technique training. Let's explore a few examples:

1   **BODY—relationships**: Ballet students explore the relationship between their feet and the floor, or between the supporting and gesturing sides of the body, or between the head and the arms. The students then identify how these relationships support their execution of different movements performed in class, such as *battement tendu, sauté, pirouette, grand battement*.[3] *What type of body relationships do you ask your students to explore in class?*

Figure 1.1 **Explore the relationship between the head and arms**

2   **SHAPE—forming**: Ballet students explore how the balletic exercises follow rhythms of opening and closing in balletic steps and exercises. For example, my students often focus on the spreading and enclosing of the legs and arms in a *port de bras, battement fondu developpé*, or *glissade*. This helps them invest in the exercises and steps as *movements* instead of as static positions.[4] *How do you teach the kinetic quality of balletic steps in your classes?*

Figure 1.2 **Explore the movements of the arms**

3   **SPACE—directions**: Ballet students explore directional ballet vocabulary, such as, *en arrière* (backward), *en avant* (forward), *en dedans* (inward), *en dehors* (outward). They also explore the directionality of their torso and limbs in space: the forward and upward pull of the upper torso, head, and arm in *first arabesque*, the backward and downward reach of the leg in *tendu derrière*, or the side-to-side counter-pull of the supporting arm and gesturing leg in *developpé à la seconde*. Exploring directionality in class clarifies spatial intent and body alignment.[5] *How do you develop your students' spatial awareness during technique class?*

Figure 1.3 Explore counter pulls in the body

4   **ENERGY—force**: Ballet students explore how use of force changes the intensity of a step. For example, executing a *grand battement devant* with a powerful thrust of the leg upward followed by a gentle descent of the leg to *fifth position* feels different than the opposite—a delicate toss upward followed by a strong descent to *fifth*. Changing the energetic quality impacts their technical and artistic execution of the movement.[6] *In what ways do you emphasize dynamic qualities, such as force, in your classes?*

5   **MUSICALITY—rhythm**: Ballet students explore the rhythms of steps through clapping: a *pas de bourée coupé ballonné* or the spotting rhythm of the head in a double *en dehors pirouette en retiré*, for example. They also explore the difference between performing a basic *barre* exercise to a 3/4 meter versus a 2/4 meter, or experiment with performing steps at different speeds.[7] *How do you challenge your dancers to develop their rhythmical skills during class?*

Using movement concepts when teaching dance is important at the upper level of ballet, primarily because the information disseminated to the students increases. Students learn new steps and the different ways that the steps can be performed in combination with other steps. They also learn how to perform the steps to different musical timings, travel the steps through space in different ways, and perform the vocabulary expressively and artistically. Overarching movement concepts, such as those explored above, serve to organize all of this information under common themes. In this way, the movement concepts act as organizational "threads" from one exercise to the next. Students learn how to apply the concepts across different contexts, which "grounds" their learning experience and helps them make sense of the dance vocabulary they practice from class to class.

In *Ballet Beyond Tradition* Anna Paskevska encourages dancers and teachers to use concepts that reveal how the body moves and forms dynamically in space regardless of the style of movement the dancer is learning. For her,

> Concepts are sign posts. They . . . guide dancers in the understanding of dynamics, effort, motivation, and the relationship of the body as it occupies and defines the space in which it moves. These concepts are fundamental to human locomotor activities, and as such are relevant to ballet technique.[8]

So, how do you know you are approaching a technique class from an overarching movement concept?[9]

> *A movement concept is applicable to different steps and exercises.*

> *A movement concept supports the development of expressive and technical balletic skills.*

> *Dancers should be able to apply the concept to their dancing in different and similar ways.*

Chances are you are already using movement concepts when you teach ballet technique. Take a moment before reading further to journal about the movement concepts you already employ in your classes. As you create your list, ask yourself:

1   *Could I apply this concept to different steps and exercises?*
2   *Does this concept facilitate the technical and expressive exploration of the balletic exercises?*

Teacher exploration 1.1: Explore movement concepts you use in class

1   List three movement concepts you focus on regularly when you teach upper-level ballet technique classes.
2   Describe how you apply each concept to different steps, exercises, and movements throughout class.

There are many sources of inspiration when looking for movement concepts to use in your ballet classes. You might choose to explore concepts from Creative Movement classes or Laban Movement Analysis, or perhaps, like Paskevska, you are inspired to apply concepts from physics and modern dance technique to balletic movement. Or, you could simply begin, as this book does, by exploring the movement concepts embedded in the French balletic terminology. *Since this vocabulary is an essential part of learning ballet, let's explore how to use it conceptually in ballet class!*

Exploring movement concepts embedded in the balletic terminology

The French balletic terminology is a wonderful source of inspiration when looking for movement concepts to explore with your students. When analyzing the definitions of the terms, one discovers a rich and descriptive landscape for describing movement. This section explores the definitions of the seven traditional movements in ballet, and identifies how to use those definitions as overarching movement concepts during technique class. Many of the balletic terms may be used in this way; I have chosen the seven traditional movements as a starting point (see Table 1.2).

The definitions for these traditional balletic movements are qualitative in nature, and are therefore applicable to multiple steps and exercises. Using the terms conceptually in class supports the development of foundational movement skills needed for performing complex ballet movements, and it deepens the dancers' understanding of the balletic vocabulary.

Table 1.2 Seven traditional movements

plier (to bend)
relever (to rise)
glisser (to glide)
elancer (to dart)
etendre (to stretch)
sauter (to jump)
tourner (to turn)

The following pages explore each of these seven traditional movements and provide examples of how to use them as movement concepts in class.

Plier—to bend

creasing   yielding   folding   suppleness   malleability

When you use *plier* as a concept, you teach students to invest in bending and yielding movement qualities. Dancers identify how their bodies fold and crease during balletic steps. *Investigate the following movement in your body from the concept of plier:*

- **Focus** on the creasing of the ankles, knees, and hips during lower body movements, such as *plié, fondu, pas de cheval, developpé,* and *pas de chat*.

Figure 1.4 Explore *plier* as a concept during *pas de chat*

- **Attend** to the suppleness of the body as it folds and inclines during large movements, such as a *port de corps,* or *penché arabesque* or *grand rond de jambe*.
- **Explore** the yielding and malleability of the lower body in *demi-plié* during *petite allegro,* consecutive *plié relevé, fouetté rond de jambe en tournant,* and so on.

How else would you emphasize the concept of plier/bending in class?

Relever—to rise

growing   ascending   expanding   soaring   inflating

When you use *relever* as a concept, you teach students to invest in an expansive use of their bodies. Dancers identify steps that soar, grow, and ascend into space.

What do you discover in your body as you investigate the following movements from the concept of relever?

- **Focus** on the quality of rising in different balletic steps, such as *temps lié, battement piqué, port de bras,* and so on.
- **Attend** to the expansiveness of the body: growing upward from a *grand plié,* soaring into space during a *chassé sauté arabesque,* feeling the breath expand the upper chest during *grand adagio.*

Figure 1.5 Explore how the body rises into space

- **Explore** different dynamic ways to rise: the difference between exploding upward during a *sauté* and raising the leg slowly during a *relevé lent.*

How else would you emphasize the concept of relever/rising in class?

Glisser—to glide

sliding   skimming   flowing   whooshing   skating

When you use *glisser* as a concept, you teach students to invest in a gliding use of their upper and lower bodies in space. Dancers identify movements that slide, whoosh, and skate. *Experiment with the following movement examples:*

- **Focus** on the sliding of the feet along the floor during steps like *chassé, glissade, balançoire, brisé,* and *pas de cheval.*
- **Attend** to the gliding or the whooshing of the limbs through space during *port de bras, renversé, rond de jambe, balancé, sissonne,* and *cambré,* for example.
- **Explore** the skimming of the tips of the toes along the floor before a *piqué en pointe,* or a *battement tendu devant* into a *tombé,* or a *pas de valse en tournant.*

How else would you emphasize the concept of glisser/gliding in class?

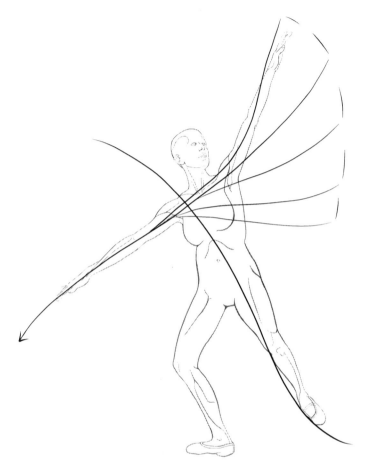

Figure 1.6 Explore the gliding quality of the arms

Elancer—to dart

dashing   *fouetté (whipping)*   *bolting*   *sweeping*   *tossing*

When you use *elancer* as a concept, you teach students to invest in a darting use of their energy. Dancers identify how their bodies burst and whip through space. *What do you feel as you play with the following movements?*

* **Focus** on the dashing of the body through space during any traveling movements, such as *failli assemblé*, *sissonne fermé*, *tombé pas de bourrée*, and *grand jeté*.

- **Attend** to the bursting or tossing nature of balletic movements at *barre*—such as, *battement frappé* and *grand battement*—and in *centre* during any turning or *allegro* exercises.
- **Explore** the quality of sweeping or whipping the arms and legs through space during a *barre* or *centre* exercise.

How else would you emphasize the concept of elancer/darting in class?

Entendre—to stretch

lengthening   elongating   extending   prolonging   allongé (outstretched)

When you use *entendre* as a concept, you teach students to invest in the elongation of their torsos and limbs in space. Dancers identify movements that stretch and lengthen. *What do you discover in your body as you investigate the following movements from the concept of entendre?*

- **Focus** on the elongation of the spine during *épaulment, cambré, attitude, grand jeté,* and *fouetté sauté.*
- **Attend** to how your legs extend downward into the floor during *rond de jambe* and *balançoire,* when rising from a *plié* or a *fondu developpé,* or when executing a *relevé* or a *pirouette.*
- **Explore** *allongé* qualities during *barre* and *centre* exercises.

How else would you emphasize the concept of entendre/stretching in class?

Figure 1.7 Explore the elongation of the body

Sauter—to jump

ballon (bouncing)   *springing*   *elastic-like*   *rebounding*   *bounding*

When you use *sauter* as a concept, you teach students to invest in the springing nature of balletic steps. Dancers identify how their bodies bounce and rebound with an elastic-like quality. *Investigate the following movement in your body from the concept of sauter:*

- **Focus** on the bouncing or spring-like quality of movements throughout class, such as *battement piqué, temps lié, sauté,* and *plié relevé.*
- **Attend** to the rebounding nature of *plié* as a transition step throughout class, and especially during *pointe* work, consecutive turns, and *allegro* exercises.
- **Explore** the elastic-like quality of *battement degagé, fondu, ballonné, sissonne,* or *faille assemblé.*

How else would you emphasize the concept of sauter/jumping in class?

Figure 1.8 Explore *sauter* as a concept during *petite allegro*

Tourner—to turn

pirouette (whirling)   *spinning*   *spiraling*   *rotation/ing*   *revolving*

When you use *tourner* as a concept, you teach students to identify movements that turn and spin. Dancers explore how their bodies rotate and spiral. *Experiment with the following examples:*

- **Focus** on the revolving and whirling nature of turning movements, such as *fouetté, pas de bourée en tournant, promenade, pirouette, chaînés,* and *soutenu.*
- **Attend** to the rotation of the hips in turnout, the arms in *second position port de bras,* the spine in *épaulment.*

- **Explore** the spiraling quality of *croisé* and *éffacé* movements in *centre*, and of *épaulment* positioning at *barre*.

How else would you emphasize the concept of tourner/turning in class?

Figure 1.9 Explore rotation of the legs at *barre*

Teachers first: embodying movement concepts

As emphasized in the previous section, a good movement concept is applicable to multiple steps and exercises and should support the technical and artistic skills needed to perform balletic steps well. Take a moment to explore this in Teacher exploration 1.2. *When used as movement concepts, how do the seven traditional movements support your technical and artistic execution of multiple balletic steps?*

Teacher exploration 1.2: Same step, different movement concept

1   Apply the seven traditional movements to your performance of each of the following balletic steps. For example, begin with *Balancé*, first performing it with the quality of *plier*, then *relever*, then *glisser*, and so on until you reach *tourner*. Then, perform the next step on the list following the same format. **It is helpful to have the names and synonyms for the seven traditional movements visible as you do this.**

Balancé
Battement degagé
Demi-plié
Glissade assemblé

Grand battement
Pirouette in retiré (en dedans or dehors)
Rond de jambe (en l'air, à terre)
Sissonne (fermée or ouvert)
Temps lié

2   Reflect:

- How does each concept affect the technique of the step?
- How does each concept affect the expressive quality of the step?
- When would you use each of the above qualities conceptually in class? What technical or artistic skills would you be exploring with your students?

I chose to discuss the seven traditional movements of ballet, but you do not need to limit your investigation to these seven terms. Many other balletic terms are also appropriate for this type of conceptual exploration. Some of my favorites include:

- *Tombé* **(falling)**: The quality of falling teaches dancers how to release their weight into the ground and move the center of weight off balance.
- *Passé* **(passed/passing)**: The quality of passing is useful when focusing on transitions between movements and steps—how does the movement "pass" from one place to the next?
- *Allegro* **(brisk, lively) and** *adagio* **(at ease, leisure)**: When explored together, the contrasting qualities of lively and leisure promote greater dynamic variety in the students' performance of the class exercises.
- *Développé* **(developing movement) and** *enveloppé* **(enveloping movement)**: The qualities of developing and enveloping emphasize rhythms of closing and opening or unfolding and folding of the arms and legs throughout class.

Teacher exploration 1.3: Using balletic terms conceptually

1   Identify three additional balletic terms to use conceptually during ballet class.
2   Define each term. What movement qualities does each term invoke?

3   How will you apply those movement qualities to different steps and exercises throughout class?

4   How do those movement qualities facilitate technical and artistic exploration of the balletic exercises?

5   How will your dancers explore these three terms as movement concepts?

Teaching your students to use movement concepts

My students have appreciated a conceptual approach to learning ballet. Many have remarked that it helps them enter class with a mindful focus and clarity of purpose. They are more adept at recognizing the movement concepts that underpin ballet technique, and they enjoy the challenge of exploring similar balletic movements from different perspectives:

A sissonne fermée from the perspective of elancer versus entendre . . .
A grand adagio from the perspective of relever versus tourner . . .
A battement tendu from the perspective of plier versus glisser . . .

Paskevska suggests making an in–class game out of finding the concepts in the technique exercises.[10] This is an excellent game! *Hide and seek with movement concepts!* presents a simple activity for doing this with your students. Students must be familiar with at least three of the seven traditional ballet movements in order to complete this activity.

Hide and seek with movement concepts!

Objective:

Strengthen the dancers' ability to identify movement concepts in the balletic exercises.

1   Identify the concepts to explore. For example, I worked on: *glisser, entendre,* and *relever.*

2   Choose a well-rehearsed *centre* or *barre* exercise (or one of each) to analyze. I used this short *petite allegro:*

Begin: *Fifth position en face,* right foot behind

Glissade right, *assemblé* right
Repeat left
Battement jeté right, then left, then right
Pas de bourée dessous traveling right
Finish: *plié fifth*, right foot behind

3   Instruct the dancers to investigate how those three concepts sup-
     port their performance of the exercise. Ask the dancers to share their
     findings with the whole class. For example, in the *petite allegro*, my
     dancers discovered:

     •   *Glisser*—the sliding of the feet in *glissade*; the skimming quality
          of the body through space in *pas de bourrée*.
     •   *Entendre*—the elongation of the body in space during *assemblé*;
          the lengthening of the *degagé* leg in *battement jeté*.
     •   *Relever*—the rising of the body in *pas de bourrée* from the last *bat-
          tement jeté*; the soaring upward of the body in *assemblé*.

These represent only some of the many discoveries possible.

The qualitative nature of the balletic vocabulary easily integrates into my
lesson plans for ballet class. I typically construct my entire class around one
concept. This provides greater focus and consistency to my verbal cueing and to
the design of my *barre* and *centre* exercises. I then explore the same concept over
multiple classes: usually 3–6 classes depending on the complexity of the concept
and of my exercises. This sustained focus on one concept over multiple classes is
helpful for the dancers. The physical and cognitive repetition helps them track
the ways in which the concept facilitates their execution of the exercises. Additionally, since we apply the concept in different ways throughout class, there is
enough variety from class to class to keep the students physically and cognitively
challenged. This balance between repetition and variation is rewarding for all.

Let's go through this planning process together in the class planning activity
Developing a concept.

Class planning activity

Developing a concept

Step 1: Choose the concept

**Choose one of the seven traditional movements of ballet to explore with
your students.**

I explored *tourner*.
Other evocative words: whirling, spinning, spiraling, rotation/ing, and revolving.

Step 2: Choose the number of classes to explore the concept

For this planning activity, I recommend 4–6 classes.

I explored *tourner* in six consecutive classes.

Step 3: Identify what to explore

What skills within the concept do you want to explore with your students? Which barre and centre exercises and steps will illuminate the concept well?

For *tourner*, I emphasized the qualities of rotation, spiraling, and turning. As I planned my classes, I placed greater emphasis on including balletic steps that turn (i.e. *promenade*, *pirouette*, and steps performed *en tournant*). I highlighted how the spine, hips, and arms spiraled and rotated in numerous balletic movements: *croisé*, *épaulment*, *écharté*, and *effacé* are just a few examples.

Step 4: Create *barre* and *centre* exercises

Create three centre exercises and three barre exercises that clearly relate to each other and to the concept.

My *barre* exercises were *battement degagé, rond de jambe, battement frappé*.
My *centre* exercises were *grand adagio, traveling waltz, allegro (medium tempo)*.

These six exercises were repeated in all six classes, which helped the students build new coordinative patterns and physical skills. They also learned to explore the movement differently in each class, which is similar to the process they employ when rehearsing the same choreography for weeks prior to a performance.

The other exercises I created for class also related to the concept, but they changed from class to class depending on the needs of the students. I kept these exercises simple in terms of musicality and sequencing.

Step 5: Scaffolding the concept across five classes

Class 1: Focus on teaching the core exercises and introducing the concept.
Classes 2 and 3: Focus on one aspect of the concept.

Classes 4 and 5: Focus on another aspect of the concept.
Class 6: Students choose the conceptual focus.

Class 1: I taught the core exercises and also focused on the joy of whirling, whipping, and spinning. Highlighting this type of dynamism when turning helped the students invest in the concept qualitatively.

Classes 2 and 3: I focused on the rotation and spiraling. In Class 2, we explored the rotation of the hips in turn out, *promenades, pirouettes,* and direction changes. In Class 3, we explored the twisting of the spine and head during those same movements and during *épaulment* movements.

Classes 4 and 5: I returned to the focus on the whirling, whipping and spinning. We explored the mechanics of turning: how one side pushes during the turn (i.e. when turning to the right, the left half of the body provides the pushing force); the rotation and spotting of the head even in quarter and half turns; and we played with creating whirling and whipping sounds with our voices as we performed the exercises. This last exploration was really useful for the dancers who turn with excessive tension in the limbs and spine—it loosened them up and made them laugh!

Class 6: I asked the dancers to choose 1–2 things from the concept *tourner* to focus on as they performed the six repeated exercises. They applied those 1–2 ideas in five places during each exercise. Some students focused on spinal spiraling and twisting, some on the rotation of the head/neck and hips, some on the dynamic qualities of turning, and so on.

Choosing which concepts to explore and how long to explore them with your students are just some of the decisions you will encounter when teaching ballet technique from a conceptual perspective. There is no perfect formula for making these decisions. One step or one exercise may be approached from multiple concepts. Additionally, it may be sufficient to explore a movement concept in one class only, or the investigation may be productive enough to continue over multiple classes. Experimentation and ongoing problem solving is important and encouraged.

Conclusion

Using movement concepts to teach dance is a foundational approach in Creative Movement classrooms. Chapter 1 applied this approach to ballet teaching and investigated the importance of conceptual learning in the education of pre-professional ballet dancers. In doing so, this chapter examined common movement concepts taught in Creative Movement classrooms, and explored how those concepts relate to the study of ballet. Chapter 1 also explored how the ballet lexicon provides a rich terrain for exploring overarching movement concepts in technique class. This facilitates greater literacy in the balletic style.

Dance educator Lorin Johnson recognizes that even though "ballet presents a codified system that simplifies the pathways to follow . . . its 'rules' do not dictate how movements are to be explored."[11] This is an important realization. A conceptual approach to ballet education teaches dancers to sense, perceive, and discern the differences between one way of moving and another. They learn how movement intentionality varies, and this strengthens their ability to make technical and artistic decisions throughout technique class. As dance researcher Paula Salosaari writes, "when the codified ballet vocabulary is explored with multiple images of content, the dancer is given a wide agenda of perceptual modes of attention to choose from ... even within the same movement."[12] A conceptual approach to ballet provides dancers with varying options for perceiving and exploring balletic movement.

This exploration is not finished, however! Creative Movement teaching practices still have much to teach. Let's continue our exploration in Chapter 2 with two more lessons learned from Creative Movement: *developing body knowledge and improvisation skills.*

Notes

1   Gilbert, A.G. (1992). *Creative Dance for all Ages.* Reston, VA: The American Alliance for Health, Physical education, Recreation and Dance, p. 3.
2   This is a fundamental premise emphasized in *Creative Dance for all Ages.* Gilbert (1992) states: "Creative dance consists of more than just exploring dance concepts. Skills must be developed, in relation to the concepts. The development of skills will improve the compositions and increase the level of creativity" (p. 4).
3   Body relationships are further explored in Part II: Balance and motion.
4   Forming is explored in Chapter 6.
5   Spatial Intent/Directions are explored in Chapters 7 and 8.
6   Force is explored in Chapter 11.
7   Rhythm is explored in Chapter 12.
8   Paskevska, A. (2005). *Ballet Beyond Tradition.* New York: Routledge, p. 5.
9   See also: Paskevska, A. (2005): Movement concepts should "reconnect ballet training to a more thoughtful physicality . . . and guide us back to a discovery of the intent of the vocabulary and the physical roots of the movement" (pp. 4–5).
10   Ibid., p. 11.
11   Johnson, L. (2011b). Teaching Ballet in Universities: How to Engage Contemporary Dancers. *Dance Teacher Magazine,* 33(9): 98.
12   Salosaari, P. (2001). *Multiple Embodiment in Classical Ballet: Educating the Dancer as an Agent of Change in the Cultural Evolution of Ballet.* Helsinki: Theatre Academy, p. 35.

Chapter 2

Drawing inspiration from creative movement

Developing body knowledge and improvisation skills

When I first began teaching Creative Movement classes as a young adult, I had not yet taken formal classes in teaching pedagogy. My experiences in dance were primarily as a performing artist in ballet; the classical ballet terminology dominated my vocabulary for describing movement. Teaching Creative Movement classes to young children broadened my vocabulary and cueing methods. I quickly discovered the importance of teaching movement through imagery and stories, and using adverbs, adjectives, and action verbs as the students danced:

softly, smoothly, lively, timidly, loudly . . .
sweeping, popping, tossing, floppy, jerky . . .
sprinkle, pounce, bounce, hop, tumble, spring, dart . . .

In later years, after taking courses in teaching pedagogy, I also learned the value of asking students to describe their own movement during class:

Do you have a name for this movement?
What do you feel when you move this way?
What do you imagine as you move?
Do you have a story for your dance?
What type of movements do you like?

I began to access their terminology, stories, and images during class, and this too broadened my vocabulary and cueing methods.

I have used Creative Movement teaching methods with beginning dancers of all ages, from young children to older adults. It is a delight to watch as the participants in these classes discover the joy of dance. For some, regardless of age or previous dance experience, this discovery happens immediately—they are delighted to play, to sense their bodies moving in space, to interact imaginatively with others through movement. For others, this discovery takes time—they need repeated opportunities to tap into their own physicality and creativity. For these students, the "spark" may happen when they perceive a change in their expressive and physical capabilities, or perform in front of their peers, or take an unexpected risk that surprises and delights them. When this happens, I know they will continue to tap into the potential of their expressive bodies long after they leave my classes.

Over the years, as I have aligned my ballet teaching methods more closely with my Creative Movement teaching methods, I have established a more holistic approach to teaching ballet.

Improvisation, experimentation, and personal expression have become equally as important as repetition, skill development, and the teaching of structured exercises.

Keeping this in mind, three overarching questions accompany me into the ballet technique classroom:

How do teachers facilitate a ballet dancer's journey into deeper sensory and body awareness?

How do dancers experiment and improvise with the balletic vocabulary in class?

What do my dancers sense, feel, and think as they perform balletic movement?

The purpose of this chapter is to address the above questions by exploring two additional "lessons" learned from Creative Movement teaching methods: **deepening body knowledge** and **developing improvisation skills**.

Deepening body knowledge

A major focus in Creative Movement classes for young children is to teach students about their bodies: how the body moves in space, how parts of the body move in different ways, how different emotions affect body shape and dynamics, and so on. Students learn these skills in multifaceted ways: through improvisation, set movement sequences created by the teacher, stories and role playing, and through the creation of their own dances. The diversity of learning experiences is intended to support the students' physical, emotional, and cognitive development, and for some students, prepare them for studies in other dance styles, such as ballet.

As any ballet dancer or teacher knows, learning about the body does not end in Creative Movement classes. Beginning ballet dancers learn numerous steps and body positions unique to ballet. Each year of training builds in complexity, and continues over multiple years before dancers reach the upper levels. At these levels, the dancers demonstrate deeper physical understanding of the balletic style and vocabulary, clearer sense of musicality, improved ability to perform complex sequences, and greater skill at observing and embodying stylistic differences between teachers.

Students at the pre-professional level learn balletic skills primarily through their performance of structured technique exercises created by the teacher. This is largely due to the increased complexity of the movement vocabulary and exercises. As a result, unlike Creative Movement classes, there are typically fewer opportunities for advanced students to improvise and experiment with ballet technique and to create their own balletic phrases during the technique class. However, this need not be the case. One lesson learned from Creative Movement is:

Body knowledge is developed in multifaceted ways.
Why multifaceted?
Because the development of body knowledge in Creative Movement classrooms involves the whole person—the thinking, feeling, and sensing dancer.

Development of body knowledge in the ballet classroom is most effective when it also involves the whole person. Body knowledge, as it is defined in this book, therefore includes a focus on developing physical and expressive skills and making purposeful decisions about one's movements (Table 2.1).[1]

Table 2.1 Developing body knowledge in the ballet classroom

Body awareness	Deepening sensory awareness of individual movement patterns and fundamental movement concepts
Personal expression	Dancing with feeling and emotion, and reflecting on the expressive content of movement
Intent	Making conscious movement choices about how to perform or think about balletic movement

Parts II and III in *Creative Ballet Teaching* apply specific movement concepts from Laban Movement Analysis to ballet technique as a way to develop a dancer's body awareness, intentionality, and expressive skills. Since the development of body knowledge is a major focus in later chapters, this section simply introduces it in the way that it is being conceived of in this book.

Let's begin by exploring the categories in Table 2.1.

Body awareness

Today's ballet dancers fluidly navigate between classical and contemporary balletic styles, as well as the "fusion-technique" styles employed by many contemporary choreographers. This is a primary reason why I teach students **fundamental movement concepts** that broaden their knowledge about the body and movement regardless of the dance style they are studying. This focus began in Chapter 1 and continues in Parts II and III.

Awareness of how the body moves—what is possible in any given movement—facilitates technical development in ballet. My students learn to ask:

What parts of the body are moving or stabilizing?
How do the parts of the body coordinate with each other?
How is the body moving through space? Where am I going?
What is the feeling-tone and dynamic quality of the movement?

Students may gather this information through my demonstrations and instructions, or by looking in a mirror, or by watching other dancers. Ultimately, however, dancers must physically sense their bodies performing the movements in order to develop sustainable changes in their technique skills. This requires them to ask: *What do I feel physically when I perform this movement?* Some questions that explore movement from this perspective include:

What parts of my feet make contact with the floor when standing in fifth position?
What does my pelvic alignment feel like in devant versus derrière positions?
How does a round shape feel physically different than a linear shape?
How do different positions of the arms affect my balance?

This type of attentiveness—**sensing and feeling the body moving**—is paramount to the development of body awareness, and ultimately of good ballet technique.

Effective education in any discipline integrates sensing and feeling in the learning process. This seems an automatic integration in dance education where students are moving, feeling, and sensing all of the time. Dance educator Matthew Henley's research is supportive of this: "Dance education immerses the student in an embodied experience by uniquely training three sensory systems: exteroception (mapping of the external world), proprioception (mapping of self-shapes and movement), and interoception (matching of bodily states to emotions and thoughts)."[2]

Let's analyze how these three sensory systems manifest in a ballet class:

Perform a battement tendu devant from fifth position with the left leg. First, establish a grounded connection into the floor from the pelvis to the heels and metatarsals of both feet. Match this downward pull into the ground with an oppositional pull upward through the lower abdominals and spine. Then, shift your weight to the derrière leg as you slide and advance the left foot along the floor, articulating from heel to toes into the extended forward position. Send the focus of your eyes outward into space as the upper spine and head lifts and rotates toward one arm rising into fifth position.

Figure 2.1 Performing a *battement tendu devant*

Perform the tendu again. Consider how you execute this relatively simple movement. Do you emphasize the expansion of the spine and limbs into space? Or, the epaulment in the upper body? Do you perform the movement slowly or quickly? Softly or firmly?

Do your physical choices conjure images or emotions as you perform the movement? If so, how do you express those?

In this one movement, you integrated awareness of body position, space, thoughts, and feelings.

As the *battement tendu* example demonstrates, there are numerous movement criteria for students to attend to during class. Attention to these criteria are not always an automatic process for dancers, however. Students learn and remember the balletic sequences with greater ease at the pre-professional level, and this increased movement facility sometimes leads to passive learning. They may begin to simply repeat their teacher's movements without thinking deeply about their technical or expressive choices. **So, even though dance education is unique in its ability to integrate sensing–thinking–feeling, teachers play an important role in consciously fostering this integration during class.**[3]

Peggy Hackney, one of my dance colleagues and mentors, stated to me in an informal conversation: teachers "don't teach sensation. Sensation teaches sensation. We don't teach feeling. Feeling teaches feeling" (personal communication, January 7, 2016). This is an important distinction to make in the dance technique classroom. I do not teach students *how* to feel or sense. Instead, my classroom exercises and verbal cueing methods provide opportunities for them to explore different bodily sensations and feeling-states during class. This increases their "proprio-intero-exteroceptive-sensory bank" while performing a variety of balletic movements in class.

Explore this in your body.

Teacher exploration 2.1: Heightening sensation

1. **Create a simple *battement fondu en croix* exercise at *barre*.**
2. **Experiment with breathing patterns.** Investigate how your use of breath changes muscular tension and feeling-tone in the *battement fondu* exercise.

    - Feel your ribs expanding and condensing as you inhale and exhale during the exercise. Every time you inhale, imagine breathing in your favorite smell or your favorite color and allow it to permeate your whole body. Every time you exhale, send scent or color into space. *How does the imagery affect your breathing and movement patterns?*
    - Explore restricting and freeing up your breath. *How does this change your technique and the feeling-tone of the movement?*
    - Perform the exercise two more times. First, emphasize the moments of inhale. Then emphasize the moments of exhale. *Does inhaling generate different sensations or images than exhaling? If so, how does this change the movement expressively?*

3. **Attend to different body parts.** Focus on different parts of the body as you perform the *battement fondu*.

    - Imagine your feet are covered in paint. As you peel one foot off of the floor to *coupé* and develop the leg into space, imagine your foot painting a colorful line in space to the *devant, à la second* or *derrière* positions.
    - Repeat the above step, but imagine the paint covers your knees and thighs. Then imagine the paint covers your arms. *How does focusing on different body parts change what you feel and sense in your body? How does it affect your technique?*

Teacher exploration 2.1 presents just a few of the many possible exercises and cueing methods to use when exploring balletic movement from different sensory inroads. The activities in *Physically sensing!* expand on this exploration with your students. These activities are easy to integrate into the regular structure of your class.

The intent of *Physically sensing!* is to strengthen your dancers' body awareness when performing balletic movement. This is accomplished primarily through visual imagery and kinesthetic and tactile sensing. Dancers learn how individual body parts move and coordinate with other parts of the body, and how intent in space affects movement efficiency. In later parts of this book, auditory sensing (through listening and vocalizing) is also used to enhance a dancer's body awareness.

Sometimes the activities in *Physically sensing!* require dancers to embody positions that stray from the classical standards or that may be perceived as incorrect. This is part of the learning process! When dancers physically feel the range of motion in their bodies, they are better equipped to discern between one position and the next. This type of knowledge is useful when working with different choreographers. An "incorrect" body position in the ballet technique classroom may be the exact alignment or position a contemporary choreographer is looking for in rehearsals.

Physically sensing!

Objectives:

Deepen the dancers' body awareness when performing balletic movement.
Provide dancers with new tools for embodying balletic steps in different ways.

Activity I: Sensing head and arm positions

Head: Use a downward and sideward focus in a *piqué arabesque* and then an upward and forward focus in the same movement. Or, look upward at the ceiling during a *grand battement* exercise at *barre*. Perform it again looking downward and again looking straight ahead. *How does head positioning affect your balance?*

Arms: Perform a *barre* exercise by placing the *second position port de bras* slightly behind the torso. Perform it again with the arms slightly in front of the torso. *How did arm positioning affect your spinal and rib alignment?*

Perform a *balancé à la second* first with the leading arm moving into *second position*, then into a *demi-second position*, and finally into a *fifth position allongé*. *Which arm positioning did you enjoy the most and why? Where else can you play with head or arm positioning in class?*

Figure 2.2 Explore different *port de bras*

Activity 2: Sensing body parts

Feet: Investigate how to move each part of the foot during different lower body movements, such as *battement tendu* or *sauté*. Or, attend to the sensation of the feet sliding across the floor in *chassé, pas de cheval*, or *glissade*, or sliding up the leg during *sur le cou de pied* or *retiré*.

(Also reference the *glisser* section in Chapter 1)

Hip joints: Explore rotation in the gesturing and supporting hip joints during *rond de jambe* or *battement fondu developpé*. Explore parallel, inward rotation, and finally outward rotation.

(Also reference the *tourner* section in Chapter 1)

Pelvis: Tip the pelvis forward (anterior pelvic tilt) during a balance in *relevé first*. Then tuck the pelvis under (posterior pelvic tilt). Repeat this a few times, each time lessening the amount of tilt until you reach a neutral pelvic alignment. *How does pelvic alignment affect the upper body? How does it change where your weight is distributed in your feet?*

Figure 2.3 Pelvic alignment affects the whole body

Spine: Emphasize the bending, twisting, and arcing of the spine during *épaulment* and *port de bras*. Or, feel the difference between shortening and elongating the spine during a *centre adagio. How do movements of the spine support your technical execution of the exercise?*

Multiple Joints: Notice how reaching the arm forward in *first arabesque port de bras* causes the shoulder blade to slide along the ribs and the spine to rotate slightly. When landing from a jump, notice how the lower body joints "ripple" from the feet to the hips. Or, notice when the pelvis and spine move as the leg lifts into *arabesque. Imaging the body as an accordion, or a fan opening and closing, or as musical notes in a scale are great images for teaching dancers how their movements flow from one body part to the next adjacent body part.*

Activity 3: Sensing through touch

Tripod of the feet: Firmly press into your first and fifth metatarsals with one hand and the inside and outside of the heel bone (calcaneus) with your other hand. Then, release the touch and explore shifting your weight through each of these bony landmarks: 1) shift into the first metatarsal and inside surface of the heel; 2) then to the fifth metatarsal and outside surface of the heel; 3) to the first and fifth metatarsals; and 4) finally to the heel bone. Explore a *battement tendu* exercise at *barre* with this awareness.

With a partner. One dancer applies the touch described above to another dancer's supporting foot. This touch is maintained while the partner performs an exercise at *barre. How do different positions of the gesturing leg (ex. derrière, devant) challenge the tripod sensation in the supporting foot?*

Feeling the shoulder blades (scapulae): Find a partner. Place your hands on your partner's shoulder blades. Maintain this touch as your partner moves the shoulder blades up and down, and together and apart. Continue this touch as your partner performs different *port de bras. What do you notice and feel in your shoulder blades as you move your arms through space?*

Tracing connectivity pathways: Ask the dancers to: 1) trace from the fingers of one hand to the fingers of the other hand passing along the shoulder blades and collarbones (clavicles); 2) trace from the toes of one leg to the fingers of the opposite (or same) arm passing through the torso; 3) trace from the legs up to the top of the head passing along the spine. Focus on one of these pathways throughout *barre* and *centre. How does this connective pathway support your movement in different exercises?*

(Also reference Chapters 7 and 8)

The activities in *Physically sensing!* are not exhaustive. *Add to this table with your own ideas and activities.* After you do this, take a moment to journal about how you facilitate sensory awareness during ballet class.

Teacher exploration 2.2: Journal about your methods

How do your classroom exercises and verbal cueing methods facilitate a ballet dancer's journey into deeper sensory and body awareness?

Personal expression

Expressive movement and artistry go hand in hand. Providing ballet dancers with opportunities to consciously integrate emotional and expressive nuance into the technique class exercises prepares them for the artistic demands they encounter in performances and rehearsals. In both contemporary and classical ballet choreography, dancers are challenged to physically embody specific feelings or emotions in order to illuminate a particular character or to tell a story. Even when the choreography does not include a focus on narrative or character, it is typically important for dancers to convey the overall mood or dynamic quality to the choreography.

While it may seem that personal expression is an automatic process when dancing, ballet teachers know that this is not always the case. I have attended and taught many classes where the students are simply "going through the motions" or performing the vocabulary precisely but not expressively. It is, of course, possible to be both technically precise *and* consciously expressive at the same time—a quality often observed in dancers during performances. When dancers practice expressing different feelings and moods during technique class, they refine their expressive skills and ultimately strengthen their overall body knowledge. Moving luxuriously or excitedly or aggressively, for example, requires different coordination patterns, muscular engagement, movement phrasing, and use of breath.

Moving expressively provides different technical challenges and leads to the development of more refined technique skills.

Dancers often experience different emotions or feelings when they dance and when they watch their peers dance. Dance educator Judith Lynn Hanna writes: "there is a close relationship between *motion* (bodily movement) and *emotion* (feelings). As we move, we move others; in observing others move—we are moved."[4] The quality of the movement—its form, energy, spatial qualities— affect how dancers interpret and understand the movements they are viewing or embodying. For example, fast movements may conjure feelings of excitement or happiness or anticipation. Strong movements may conjure feelings of determination or confidence or celebration.

Asking dancers to reflect on how movements make them feel throughout a technique class is an effective and simple way to facilitate the connection between motion and emotion.

- *What qualitative words do they use to describe different movements?*
- *Do their words and images invoke specific moods or feeling-tones?*
- *Do particular movements conjure different images or emotional associations—a slow and smooth rond de jambe versus a sharp and sudden battement frappé, for example?*

It is also important for dancers to understand how their physical choices—body positioning and use of energy and space—impact the expressive content of their movement.[5] This teaches dancers to perceive balletic movement as meaningful.

Experience this in your body:

How does changing the focus of the head and face change the mood of the movement?

Figure 2.4 Explore different head positions

How do linear arm positions carry different feeling-tones than curved arm positions?

Figure 2.5 Explore linear and curved *port de bras*

How do different levels in space change the feeling-tone of the movement—movements of the limbs that happen at a low level versus a high level, for example? (See Figure 2.2)

How do different movement or musical dynamics (i.e. fast, slow, contained, powerful, soft, etc.) affect the emotional quality of your movement?

Dancers can journal about or verbally discuss their answers to questions, such as these, during class. Listening to other students' responses to these questions is important because there will likely be varied responses among the dancers. This teaches them to interpret the codified vocabulary in personal ways, which facilitates artistic development.

Dancers in my classes are more willing to approach movement expressively in class when I cue and demonstrate movement in expressive ways. There are many ways I do this:

- Asking reflective questions such as those listed on the previous pages.
- Creating stories for my exercises.
- Sharing my images for movements or sharing how different movements make me feel.

- Using varied dynamic tones and sounds in my voice as I demonstrate movement.
- Using characters from story ballets, contemporary ballets, books, or popular culture as inspiration for my exercises in class.[6]

Teacher exploration 2.3: Journal about your methods

How do you verbally or physically demonstrate different moods, feeling-tones, or emotions when teaching balletic phrases in class?

Expressing skills, skillfully expressing! presents four activities for facilitating expressive movement in technique class. I typically use these activities in class when I explore movement dynamics and personal expression with my students. Many activities in Part III: Deepening dynamism also approach balletic movement expressively and emotionally, so the intent of the activities in *Expressing skills, skillfully expressing!* is to simply get started with this investigation. Similar to *Physically sensing!* these activities are easy to integrate into any of your *barre* or *centre* exercises.

Expressing skills, skillfully expressing!

Objectives:

Deepen a dancer's expressive connection to balletic movement.
Strengthen a dancer's ability to imbue movement with feeling and emotion.

Different choice, different expression

Activity 1

1   Teach a *barre* or *centre* exercise to a piece of music that has a clear dynamic tone. (For example, I taught a traveling *balancé/pirouette* to "*Air On the G String*" by Bach.)
2   After the dancers are familiar with the exercise, ask them to: *generate a list of evocative words, images, and feelings for this exercise.*
3   After a few classes, teach the same exercise to a contrasting piece of music. (For example, I taught the same *traveling balancé/pirouette* to *Hungarian Dances: No. 5 in G Minor* by Brahms.) Follow the same reflective process as Step 2.

Activity 2

1   Teach a simple *barre* exercise with non–syncopated, even musical phrasing and subdued movement dynamics.

2   Cue the dancers to: *imagine your favorite color. Imagine that color soaring through your body every time you inhale. It permeates your limbs and torso, filling your body with any images and associations you have with that color. Every time you exhale, imagine that you send that color into space, all around your body. Notice how your limbs trace that color in space.* Encourage the dancers to embody their own dynamics, timing, and rhythm as they perform the exercise with that color in mind. Be prepared to demonstrate an example of this in your own body.

3   When they repeat the exercise on the other side, ask them to follow the same process as above, but with a contrasting color. *What feelings and sensations did each color offer? How did your performance choices change as the color changed?*

Playing with characters

Activity 1

1   Choose one of your favorite characters from a story ballet, book, or movie.

2   Create a list of personality characteristics for that character. Consider the character's posture, emotional and dynamic qualities, use of space, movement patterns, and so on.

3   Create a *centre* exercise that embodies some of the qualities you listed. For example, if your character is bold and confident and enjoys large movement, you might create a *grand allegro* exercise. How does your character inspire your selection of music, balletic steps, and *port de bras* for this *grand allegro*?

Activity 2

Bring props or parts of costumes to class—for example, different hats, capes, hand held props, fabrics, and so on. Props and costumes are playful additions to the classroom environment and tend to create an uplifting mood in class.

•   **Fabric:** encourage the dancers to "wear" the fabric in different ways. They can tie the fabric around different parts of the body or wrap the fabric around their torsos. Fabrics with different textures, colors, and weights inspire different movement qualities. For example, heavy fabric causes my dancers to move with greater force; light-weighted fabric invokes a more ethereal movement quality; brightly colored/patterned fabric tends to promote more "zest" in their movements, and cool colors create a serene movement quality.

- **Hand held props**—scarves, fans, swords, streamers, etc.—expand the dancers' use of space, and in my experience the dancers vary their movement dynamics in order to manipulate the props as they dance.
- **Capes** are exciting to use in class because they create volume around the dancers' bodies. The dancers can play with wrapping themselves into the capes during movements that close inward toward the body and whipping the capes in different directions when their movements expand into space.
- **Hats** inspire different personalities—top hats, pill box hats, large brimmed hats, hats with ostrich feathers, fedoras, funky winter hats, and so on. When your dancers wear hats in class, ask them to: *create a list of personality characteristics for the "person" wearing the hat. Then, incorporate those qualities into 3–5 places during an exercise. Describe the choices you made.*

Similar to the activities in *Physically sensing!* the above activities are not exhaustive. *Add to this table with your own ideas and activities. How else might you explore characters and contrasting movement expressions in class?*

Intent

Intent involves determination and mindfulness. Fulfilling intent requires dancers to learn how to make conscious decisions about what to focus on and experiment with during class. Each ballet dancer demonstrates unique patterns of moving, thinking, and feeling: "the musculoskeletal structure of one dancer is different from that of the next, and every dancer moves in his or her own unique way expressing individual feelings and understanding of technique within the same classical ballet vocabulary."[7] **Since no two dancers are physically or expressively the same, the ballet classroom provides an ideal learning environment for teaching dancers there are many ways to think about and perform the balletic movement.**

A dancer may choose to focus on the upper body during an exercise while another dancer focuses on the lower body. Or, as emphasized in Chapter 1, a dancer may embody the concept of *glisser* during a *developpé devant* while another embodies the concept of *entendre* in the very same step. When dancers have the freedom to perform a movement with a different dynamic quality, one may choose to perform it softly and quickly, while another performs it powerfully and slowly. Dancers also use different images for the same movement, and even when using the same imagery, they imagine and feel it differently in their bodies.

Dancers (of all ages and levels) learn to exercise choice and intent in the ballet class when they are given the opportunity to experiment with the movement concepts, sense their movement in different ways, and interpret movement personally. Dance educator and choreographer Soili Hämäläinen writes: "Sensations and feelings can lead to new movement but movement can also lead to a new sensation and feeling. They work together constantly. They and their interaction form a central source in a creative process."[8]

This process of "developing the skill and discipline to follow through on such inner direction, connects inner sensory awareness with conscious thought."[9] Making choices and following through with those choices teaches dancers about their movement preferences and it deepens their understanding of the balletic style. It also prepares them for the contemporary dance field. Increasingly, choreographers and artistic directors seek dancers who move with clear intent and purpose, know how to work collaboratively, and generate novel ideas during the dance-making process.

Intent is a major theme in *Creative Ballet Teaching*. It was addressed in the last chapter and previous two sections, and continues as a theme in the following chapters. The class activities in this book consistently challenge dancers to ask:

What is my motivation or intent?
What do I want to focus on in this exercise?
What do I see or hear in the space around me?
Who is moving with me in the room?

Designing a classroom environment that increases the dancers' awareness of their motivations and the space around them organizes the body-mind and facilitate their ability to move in space with greater clarity.

Developing improvisation skills

Improvisation is comprehensive tool for developing body knowledge in the ballet technique classroom. As dancers improvise with technique concepts, they strengthen their body awareness, practice personal expression, and learn to make clear movement decisions. Many of the pre-professional ballet dancers in my classes do not initially identify improvisational skills as necessary to ballet training. Improvisation is an activity they associate with studying jazz, hip-hop, and modern/contemporary dance technique styles, likely because they first experienced formal classes in "dance improvisation" when they began studying these technique forms. Some also remember using improvisation as young dancers in Creative Movement classes. So, movement improvisation is also something they associate with dance classes for little kids.

I use improvisation in my ballet technique classes regularly. One challenge I face is convincing students that improvisation benefits their technical and artistic development in ballet. A question I often ask my students is:

Since most ballet dancers receive training in improvisation in other technique styles, is it important to develop improvisational skills in ballet technique classes?

I typically begin this conversation by asking my students to reflect on the importance of improvisational skills during live performances. They improvise when dancers miss entrances and the onstage dancers must "fill in," when there is a mistake in the live or recorded musical accompaniment, when someone gets injured and another dancer has to step in, when a prop or piece of costuming falls off, and so on. In each of these onstage "hiccups," the dancers make intelligent, in-the-moment movement decisions. These scenarios are immediately recognizable to the dancers in my classes, and it does not take long for them to recognize that they do, in fact, make many improvisational choices during live performance.

Good improvisational skills also underpin the artistic decisions dancers make during live performances. Even though dancers perform set choreography similarly from one performance to the next, their performance of the choreography is never the same. Their focus, physical and affective readiness, and understanding of the choreography changes and evolves each time they perform the same piece. In part, this is what makes live performance exciting for the audience members. The audience is also "involved in watching and appreciating the process of improvisational artistry that takes place during a performance-in-progress."[10] Together, the audience and the dance artists participate in an unrepeatable, unfolding sequence of real-time events where anything can happen.

When my dancers and I discuss this aspect of improvisation in performance, I often ask them the following questions:

In what ways do you experiment with your performance during a dance concert?

How does your performance of a piece change spontaneously from one performance to the next?

In his 2000 article, *Improvisation in Dance*, Curtis Carter traced the role improvisation has played in the development of theatre dance. Specifically, in relationship to classical ballet, Carter stated:

Despite the dominance of set choreography in the evolving history of ballet . . . there remained a place for improvisation, most notably in the performances of principal dancers such as Fanny Elssler, Marie Taglioni, and Anna Pavlova, and their successors whose special interpretive gifts allowed for the improvisational embellishments of the ballets in which they performed. Improvisation in the context of the performance of traditional ballet relies primarily upon the dancer's individual display of dramatic character and attitude. It is based on technical virtuosity and the unique features of the dancer's specialized imagination and body.[11]

Improvising with artistic choices during a performance often reveals the performer's unique style, characteristics, and technical strengths. A dancer might linger in a balance a split second longer, attack a movement phrase with more gusto, or accentuate a gesture in order to communicate the emotional content of the piece. In this way, "improvisation allows a performer to share the creation of what is happening and to offer a personal contribution to the performance."[12] When dancers repeat choreography over many performances, it is not uncommon for them to make improvisational performance choices that integrate the choreographer's intent with their own interpretive lens.

So far, this discussion has focused on the importance of improvisational skills in live dance performance. But, there is another reason why developing good improvisation skills in the balletic style are useful to dancers. Increasingly, ballet choreographers employ collaborative and creative methods during the choreographic process. These methods rely on a dancer's ability to improvise with balletic movement as a way to generate choreographic phrases. In reflecting on the methods of George Balanchine and William Forsythe, Carter describes:

> Balanchine's method of working often consisted of creating dance steps "on the spot" in collaboration with his dancers and with the result that his dances might incorporate incidents that occurred spontaneously or even accidentally in the process of testing his concepts ... Other contemporary choreographers have extended the vocabulary and theatrical context for ballet through their experiments with improvisation. William Forsythe . . . combines improvisational movement with "language, song, film, video, sculpture, . . . electronic sounds, as well as amplified noises produced by the dancers."[13]

Many other contemporary ballet choreographers and ballet companies employ improvisational and collaborative choreographic methods with their dancers.[14] It has become commonplace in today's professional dance world. When I choreograph on pre-professional ballet dancers, I rely on their creative contributions to the choreographic process. The dancers improvise with movement ideas in most rehearsals and they use those improvisations to create small movement phrases with their peers. They also have the freedom to experiment with the choreography in different ways from one rehearsal to the next. Their explorations in the balletic style merge with mine, and collaboratively we create contemporary ballet choreography that represents everyone's ideas.

Improvisation as a way to improve technique and artistry

Thus far, we've established that well-developed improvisational skills are important during dance performances and when working with contemporary choreographers. There is, however, an additional benefit for developing a ballet dancer's improvisation skills:

Improvisation helps dancers strengthen their technical and artistic skills and their understanding of ballet.

Before discussing ballet education, let's first explore improvisation in Creative Movement classrooms. I use improvisational dance activities to:

*   promote creative thinking and self-expression;
*   develop new physical skills;
*   teach movement concepts and assess whether or not the students understand them.

So, how does improvisation develop these skills? Here's a brief description of a Shape-focused lesson I often use with Creative Movement students.

I first teach the students different categories of shapes—round, long, big, small, angular, twisted, and so on. We embody these together, and we embody the shapes of different objects found in our dance classroom. We then practice all of these different shapes at different levels and with different body parts. These first improvisational explorations serve to increase the students' physical vocabulary.

Next, I play music and ask the students to improvise freely on their own. As they improvise, I cue them to explore the shapes that we learned and to make new shapes with their bodies. In this way, the improvisation presents the opportunity for them to practice their new movement skills, while also creating shapes that are different from those we practiced at the beginning of class. Finally, the dancers compose short "shape dances." This challenges them to turn their improvisational explorations into movement phrases that can be repeated and shared with others.

Observing Creative Movement students improvise freely to music gives them the opportunity to focus on the concept in their own way and it gives me the opportunity to assess their understanding:

Which shapes do they choose?
How do they use their bodies to make different shapes?
Do they create new shapes or experiment with the shapes in different ways?
Do they play with the shapes at different levels?
And so on.

All of this helps me gather information about which movement skills I need to teach in order for the dancers to embody the shapes clearly and creatively. I might need to teach them how their spines or limbs change shape. Or, we might need to explore different images for the shapes or create stories that accompany our shape dances so they learn how to move expressively when performing and improvising.

Using improvisation as a teaching tool in ballet classes has similar benefits to its use in Creative Movement classrooms. Improvisation is an effective way to help ballet students problem solve about the movement they are learning. According to Dance Educator Jan Erkert, "Improvisation encourages unique movement choices and opens up the movement palette. Improvisation reinforces technique. While technique removes the rough surfaces, improvisation cherishes the coarse textures."[15]

This is especially important as dancers progress to higher and higher levels in ballet. As the technical concepts in ballet class increase in difficulty and specificity, the need to problem solve and experiment with the movement increases. Improvisation provides a balance between structured and unstructured learning, and therefore between specificity and experimentation. The potential for personal discovery is high both technically and artistically.

Take a moment to experience this type of improvisational problem solving in your body.

Teacher exploration 2.4: Improvise with movement concepts

1   Create a short *centre floor* ballet exercise.
2   Perform the exercise a few times until you feel familiar with the sequence.
3   Explore: *Recall Chapter 1. Choose one of the seven traditional movements to focus on. How is that concept embedded in this exercise? How does it support your performance?*

4   The next time you perform the sequence, add approximately 24–32 counts of improvisation at the end to explore the concept you chose in Step 3. Use (or don't use) movements from the exercise as you improvise. You decide!

5   *How did the improvisation support your understanding of the exercise? How did the improvisation support your technique or artistry?*

Improvise with balletic steps! presents improvisation activities to use in class when exploring balletic steps and technical concepts. The activities progress from simple to complex, more restrictive to less restrictive. It is important to begin with simple, highly structured improvisations, especially if improvising during ballet class is new for your dancers.[16]

Improvise with balletic steps! requires knowledge of balletic steps. In my experience, my students' familiarity with the ballet lexicon makes the improvisation less daunting. There are clear physical tasks for them to perform (the balletic steps) and a structured improvisational "score" to follow. Starting with this activity helps students build confidence in their improvisational abilities in ballet.

Improvise with balletic steps!

Objectives:

Deepen a dancer's knowledge of the balletic vocabulary.
Strengthen the dancers' technical execution of the balletic steps.

Preparation: Create and teach a 16–32 count *centre adagio* (one side) to your students.

Note: Any exercise from class may be used for this activity. I chose *grand adagio* as a starting point because the slower tempo lessens the pressure on the dancers to generate a lot of movement during the improvisations.

Foundational balletic steps

1   Ask your students to identify where *battement tendu* occurs in the *grand adagio*: as an actual step or as a movement that another step passes through (e.g., *relevé lent, degagé, temp lié,* and so on).

2   Instruct them to take 16 counts at the end of the *grand adagio* to improvise with *battement tendu* using movements from the *adagio* or playing with *battement tendu* in their own way.

Note: I chose *battement tendu* because it is a foundational balletic step. My dancers often need to revisit how basic steps, such as *battement tendu*, underpin complex movements. I also enjoy focusing on *port de bras* or *developpé* or *promenade*. *What foundational steps do you want to emphasize with your students?*

Categories of balletic steps

1   Ask your students to identify how transition steps are used in the *adagio* (e.g., *glissé, plié, pas de bourrée, tombé, coupé, temps lié, passé*, and so on).
2   Instruct them to take 16 counts at the end of the *adagio* to improvise with the transition steps from the adagio.

Note: I chose transition steps because the students often need opportunities to practice identifying the "in-between" moments in an exercise, especially *adagio*. Any category of balletic steps will work for this activity: preparatory steps, turning steps, *port de bras, grand* or *petite* steps, and so on. *What categories of balletic steps do you want to emphasize with your students?*

Dancer's choice

Ask your students to take 16 counts to improvise with their favorite steps or the most challenging steps from the *adagio*. In either case, encourage them to use the improvisation as an opportunity to explore parts of the *adagio* in their own way.

The following cues may be helpful in all three activities:

*   *You may choose to play with one step repeatedly or multiple steps from the combination. They need not be steps that occur in succession in the exercise.*
*   *You may play with performing the steps with different dynamic qualities— slowing them down or speeding them up; moving them softly or powerfully; performing them with momentum or with greater control.*

The ballet technique class provides the ideal structure for developing improvisation skills. As the above activities demonstrated, it is easy to add 16–32 counts at the end of the exercise for the dancers to improvise with steps or difficult parts of the exercise. As another possibility, dance educator William (Bill) Evans uses improvisation as a way to transition between different groups of dancers in an exercise. The dancers improvise with the "themes" or movement concepts within the exercise as they exit or enter the dance space.[17] This is a fabulous method for teaching dancers how to enter and exit the performance space with mindfulness and creativity.

The next class activities table, *Improvise with movement concepts!* requires knowledge of movement concepts. My dancers initially find these improvisation activities difficult even though they are familiar with the movement concepts we explore. Improvising with movement concepts is a less structured activity because the concept applies to multiple steps. They must therefore generate the steps and physical actions that illuminate the concept in their improvisation. Over time, the dancers appreciate the freedom these activities offer. When first introducing these activities to your students, however, provide them with clear instructions and encourage them to use movements from the class exercises.

Any movement concept may be used in these activities. As a continuation of the explorations in Chapter 1, the following activities challenge the dancers to improvise with the seven traditional movements in ballet.

Improvise with movement concepts!

Objectives:

Deepen a dancer's knowledge of movement concepts applicable to ballet technique. Strengthen the dancers' technical execution of the balletic steps.

Preparation: Any exercise from class may be used, but for the sake of consistency, the following activities use the same *centre grand adagio*.

Seven traditional movements in ballet

Cue your students to improvise with the concept of *relever* for 16 counts at the end of the combination. Play with the qualities of growing, ascending, expanding, and soaring.

Note: Any of the seven traditional movements may be used in the *adagio* improvisation, even *sauter* and *elancer*. *Sauter* promotes experimentations in rebounding and elasticity. *Elancer* promotes a more varied use of movement dynamics.

Dancer's choice

This activity is similar to "Hide and seek with movement concepts" from Chapter 1, except we are now adding improvisation to the activity.

Ask your students: *What are the major concepts embedded in the grand adagio? Which of the seven traditional movements support your performance?* Create a list from their answers. Ask the dancers to: *Choose a concept from the list and improvise with that concept at the end of the adagio.*

Note: This activity works best when your dancers have deepened their knowledge about what movement concepts are, and therefore have a variety of movement concepts to choose from. Parts II and III in this book also present numerous movement concepts to use in class, so return to this activity as you progress through the book.

Options

Ask your students to share key moments from their improvisations with other students in the class. This builds confidence for the dancers who are nervous about improvising. They learn that there are multiple ways to approach the improvisational activities. Sharing in this way also builds the community "bank" of knowledge about movement concepts.

Collectively, the activities in the above tables develop a ballet dancer's technique, understanding of balletic steps, and awareness of how movement concepts support their performance of complex exercises. Additionally, the freedom to improvise with movements on their own provides them with the time and space to practice specific steps and concepts in their own way.

Similar to my experience teaching Creative Movement classes, the above activities are effective methods for assessing the students' understanding of the balletic vocabulary and the supporting movement concepts. As I watch them improvise, I learn what they mentally and physically understand about the balletic steps or technical execution of those steps. I also develop insights into the creative thinking processes they employ when improvising. Finally, I learn how they experiment with movement both technically and expressively. All of this helps me to design future classes that address their technical and artistic needs.

Your dancers will become more expressive and creative improvisers in ballet if they experience consistent exposure to improvisation in class. Improvisational activities, like those described above, deepen concentration and self-perception, and sharpen a dancer's in-the-moment decision-making skills. This facilitates their ability to become more nuanced and expressive ballet artists.

Conclusion

Holistic development of body knowledge influences the focus of the ballet technique class: sensory and perceptual awareness, personal expression, and intentional action become the methods for learning ballet technique and experiencing one's movement potential. Through this approach, students learn how to uniquely perform and interpret the balletic vocabulary, which in turn, enhances their technical skills and capacity for creative self-expression.

Chapter 3 "Drawing inspiration from teachers," builds on the information from Chapters 1 and 2. Deepening your dancers' movement intentionality, technical skills, and potential for creativity continues to be paramount. Chapter 3 also presents new activities and approaches that develop your dancers' creative and critical thinking skills: dancers learn to create movement exercises and use your teaching tools to analyze their movement.

Notes

1   This perspective is also influenced by my practice as a Registered Somatic Movement Therapist with ISMETA and a Certified Laban/Bartenieff Movement Analyst.
2   Henley, M. (2014). Sensation, Perception, and Choice in the Dance Classroom. *Journal of Dance Education*, 14(3): 96.
3   In support of this, Henley states: "Perception, action, and emotion . . . are unified, and, if properly fostered by a dance educator, become a powerful tool for accessing critical thinking through embodied experience." Ibid., p. 96.
4   Hanna, J.L. (2015). *Dancing to Learn: The Brain's Cognition, Emotion, and Movement*. Maryland, MD: Rowman & Littlefield, p. 39.
5   See also: Gilbert, A.G. (1992). *Creative Dance for all Ages*. Reston, VA: The American Alliance for Health, Physical education, Recreation and Dance. Gilbert advises teachers to

> ask your students . . . how moving to certain music makes them feel; how contrasting movements create different feelings; how people feel differently doing the same movement; how people react differently watching the same set of movements and so on . . . share your own feelings, too (p. 46).

6   Reference *Dance the classics!* in Chapter 11.
7   Foster, R. (2010). *Ballet Pedagogy: The Art of Teaching*. Gainesville, FL: University Press of Florida, p. 118.
8   Hämäläinen, S. (2007). The Meaning of Bodily Knowledge in a Creative Dance-Making Process. In L. Rouhiainen (ed.), *Ways of Knowing in Dance and Art*. Helsinki: Theatre Academy, p. 74.
9   Stinson, S. (2004) Lessons from Dance Education. In L. Bresler (ed.), *Knowing Bodies, Moving Minds: Towards Embodied Teaching and Learning*. Dordrecht: Kluwer Academic, p. 157.
10   Bresnahan, A. (2014). Improvisational Artistry in Live Dance Performance as Embodied and Extended Agency. *Dance Research Journal*, 46(1): 88.
11   Carter, C.L. (2000). Improvisation in Dance. *The Journal of Aesthetics and Art Criticism*. 58(2): 183.
12   Biasutti, M. (2013). Improvisation in Dance Education: Teacher Views. *Research in Dance Education*, 14(2): 135.
13   Carter, C.L. (2000), p. 183.
14   Some such companies include: Crystal Pite's *Kidd Pivot*, Alonzo King's *Lines Ballet*, Netherlands Danz Company, Cassa Pancho's *Ballet Black*, Dwight Rhoden's and Desmond

Richardson's *Complexions Contemporary Ballet*, James Hampton's and Ashley Roland's *Body Vox*.

15 Erkert, J. (2003). *Harnessing the Wind: The Art of Teaching Modern Dance*. Champaign, IL: Human Kinetics, p. 15.

16 Biasutti, M. (2013), p. 131.

17 I was exposed to this teaching practice as a guest teacher in the *Bill Evans Dance Teachers Intensives*.

Chapter 3

Drawing inspiration from dance teachers

Teaching students how to use your "tools"

There are many ways ballet dancers deepen their knowledge about ballet and improve their technique skills. They might read books or write about ballet technique, watch live ballet performances, study at summer ballet programs or with guest artists, or take classes in other subjects that support ballet training, such as human anatomy, conditioning, or music theory. One of the best ways to achieve greater knowledge about the discipline, however, is through their daily classes with you. Your students spend numerous hours in the dance studio with you, and this consistent interaction creates the potential for deep and comprehensive learning.

Chapter 3 therefore draws inspiration from us—the dance educators. One thing I have always enjoyed about attending dance education conferences and workshops are the dance educators! It is inspiring to listen to and physically experience another teacher's approaches and methods. It sparks my own curiosities and imagination, which is especially helpful when I feel stagnant in my teaching. Through this process, I acquire new words, images, activities, and methods for teaching ballet.

This chapter therefore explores the following question:

What are our methods, or "tools," for teaching ballet technique?

When I use the word "tools" I am simultaneously referring to the methods, techniques, and activities dance educators use to teach ballet technique. These three things—methods, techniques, and class activities—integrate in important ways, and our students experience that integration during class. If, for example, a teacher values imaginative learning as a method for teaching ballet, it would not be surprising to observe that teacher using imagery or storytelling when teaching exercises and providing feedback to dancers. The students in this class might also embody different characters or personalities when performing the class exercises. Chapter 3 focuses on how teaching tools, such as these, enrich your students' understanding of ballet technique.

In the Introduction, I presented the subject-centered teaching model, and explored how this model requires students to "step up" and learn how to think, act, and create like ballet teachers. Think about this a moment: *didn't you become a better dancer when you began to teach ballet to others?* I know I certainly did. I experienced technical and artistic growth as I practiced communicating my knowledge of ballet to my students. Your students will experience similar benefits. Chapter 3 therefore also explores the following question:

How do students learn to use the teacher's "tools" to direct their own learning and coach their peers?

Identifying our teaching tools

I imagine, like many dance educators, your "bag" of teaching tools is large. I know mine is. The dancers in my classes learn in a myriad of ways, and as a result, I must use a myriad of methods, techniques, and activities when teaching ballet technique. *What tools do you use when teaching ballet technique to your students?*

Do you use imagery, or anatomical cues, or rhythmical sounding and singing?
Do you tell stories or use poetry or inspirational quotes?
Do you improvise or experiment with movement concepts?
Do you ask students to work with each other during class?
Do you draw on knowledge from other disciplines?
Do you use touch or visual tools, such as photographs or videos or props?

Styles
of
Teach-
ing

It is not until the end of technique class that I become aware of the energy I exerted while teaching. It is in this first quiet moment, after the dancers have left the dance studio, when I begin to feel the subtle (or sometimes not so subtle) fatigue seep into my muscles and vocal chords. For me, this fatigue is usually positive, an outcome of using my body and voice actively throughout class.

A dance teacher's demonstrations and explanations are the most common ways students learn how to perform ballet technique. These are two of our most important teaching tools. According to dance educator Tanja Råman, physical demonstration, in particular, helps dancers "gain a large amount of information about a movement within a short period of time ... [and] create a mental image of the movement that can be used to self-monitor the performance of a particular skill."[1] Simply put, dancers capture the physical essence of the movement through our demonstrations.

I have taken classes from numerous ballet teachers of varying ages and physical abilities, and physical demonstration was essential in all of them. Even when a teacher's range of motion was limited, his/her body and gestures conveyed important information about movement qualities, body facing, musicality, and sequencing. The importance of physical demonstration to the experience of learning ballet is one reason why this book emphasizes embodied exploration in many of the teacher exploration activities. Your physical and expressive development is just as important as the students'.

Dance teachers also use varying sounds and words to explain movement concepts and provide feedback to their dancers. We describe the actions of the body, voice the musical counts, use balletic and anatomical vocabulary, verbally analyze technique concepts, convey imagery, sound rhythmically, sing with the musical phrasing, and so on. And, usually we integrate these "tools" of the voice with our physical demonstrations in order to provide the dancers with a more layered understanding of technique concepts, movement sequencing, and artistic nuance.

As you know, different dance teachers demonstrate movement and explain ideas in the different ways. This is the joy of experiencing someone else's technique class! You are exposed to new ideas and artistic influences. So, experiment with the many ways you convey your understanding of ballet to your dancers. Additionally, physical demonstration and verbal explanations are not the only tools we use to teach ballet. For example, I also use touch, props (i.e. balls, scarves); visual media (i.e. photographs, videos); and writing (i.e. group concept mapping, journaling) in my classes; and when planning my classes, I spend time designing exercises and experimenting with movement, two teaching tools that help me create artistically and technically challenging classes for my students.

example   Table 3.1 lists many of the teaching techniques and methods mentioned in the previous paragraphs. This is not an exhaustive list, however. As you read this list, think about what's missing. *What would you add?*

Table 3.1 Sample list of teaching tools

Analyzing technique concepts
Describing the actions of the body
Designing exercises ✓
Group concept mapping
Imagery ✓
Journaling ✓
Movement experimentation
Physical demonstration ✓
Props ✓
Providing verbal and touch feedback to dancers
Rhythmical sounding
Singing the musical phrasing
Speaking the musical counts
Using specific vocabulary (i.e. balletic, anatomical) ✓
Watching videos that illustrate movement concepts

Before moving on to the next section, journal about some of the teaching tools you use to teach ballet technique.

Teacher exploration 3.1: Journal about your teaching tools

List five of your favorite teaching tools (activities, methods, and/or techniques).

Why do you use them?
When do you use them?
How do they assist your teaching of ballet?

Teaching students to use our tools

Many of the students who take my upper-level ballet classes are skilled at learning exercises quickly, attuning to musicality, and applying my feedback to their dancing. They are, however, less skilled at experimenting with movement concepts on their own, and they tend to rely on my feedback in order to initiate technical and artistic changes in their dancing. So, one question I have explored over the years is:

How do I help students develop the skills to direct their own learning?

Learning how to use the teacher's methodological tools is one way to develop these skills. It increases their movement literacy and body knowledge and diversifies their self-coaching strategies. In my own experience, my knowledge about ballet (and about movement, in general) developed as I explored different methods for teaching ballet technique. I learned how to communicate my understanding of ballet technique and performance in different ways, which expanded my problem-solving skills and cueing methods when coaching dancers. It also enhanced my ability to assess my own movement patterns and technique skills. **Simply put: as I developed my ability to communicate my knowledge to others, I increased my capacity to direct my own learning.**

As students learn to engage in the same critical thinking processes we engage in as dance educators, they too will learn to ask and answer the following questions:[2]

- *Why do I execute certain exercises and movements in ballet class? What are they for and what do I feel when I perform them?*
- *What strategies or methods do I use inside and outside of class to develop my understanding of class exercises and concepts?*
- *How do I use different learning approaches to practice the same movements? How do I experiment or "play" with balletic movements in different ways?*

These questions may sound similar to the questions you pose to yourself when planning your classes, problem solving about how to explain technique concepts to your students, and investigating new ways to approach the class exercises. Consequently, you have developed (or are developing) many teaching "tools" and strategies for addressing these questions, and you have likely deepened your ability to communicate your intentions to your students.

Your students, on the other hand, will have difficulty answering these questions until they acquire their own tools and strategies for doing so.[3] This happens as they develop a broad knowledge base about ballet technique and more diverse problem-solving strategies for improving their technical and artistic skills.[4]

Table 3.2 includes a sample list of ten teaching tools I use regularly in the classroom and describes how my students also use those tools to explore ballet technique. Using these tools ensures that my students experiment with different ways to think about and perform the movement, as well as engage comprehensively in the movement exercises.

All ten tools listed in Table 3.2 are explored throughout this book. Teaching tools 4, 9, and 10 are discussed in greater detail below. Before moving on to that discussion, however, take a moment to explore how your students actively use your teaching tools.

Teacher exploration 3.2: Journal about how students use your teaching tools

Recall the five teaching tools you wrote about in Teacher exploration 3.1.
   How do your students use these tools to direct their learning or coach their peers during technique class?

Table 3.2 Ten teaching tools students can use in ballet class

Tools the teacher uses to teach ballet	Students use the teacher's tools to deepen their understanding of ballet
1. Musicality and rhythm	Students generate their own rhythms and timing for specific exercises or change the rhythms and timing in the exercises you created. See Chapter 6 for more ideas about musicality and rhythm.
2. Anatomical cueing	Students identify specific muscles or bony landmarks on their bodies, or explore the actions of a joint or muscle during an exercise. Chapters 7 and 8 explore basic anatomical knowledge.
3. Acting and role-playing	Students create characters, scenarios, narratives, or stories for the class exercises. Part III: Deepening dynamism explores this.
4. Imagery and metaphor	Students create their own images or metaphors for movements and they embody different images for the same movements. This idea is discussed below and throughout this book.
5. Applying knowledge from another field	Students apply concepts from another dance style (i.e. jazz, modern, hip-hop), or from another discipline (i.e. Yoga, Alexander Technique), to their performance of ballet technique. Applying Laban Movement Analysis to ballet is the focus of Chapters 5–14.
6. Reflection	Students reflect on their own movement or a peer's movements verbally in class or through journaling and drawing. Student reflection is explored throughout this book.
7. Providing feedback	Students provide a peer with affirmations and suggestions during class. This is the primary focus of Chapter 4.
8. Dynamic sounding or singing	Students create their own sound and song cueing for steps, or experiment with different sounds for the same step. See Chapters 6, 8 and 10 for more information about dynamic sounding/singing.
9. Movement experimentation	Students experiment with different ways to perform an exercise or step. This idea is discussed below and throughout this book.
10. Designing exercises	Students practice creating movement exercises individually and together. This idea is discussed below and in subsequent chapters.

Teaching tool #4: Imagery and metaphor

Imagery and metaphor are essential to the artistic experience of learning dance. As dance educators, we use imagery poetically to emphasize specific technique and performance principles:

The grand battement is a gust of wind!
Your arms are fluffy clouds floating from one shape to the next.
The supporting leg sends deep roots into the earth during the developé devant.
Your center is the sun and its light radiates from the center through each limb.
Fill the space with color as your limbs "paint" the space around you.
Your arms and torso expand into the space like peacock feathers as you move your
    arms into second position port de bras.

In these examples, the images and metaphors enhance the dancer's connection to the dynamic, expressive, and subtle qualities of dance technique. The first image encourages the embodiment of force and momentum in a *grand battement*, whereas voluminous delicacy is inspired in the second image. The third and fourth images promote grounded stability. The fifth and sixth images encourage an interactive relationship between the dancer's body and the space around the body.

Different imagery creates a different kinesthetic experience. *Take a moment to explore this on your own in Teacher exploration 3.3.*

Teacher exploration 3.3: Play with imagery

Embody the list of images at the beginning of this section.

Questions:

*   How did each image affect your technical execution of the steps or movements?
*   How did each image affect your expressive execution of the steps or movements?

Alter the imagery:

The grand battement is a rubber band that stretches in and out.
Your arms are bouncy balls rebounding from one shape to the next.
The supporting leg is perched upon a fluffy cloud during the developpé devant.
Your center is a pinwheel of energy spiraling outward to each limb.

Your limbs are submerged in water as you move in space.
Your arms and torso condense like a shrinking balloon as you move your arms
    into second position port de bras.

Questions:

- How did the technical or artistic quality of the movement change as you embodied these new images?
- How did your personal connection to each movement change?

Next, reflect on the imagery you use with your students. *Why do you use those images? How do they support the technical and artistic goals you have for your students?*

Teacher exploration 3.4: Analyze the imagery you use in the classroom

List three of your favorite images you regularly use in the classroom. Then, write about how these images support the technical and artistic concepts you explore with your students.

Example:

Image #1:_____

Technical/artistic concepts: _____

When you use the images from Teacher exploration 3.4 in class, your dancers likely embody the movement with greater clarity. It is also likely that their embodiment varies. In Salosaari's research with ballet dancers, "images offered tools for intentionality in the formal ballet vocabulary, suggesting what could be engaged with in the dance, but did not impose a pre-determined end product."[5] She noted that a dancer "embodies the image and pays attention to it in a personal way."[6] I often observe this in my classes. My dancers make different movement choices when I use an image that can be applied to any part of the body or anywhere in the exercise. And, even when my imagery is step or body specific, they make different qualitative choices to physically express the image. I enjoy watching the variety of physical responses in my dancers' movements. When I notice these differences, I often ask each dancer to demonstrate to the entire class how they embodied the image. As they watch each other, they learn that there are different ways to perform the movement correctly. This is a fundamental realization for them, one that underpins their artistic development.

Sometimes the imagery I use in class creates physical responses that are counterproductive to the technical and artistic goals I am working on with my dancers. When this happens, I share more than one image for the same technical or artistic goals. It is for this same reason I enjoy using Dance Educator Eric Franklin's books with my students.[7] Students enjoy sifting through the multitude of images he offers in his texts and choosing those images that seem to impact their technique the best.

Since images affect each dancer uniquely, the use of more than one image illuminates the same technical and artistic goals in different ways for different dancers. I therefore collect a "bank" of images for the same technique concept. Over time this has diversified my verbal cueing. Take a moment to practice creating your own imagery "bank" in Teacher exploration 3.5.

Teacher exploration 3.5: Create different images for the same concept

Reference the technical and artistic concepts you listed for each image in Teacher exploration 3.4. Generate three more images for each concept so that you have a "bank" of images to use for those technical and artistic goals.

Example:

Technique or artistic concept #1:_____

    Image: _____

    Image: _____

    Image: _____

Now that you have brainstormed about your use of imagery in class, let's explore how your students learn to use this teaching tool. Dancers learn how to think in increasingly imaginative, intentional, and meaningful ways about ballet technique as they practice generating their own images during class. According to dance educator Eeva Antilla, "listening to the body and deriving meanings from bodily experiences [something which imagery facilitates] can support young dance students' self-understanding and personal growth as dancers, artists and human beings."[8] Creating images during technique class is an easy and fun way for dancers to connect their bodily experiences to their performance of the balletic vocabulary:

Begin this process by simply asking the dancers to share an image for a movement that you have been exploring in class. If this process is new for them, first provide them with one or two images that you created. Then, ask them to practice the movement using those images. Finally, ask for volunteers to contribute a new image for the movement. In most cases, at least one person in the class will share an image.

Since images illuminate performance qualities and technique principles in different ways, it is productive to ask students to verbally share the images they generate during class. Each image contributes to the collective knowledge of the class, and teaches students to approach the vocabulary and technique concepts from different perspectives. My students often come up with images that are specific to their generation (i.e. references to popular culture, songs, or products). Using images like these may be more tangible to their peers and therefore more helpful in improving overall understanding of the balletic concepts. Some of your students will struggle with generating images for balletic movements. This is normal. This is another reason why it is important for students to share their images out loud. Doing so will help the less confident students gain confidence over time.

Different image, same movement! presents a simple and quick imagery activity to use in class. This activity focuses on imagery and metaphor, but I often ask students to embody "characters" or "stories" too. This is especially fun for younger dancers.

Different image, same movement!

Objective:

Dancers learn to generate images as a way to enhance their technique and artistry.

Ask 3–5 students to share an image for the same movement or movement phrase in an exercise. Each time a student shares an image, instruct the entire class to perform the movements to that image.

Example: *grand rond de jambe en dehors*

Student 1: *I imagine red finger paint on my head, fingers, and toes. As I perform the grand rond de jambe en dehors I imagine I am painting the space with red paint.*

This image facilitates active reaching into space through the distal ends. It also helps the students feel the forward weight shift in the upper body, neck, and head as the leg and arm move from *à la seconde* to the *arabesque* position. I sometimes instruct students to imagine paint on their knees, elbows, hips and shoulder joints. This promotes greater activation of the entire limbs (arms and legs) into space (explored further in Chapter 7).

Student 2: *My legs and arms are snowflakes. As I perform the grand rond de jambe en dehors I imagine a soft winter breeze is blowing the snowflakes through the space.*

This image facilitates a light and buoyant quality in the arms and legs and an easeful sweeping of the legs and arms through the space. This may be especially useful for students who "muscle" their arms and legs through the space when they perform this movement (explored further in Chapters 10 and 11).

Student 3: *I imagine my gesturing leg is gliding across the top of a table as I move toward the arabesque.*

This image facilitates a clear pathway for the leg as it moves from *devant* to *à la seconde* to *derrière*. This is helpful for students who experience difficulty maintaining the level of the leg in space (explored further in Chapter 8).

Ask them: *How did each image change the technical and artistic demands of the movement?*

Teaching tool #9: Movement experimentation

Challenging students to experiment with movement and technique concepts is a fundamental focus of this book. *In what ways do you experiment with movement as you create exercises for your students?* Take a moment to journal about this in Teacher exploration 3.6.

Teacher exploration 3.6: Journal about movement experimentation

• How do you experiment with movement as you create your balletic exercises?

Examples: Do you play with musicality and rhythm? Or, perhaps you experiment with the sequencing of balletic steps? Or, maybe you play with different images?

- Journal about why you experiment with movement in these ways. *What are your goals? What are you attempting to discover or achieve?*

I constantly experiment with movement when I create exercises for my ballet technique classes. My choices are dependent on the technical and artistic goals I have for a particular class or a larger curricular unit. I play with using different musical timing, movement phrasing, dynamic qualities, and *port de bras* for the steps in the exercises. I also experiment with different transition steps to use in between larger steps (i.e. using a *pas de bourée* versus a *chassé* or a *pas de basque*), and I make choices about the larger steps to include in the exercises (i.e. a *cabriole* versus a *jeté entrelacé* versus a *fouetté en tournant*). Experimenting with balletic movement in this way teaches me about the stylistic and technical nuances of the art form.

Students, too, can experiment with the timing, dynamics, or phrasing of an exercise, or they might simply apply a concept from class to the exercise in their own way. In these approaches, the steps in an exercise often remain the same, but the students play with *how* the steps are performed (see also: Chapter 1 class activities). When experimenting with technique concepts, for example, one student might explore the concept of *glisser* as they perform an across-the-floor waltz while another student explores the concept of *entendre*. When experimenting with dynamics, movements that were controlled may be performed with momentum, and those phrased quickly may become sustained. When experimenting with movement phrasing, what used to be one movement phrase—a *développé croisé devant* into a *chassé en arrière* into a *piqué arabesque*—may become two phrases—the *développé devant* is held in a balance and the *chassé* and *piqué arabesque* are still linked. Ultimately, these approaches teach students to use the methods of experimentation and curiosity to initiate technical and artistic changes in their dancing.

Learning how to experiment with movement is also important to use artistically during rehearsals and performances. For example, I often ask dancers to manipulate the movement phrasing or dynamics in a solo. This may result in their decision to linger in a balance or to perform a series of movements with a syncopated rhythm. I also encourage them to do this during live performances when I know they have interpretive liberty with their artistic choices. Learning to play with movement in this way provides dancers with opportunities to increase their artistic sensitivity when performing set choreography and leads them to develop sophisticated performance skills. This is a fundamental focus of Part III: Deepening dynamism.

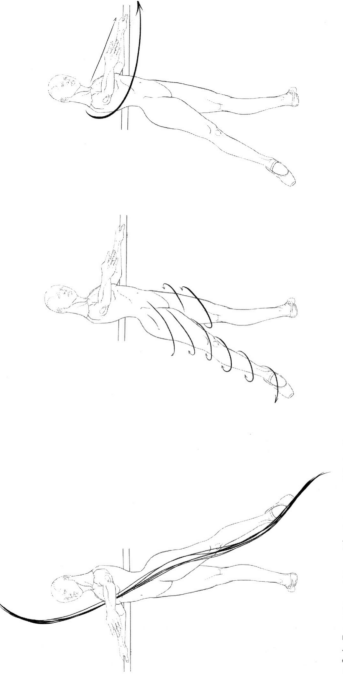

Figure 3.1 Experimenting with movement intent

Since movement experimentation involves the ability to make purposeful, conscious decisions about movement, it is also a good method to use for developing body knowledge. *Experimenting with movement propensities* presents two approaches for exploring this in your classes.

Experimenting with movement propensities

Objective:

Dancers recognize and broaden their movement patterns and preferences.

Experiment with movement preferences

Ask your students to brainstorm about their favorite parts of ballet class. Here are some examples of questions to ask:

General questions: *What are your favorite parts of class or favorite exercises or steps to perform? Why are those your favorite?*

Specific questions: *Do you like to travel or stay in place? Do you like small or large movements? What parts of your body do you like to use to express your movements (i.e. eyes, face, arms, legs, torso, etc.)? Do you like fast or slow movements? Do you enjoy movements that are controlled or unrestricted? Do you like to move powerfully or delicately?*

After they generate a list of personal movement preferences, ask them to experiment with those preferences during an exercise.

Examples:

If they enjoy movements that travel, ask them to amplify the traveling movements during *barre* exercises.

If they enjoy movements that are powerful, ask them to experiment with powerful and firm movement dynamics throughout class.

If they like using their arms, head, face when performing, ask them to explore the expressive use of their upper body throughout class.

Experiment with movement challenges

Ask your students to brainstorm about movements or parts of class they struggle with. Use the following questions to get them started. Also reference the "specific questions" above.

General questions: *What do you struggle with in class? What steps, exercises, or technique concepts are difficult for you? What movement qualities or technique concepts challenge your habitual movement patterns? What movements make you feel uncomfortable, silly, or vulnerable?*

Next, ask them to experiment with their list of movement challenges during specific exercises from class. *Note:* This activity typically works best when they are familiar with the exercises.

Examples:

If they avoid movements that are gentle and soft, ask them to experiment with these movement dynamics during a *grand battement* exercise.

If they avoid paying attention to small or subtle movements, ask them to emphasize the enclosing of the arms or legs during an *adagio*. Or, possibly this student emphasizes the *battement tendu* before *relevé lent* or the *sur le cou-de-pied* before the leg lifts into *passé*.

If they avoid changing the focus of the head and eyes when performing, ask them to experiment with different foci during exercises throughout class.

Many of the class activities presented in the following chapters use movement experimentation as a primary approach for developing body awareness, intent, and artistry. Dancers of all ages and levels will learn to exercise choice and autonomy in the ballet class when they are given the opportunity to experiment with the movement themes within a particular class. As dancers learn to follow through with their movement choices, they develop greater intentionality.

Teaching tool #10: Designing exercises

Creating sophisticated movement exercises is a primary activity for dance educators. Well-designed exercises typically contain:

- *focus*, to effectively introduce dancers to new vocabulary and steps;
- *rigor*, to challenge dancers to refine their technical skills;
- *creativity*, to teach dancers how to sequence movements together in different ways and to provide new technical challenges;
- *artistic nuance*, to diversify the dancers' expressive range and to provide them with different artistic challenges.

I use these four categories to analyze the ways in which my exercises provide dancers with different artistic and technical challenges. Do my exercises contain different musical rhythms and movement dynamics? Do they introduce the dancers to new ballet vocabulary or new ways of using the vocabulary? Do they challenge the dancers' neuromuscular patterns?

Take a moment to explore and analyze the exercises you create for your students in Teacher exploration 3.7. *In what ways do your exercises challenge your students to develop as artists and technicians?*

Teacher exploration 3.7: Analyze your class exercises

Think about a new or less practiced balletic step you want to use in class with your students. For this exploration, choose a step you use in center combinations—a *jeté entrelacé, sissonne ouverte, pirouette attitude derrière en dedans*, or *fouetté rond de jambe en tournant*, for example.

1   *Focus*: In what ways do your *barre* or *centre* exercises prepare dancers for this step? How do you build up to the new vocabulary throughout class?

2   *Rigor*: How do you change the way you practice this step in subsequent classes? Do you change how your exercises prepare the dancers for the step, or does the preparation remain similar from class to class? In what ways do you deepen the exploration?

3   *Creativity*: How do your *barre* and *centre* exercises use the step in different ways? You might experiment with the steps that come before and after this step. Or, you might change how the step is used in the exercises—it might reverse, or be performed *en dedans* instead of *en dehors*, or face a different direction.

4   *Artistic nuance*: Do your exercises challenge the dancers to embody the step with different movement dynamics or musical rhythms? Do you use imagery? Observe how the step is performed in contemporary or classical ballet choreography, and incorporate those expressive qualities in your class exercises.

Challenging students, including younger dancers, to create their own movement exercises or movement phrases within the class period is an effective way to assess their understanding of ballet technique:

Do they know how to create movement phrases that explore specific balletic steps?
Do they know how to link those steps together in different ways?

> *Do they know how to create dynamic, expressive, and rhythmically diverse movement phrases?*

For example, when I assess my students understanding of:

- *Balletic steps and vocabulary,* I instruct them to create exercises that focus on balletic categories from class—creating a *barre* exercise or a turning or jumping combination, for example—or on particular balletic steps—creating an exercise that explores *grand battement* or *pirouette*, for example.
- *A technique concept*—efficient use of turn out, for example—I instruct them to create a *barre* or *centre* exercise that explores the rotation of the hip joints during various steps and positions.
- *An artistic concept*—embodying a character when they dance, for example—I instruct them to create a *barre* or *centre* exercise with a particular character or personality in mind.

Creating ballet exercises! explores these three approaches. Asking students to create movement exercises takes up time in class. So, it is important to identify when in the curriculum this is necessary and how much movement you are asking the students to create. For example, if I am pressed for time, I sometimes ask students to simply create 4–8 counts of set movement to include at the end of an exercise. Or, instead of *reverence*, I sometimes ask students to create 8–16 counts of movement that parallels something we focused on in class that particular day. This option is particularly useful if I need to assess their understanding of the class concepts. *Creating ballet exercises* provides both simple and complex options to use in class.[9]

Creating ballet exercises

Objective:

Dancers demonstrate their knowledge of ballet technique and artistry as they create barre and centre exercises.

"Add a pearl" ... how to string together balletic steps

This activity requires students to create exercises by stringing together balletic steps. For example, in a *battement tendu* at *barre*, ask one student to come up with the first 4 counts of movement. Then, the next student adds on 4 more counts. They continue "Adding a pearl" of 4 counts until every student has contributed movement to the exercise. This is a fun and simple way to create exercises for any part of class. My students especially enjoy the "Add a pearl" activity for traveling turns from the corner.

Simple application: If my class is large, the students take turns creating the movement—8 students create the exercise (32 counts) one day and then 8 more the next day, and so on.

How a movement concept becomes an exercise

Part I: Brainstorming. Students must understand the movement concepts you are exploring in class in order to successfully create exercises based on those concepts. Therefore, first ask them to brainstorm as a class about a movement category. For example, when I explore technique of the lower body in class, I ask my students to share what they know about using the lower body in ballet technique. Many ideas are generated: efficient use of turn out, articulation of the feet, alignment, propulsion, the seven traditional balletic movements, and so on.

Part II: Choose a concept. If this activity is new to your dancers, choose one idea to explore from the brainstorming process: for example, everyone explores *entendre*. If they are used to this activity, however, ask them to choose their own criteria from the brainstorming discussion. One dancer might explore propulsion while someone else explores *plier* as a concept, and so on.

Part III: Choose a common exercise, musical meter, and tempo for the exercise. Do you want the students to create a *rond de jambe* at barre or a *centre adagio*? Or, possibly a *petite allegro* or a *port de bras* exercise? Since each dancer is creating movement individually, deciding on a common exercise, musical meter, and tempo keeps the class more organized. Make sure the music is playing as they create their exercises.

Part IV: Create the exercise. I ask the students to create a 16–32 count exercise. The number of counts depends on the exercise. If it's a *petite allegro*, for example, 16 counts is likely sufficient. If it's an *adagio*, 32 counts may be more appropriate.

Part V: Perform the exercises. The students practice their exercises during the next 2–3 classes. It is fun to have them perform their exercises in small groups (even if it is a *barre* exercise) so that they have the opportunity to observe each other's exercises.

Simple application: If you are pressed for time, ask your students to create a shorter phrase of movement (8 counts). Or, ask them to add 8 counts of movement to the end of an exercise you already taught them.

Using a character to create an exercise

Repeat the same 5-step process used in Activity 2. But, instead of focusing on a technique concept, ask the students to explore a character when creating their exercises. During Part I: Brainstorming, ask the class to brainstorm about a character. I often choose one from a classical or contemporary ballet they are familiar with, but you may find they also enjoy brainstorming about a character from popular culture. Then, generate evocative language to describe the character. For example:

Is the character demanding or passive? Gentle or powerful? Indirect or straightforward? What parts of the body and facial expressions does this character utilize? Is this character a large or small mover? Does the character travel or stay in one place?

There are many questions you can ask your students when thinking about characters. Students are quite good at generating answers to these questions, especially if they have watched or performed story or theatrical ballets. Once they have generated ideas, images, and evocative words for the character, ask them to begin using those images and words to create their exercises.

Conclusion

The activities and concepts presented in this chapter challenge students to engage reflectively, imaginatively, and decisively throughout the technique class. Learning to use the teacher's methodological tools is an easy subject-centered approach for developing a student's depth of knowledge and creative potential. According to educational researcher Mike Radford:

If we are to encourage creative intelligence, pupils need to be given the opportunity to generate new explanations, new constructions, new ideas and forms for expression . . . They need to be given the opportunities to think, hypothesize, and "play" at the boundaries of sense.[10]

When students are given opportunities to generate their own images, experiment with movement, and create movement exercises during class, they develop a more comprehensive understanding of the balletic style.

While this chapter focused on how students use your methodological tools to direct their own learning, the next chapter explores how they use these tools to educate each other. *How do students inspire each other? And, how are we, as dance educators, inspired by the knowledge our students generate during class?*

Notes

1 Råman, T. (2009). Collaborative Learning in the Dance Technique Class. *Research in Dance Education*, 10(1): 78.
2 Ibid., p. 77. Råman asks: "should not efficient dance technique training actively encourage dance students to engage in the movement material and to explore and to question how they perform it?"
3 See also: Bailin, S., Case, R., Coombs, J.R., and Daniels, L.B. (1999). Common Misconceptions of Critical Thinking. *Journal of Curriculum Studies*, 31(3): 285–302. According to Balin et al. "critical thinking is not promoted simply through the repetition of 'skills' of thinking, but rather by developing the relevant knowledge, commitments and strategies and, above all, by coming to understand what criteria and standards are relevant" (p. 280).
4 Ibid., pp. 281–282. The researchers note

> a variety of means may be employed [by the educator] to promote such development, including direct instruction, teacher modeling, creation of an educational environment where critical inquiry is valued and nurtured, and provision for students of frequent opportunities to think critically about meaningful challenges with appropriate feedback.

5 Salosaari, P. (2001). *Multiple Embodiment in Classical Ballet: Educating the Dancer as an Agent of Change in the Cultural Evolution of Ballet.* Helsinki: Theatre Academy, p. 82.
6 Ibid., p. 82.
7 Eric Franklin's research focuses on the use of imagery in understanding anatomy, dance technique, and dance performance. Readers are encouraged to reference Franklin's *Dance Imagery for Technique and Performance*, 2nd edn. (2013) and *Dynamic Alignment through Imagery*, 2nd ed. (2012) for more information and guidance about the use of dance imagery when teaching technique classes.
8 Anttila, E. (2007). Mind the Body Unearthing the Affiliation Between the Conscious Body and the Reflective Mind. In L. Rouhiainen (ed.), *Ways of Knowing in Dance and Art*. Helsinki: Theatre Academy, p. 96.
9 "Add a pearl" is an activity I experienced in my L/BMA Certification Training. My colleague Janice Meaden used this activity to teach students how to create Bartenieff Fundamentals movement sequences.
10 Radford, M. (2004). Emotion and Creativity. *Journal of Aesthetic Education*, 38(1): 63.

Chapter 4

Drawing inspiration from dance students

Learning from peers

During live performances, dancers move and interact with other dancers, physically communicate to multiple audience members, and act as their own teachers. During technique class, however, dancers typically stand as "soloists" facing the same direction during *barre* and *centre* exercises and maintain focus on their own bodies even when traveling across the floor with other dancers. Their performance energy is directed toward imaginary audiences at the front of the room with the teacher and the mirror serving as more tangible audience members.

How do we, as teachers, design a class structure that parallels and prepares dancers for the communicative and relational aspects of theatrical performance?

Using peer interaction and education during the technique class is one way to achieve this.

Peer education promotes critical thinking and enhanced body awareness during the technique class, and it is a fundamental component to creating a collaborative subject–centered classroom. As your students develop body knowledge (Chapter 2) and become more familiar with using your methodological tools in the classroom (Chapter 3), they develop foundational understanding needed for effective collaborative learning with their peers. While Chapter 3 focused on developing collaborative learning approaches between you and your students, this chapter focuses on teaching students how to collaborate with each other during the technique class.

Effective peer engagement teaches dancers how to be more physically and verbally intentional, relational, and communicative. Dance educator Tanja

Råman notes that collaborative work among peers acts "as a motivator, stimulating students' curiosity and encouraging them to work harder," and broadens their "experience by serving as a source of self-awareness."[1] When students share their observations with each other, they learn there are multiple ways to think about the technique exercises; this deepens their understanding of the balletic vocabulary and it confirms that their movement choices are stylistically varied and communicate different feeling-tones and attitudes.[2] As dance educator Sondra Fraleigh notes: even though "a dance usually has an objective, repeatable structure (it can be performed by several people), it is subject of individual interpretation and dependent upon the individual body aesthetic of the particular dancer."[3]

Peer interaction requires student dancers to become active participants in the learning process. Of course, when observing your dancers in class, it may seem as though they are already physically and mentally "active." After all, learning and executing the balletic exercises requires complex mind-body concentration, coordination, and problem-solving skills. This type of physical and mental engagement provides a good foundation for more fully invested, active learning among your dancers. The active learning approaches in this chapter challenge students to also become producers, not just reproducers, of knowledge in the classroom. In order for this to happen, students must develop their skills as autonomous and creative thinkers and movers.

The following pages present a series of methods and activities for developing your students' peer education and interaction skills. There are, of course, many ways to do this.[4] Before reading further, take a moment to reflect on the methods you already employ in your classes.

Teacher exploration 4.1: Journal about peer interaction in your classes

How do students interact with each other during your classes?

Developing communication skills

Effective communication is necessary in peer education. There are many ways dancers develop their communication skills during ballet class. They might:

- verbally answer questions posed by the teacher;
- share their artistic or technical intentions for an exercise with a peer;
- generate images or stories for movement exercises;
- write about their movement experiences in a journal.

Take a moment and add to this list: *What other methods do you employ to develop your students' communication skills during ballet class?*

- _____
- _____
- _____

Dance educator Dale Johnston highlights the importance of personal reflection and verbal communication during ballet class because it helps "organise and integrate many disparate aspects of children's functions, such as perception, memory and problem solving."[5] Johnston's research cites the importance of incorporating many forms of personal and social communication in ballet classes. Some examples include: private speech, journal writing, drawing, group concept mapping of technique concepts, verbal communication and other forms of social communication, such as sign language. Encouraging students to use communicative and reflective learning methods, such as these, *during* the technique class not only develops the students' knowledge of ballet technique but it also provides them with a foundational skill-set needed for peer-to-peer learning.

Dance educator Gretchen Alterowitz uses "speaking and guided inquiry projects" in the ballet classroom as an assessment tool, noting that these types of "projects offer students different ways of exhibiting knowledge and engagement with class material than physical demonstration, which is generally students' only means of transmitting understanding in a ballet technique class."[6] Guided inquiry projects and speaking about technique concepts with peers are useful for all students, but especially for those students who struggle with physically reproducing the exercises. These types of activities provide opportunities for teachers to assess their students' cognitive understanding of the technical and artistic concepts from class, regardless of their ability to physically reproduce the material. Ultimately, however, when dancers deepen their cognitive understanding about the body and movement and learn how to communicate that understanding to others, they develop greater movement intentionality and clarity. As teachers of ballet, this shouldn't be surprising! *Didn't your movement clarity and intentionality improve as you began to teach ballet technique to other people?*

As teachers, we develop our verbal and physical communication skills every time we explain and demonstrate movement concepts to our students and coach our dancers for greater technical and artistic clarity. Students need these same opportunities; they, too, will develop their communication skills as they learn to articulate their ideas in private journals and to their peers during class. My dance colleague Anne Burnidge wrote:

> The teaching and learning atmosphere I seek to create is one in which each individual is expected to be an active participant, every voice is encouraged to become an integral part of the educational fabric of the class, individuals

are supported to take responsibility for their own learning and growth, and opportunities are presented for engagement in deep personal inquiry and open dialogue.[7]

Ultimately, both students and teachers enter the classroom with insights and observations worth hearing and sharing during class. Taking time to listen to what students have to say to you and to each other not only helps you assess their understanding of ballet technique, but it also improves your students' understanding of ballet and creates a collaborative teaching and learning environment.

Use Burnidge's description of her classroom environment as a "springboard" to explore ways in which your teaching methods promote personal accountability, reflection, and peer dialogue. After you have reviewed Burnidge's statement, take a moment to reflect on the questions listed in Teaching exploration 4.2.

Teacher exploration 4.2: Journal about your classroom practices

Personal accountability

What methods do you use to encourage students to take responsibility for their own learning and growth in your classes?

Assessing student learning

In what ways do your students demonstrate their learning to you? Physical practice? Journal writing? Answering questions? Working with peers?

Peer dialogue

When do you (or would you) encourage open group dialogue about technique concepts in your classes? In what context does this (or would this) happen? What are (or might be) the benefits of this approach?

Creating a classroom environment for positive peer interaction

Unhealthy competition, feelings of jealousy and inadequacy or superiority and entitlement are commonplace in pre-professional ballet training. Differences in technique abilities, perceived favoritism from teachers and choreographers, competition for performance roles, and membership in youth ballet companies are just some of the many factors that may contribute to negative interactions among dancers. For example, younger dancers who are promoted to higher technique levels or who receive a lead role in a ballet sometimes experience resentment and jealousy from older dancers, which often leads to unhealthy competition in the technique class. Similarly, dancers who struggle to embody technique concepts correctly sometimes experience rejection from their class-mates, especially when they are in the same class level. These types of interactions are unavoidable because students demonstrate different physical abilities, and therefore they are placed in different technique levels and awarded different performance roles. But, the methods teachers employ in technique class may lessen the negative interactions that occur among students inside and outside of class.

Before discussing some of these methods, however, take a moment to first reflect on times when you have experienced negative and positive interactions with ballet peers.

Teacher exploration 4.3: Positive and negative interactions between students

1   Think of a time during your ballet training when you experienced and/or observed healthy competition or positive interactions with other dancers.

   •   Describe the interactions. Why were they positive? How did you contribute to those positive interactions?
   •   Did your dance teacher notice the positive behavior? If so, what methods did the teacher employ to facilitate a positive commu-nity environment?

2   Think of a time during your ballet training when you experienced and/or observed unhealthy competition or negative interactions with other dancers.

   •   Describe the interactions. Why were they negative? Were there ways you may have contributed to the negative interactions?
   •   Did your dance teacher address the negative behavior? If so, what methods did the teacher employ to create a positive community environment? If not, why was the teacher unable to address the situation?

Based on your answers to # 1 and 2, *what methods would you employ (or methods do you currently employ) to promote positive interactions between stu-dents during technique class?*

One thing I can count on when I walk into a class with a new group of dancers is that each dancer will present unique capacities and challenges regardless of the technique level I'm teaching: some dancers are skilled at *adagio* while others enjoy *grand allegro*; some demonstrate impeccable technique in *pirouettes* while others master quick footwork in *petite allegro*; some struggle with the technical nuances of ballet while others easefully execute it; some enjoy working independently while others enjoy peer engagement; some love experimenting with artistic nuance while others work diligently to master the smallest technical details.

Do these descriptions resonate with you?

Observing each dancer's differences and preferences influences my verbal cueing and feedback and the way I design my classes. I notice who responds to imagery or to body part cueing or to rhythmical sounds or counts. I make choices about when to push the dancers towards new technical and artistic challenges and when to affirm technical changes. I analyze how my combinations challenge dancers differently so that each student experiences unique challenges and accomplishments by the end of class.

Recognizing how students learn and process information differently is the first step in setting up a classroom culture that supports the diversity of experiences and preferences in the classroom. If your students experience varying feedback and approaches to learning exercises, they will be more likely to draw on those experiences as they begin to provide feedback to one another. Over time, **this type of classroom culture also teaches students there are multiple ways to succeed, to show aptitude, to take risks, and to be challenged in the ballet technique classroom.** This is important, especially when cultivating a classroom culture that promotes positive peer education.

Teacher exploration 4.4: Journal about your students

Reflect on the dancers in your classes. Create a short list of each dancer's capacities, preferences, and challenges.

Every dancer in a technique class will experience feelings of failure and success (albeit in different proportions) regardless of their overall technical or artistic abilities. It is easy for dancers to focus on their own and each other's failures, but only focusing on this leads to a negative classroom environment. It is important for dancers to also identify the many ways proficiency is demonstrated in the ballet classroom.

Parts II and III of this book teach dancers how to observe balletic movement from multifaceted perspectives, which strengthens their ability to observe aptitude in their peers' movements. But, they can begin this process now by observing how you do this in class. When you, as the teacher, verbally confirm each dancer's capacities, your dancers will begin to expand their observations of each other to also include those capacities. Affirmative feedback is especially beneficial for those students that struggle learning the balletic style, but all students will benefit from this approach. There are many opportunities to provide positive affirmations in class—when someone:

- contributes a unique image or movement for an exercise;
- embodies a technique concept you were just working on;
- makes an interesting performance choice in an exercise;
- takes a risk performing a particular movement even if they make technical mistakes;
- responds to rhythmical or musical cueing in novel ways;
- asks an important question;
- helps a peer learn a movement effectively;
- [add your own example]:_____;
- [add your own example]:_____;
- [add your own example]:_____.

Reference the list of capacities, preferences, and challenges that you wrote down for each of your students in Teacher exploration 4.4. These lists include potential affirmations to use in class. Challenge yourself to provide each of your dancers with a positive affirmation publicly in class within a two-week period. Vary the positive feedback so that dancers hear different affirmations. This will ensure that everyone receives diverse positive feedback regularly.

Notions of "right" and "wrong" and "good" and "bad" are also important to address in the ballet classroom. This type of polarized thinking has the potential to lead to a negative classroom environment—students begin to assess each other as "right" or "wrong" or to label each other as "good" dancers and "bad" dancers. This is counterintuitive to the type of classroom culture needed for effective peer education.

Additionally, the contemporary dance environment requires dancers to be familiar with numerous dance styles and to work with varying choreographers. What is deemed "good" in the ballet classroom may not be "good" in a different technique form—in modern dance, or tap, or hip-hop forms, or Afro-Caribbean styles, for example. Similarly, what is deemed "right" for one choreographer may change drastically when working with a different choreographer. This does not discount that there are stylistically preferred ways to execute ballet technique, but dancers learn that those stylistic preferences are just one of many choices they can make in their bodies when dancing.

Choosing different dancers to demonstrate movements from class to class is a great way to dispel stereotypical notions of "good" and "bad" and "right" and "wrong" in the ballet classroom. Also attend to the language you use when providing feedback.

For example, instead of saying, *"This is the right position for your pelvis when you perform the relevé sous-sus,"* I typically use one of the following options:

- *What if you moved your pelvis into this position [I show the position] when you perform the relevé sous-sus? How does that feel different?*
- *Play with adjusting your pelvis in three different positions when performing the relevé sous-sus [I show three different positions]. How does each position affect your movement differently?*
- *In ballet, we typically place the pelvis here [I show the position] in a relevé sous-sus, but we can also move the pelvis in many other ways. Let's experiment with how the pelvis moves and identify when we use those movements in balletic movement and other dance styles.*

Providing inquiry-based corrections and feedback teaches the dancers there are many ways to move the body. This develops their overall body awareness, which ultimately facilitates their ability to give feedback to each other in class.

Teaching students to educate each other: a five-step process

All dancers have the potential to contribute to the classroom learning in positive and novel ways regardless of their technique level. This does not mean all dancers contribute in the same way—some are verbal, some introspective, some enjoy analyzing exercises, and some enjoy opportunities to generate imagery, or characters, or movement. It is exciting to help students discover how they approach their learning and embodiment of ballet in unique ways. Furthermore, these differences are precisely why peer education is so valuable in the classroom. As the dancers interact with each other, they share their capacities and unique learning approaches. This, along with the approaches discussed above, creates a positive learning environment.

Table 4.1 presents five methods for using peer education activities during class. Collectively, these five approaches to peer education teach dancers how to observe differences in movement choices, to communicate those observations, and to feel kinesthetically a peer's movement choices. These methods also allow you, as the teacher, to "step back" and take in the learning of your students. You will notice what your students do and do not know as you observe them working with each other.

These five methods progress from beginning to advanced. If peer interaction is new for your students, focus on methods 1–3 until your students are ready to move on to methods 4–5.

#1: Dance with others   Sensing

Simply asking students to face each other when performing *barre* and *centre* exercises is an easy and fun way to introduce peer observation and interaction

Table 4.1 Ways to incorporate peer education and interaction in technique class

Task for students	Pedagogical benefits
1. Dance with others	Students learn how to interact and perform with a peer while dancing.
2. Review class exercises with a peer	Students collaborate with each other to learn the class exercises.
3. Observe and embody a peer's movement choices	Students learn how to observe and to be observed by others, and they experience different ways of moving.
4. Teach movement choices	Students develop their verbal and kinesthetic communication skills.
5. Provide verbal feedback	Students learn how to provide critical feedback, both affirmations and suggestions, to their peers.

to your students.[8] It reminds students that ballet technique is relational; the movement is intended to be communicative and performed for live audiences. This is also a great approach to use when you observe your dancers "zoning" out or moving with excess tension.

Excess tension in the body results in restricted locomotion during traveling phrases, a smaller physical reach space with the limbs, and difficulty projecting energy into space. When dancers face each other during *barre* and *centre* exercises, they serve as audience members for each other, which teaches them to direct their focus and energy to someone tangible. This lessens bodily tension and expands their physical and psychological reach into space.[9]

Dancing with others! presents three simple ways to use this approach in class. Activities, such as these, are incorporated throughout this book.[10] *What technical and artistic improvements do you observe in your dancers' performance when you use Dancing with others! in class?*

Dancing with others!

Objective:

Dancers move more communicatively, easefully, and relationally.

Face a partner at *barre*

1   Ask your dancers to face each other at *barre* during simple exercises, such as *battement degagé* or *tendu*, and during more complex exercises, such as *rond de jambe* and *battement frappé*.

2   Encourage them to reach their limbs in space by cueing them to reach for their partner's toes during a *battement tendu devant* or for their partner's fingers during a *arabesque port de bras*. Also cue them to expand and widen their limbs in space together during *à la second* movements, and to advance and retreat from each other during *en arrière* and *en avant* movements.

Face a partner during *grand adagio*

1   Divide the class in half during *grand adagio* and ask each half to face the center of the room.
2   Instruct the dancers to stand directly across from a dancer in the opposite group. One partner starts the combination with the left side/leg and the other partner starts with the right side so that they mirror each other.
3   Ask them to exaggerate their movements toward and away from their partner, and to spot each other during turns and promenades.

Stand in a circle

This activity creates community cohesion and increased awareness of how the students use their bodies to communicate to others in the space. I begin all of my ballet classes this way. It's a great way to initiate class!

1   Instead of starting class at *barre*, ask the dancers to begin standing in a circle facing each other during *demi* and *grand plié*.
2   As they perform *demi* and *grand plié*, ask them to look at each other and to direct their arms and legs to different dancers along the circle.

#2: Review class exercises with a peer

Class exercises become increasingly complex at the upper technique levels. As a result, students typically need more time to review and practice the exercises during class. Students may review exercises together without the aid of the teacher. This is a simple way to promote peer interaction, and according to Råman's research, students reported "they could learn the order of the movement material with greater detail and more quickly by comparing their own knowledge of the movement combination with their peers' versions."[11] Similarly, students perform the exercises with greater intentionality when they have the opportunity to review the material verbally and kinesthetically with their peers.

Initially, if the exercise under review is new to the students, invite them to simply review the sequencing of the steps. As they become more familiar with the exercise in subsequent classes, ask them to review the technical concepts required to perform the movement accurately, or even the artistic nuances of the balletic phrases. In order to reach this deeper level of discussion and review, I recommend repeating class exercises over multiple classes.

Reviewing exercises together! provides a step-by-step process for employing this approach in your classroom.

Reviewing exercises together!

Objective:

Dancers learn to talk about the details of an exercise: steps and sequencing, specific technical concepts, and artistic performance.

Ask your students to review a *centre* combination with a partner. I recommend repeating this combination over five classes.

Class 1: Ask the students to work with a partner to review the sequencing and steps. This gives them the opportunity to practice speaking the ballet vocabulary and to clarify sequencing.

Classes 2 and 3: Ask the students to work with a partner to review the technical concepts for the exercise. For example, if the class is working on *entendre* in the upper body, they might review how the arms move in space or how to engage the head and upper torso during the exercise. As another example, if the class is working on rhythm, they might review how the timing of the legs is different or similar to the timing of the arms.

Classes 4 and 5: Ask the students to work with a partner to discuss their artistic performance of the exercise. For example, they might discuss how they use their eyes and face, or emphasize some movements more than others, or use different dynamics or imagery.

#3: Observe and embody a peer's movement choices ~Thinking~

The previous two sections present entry-level approaches for fostering student interaction during class. When your students have established comfort with this level of interaction, challenge them to observe each other during large *centre* combinations. If observing others during these exercises is a new experience for your students, guide their process by instructing them to look for a particular technique concept you have discussed in class. If your students are already comfortable observing each other, however, instruct them to look for anything that strikes them about their peers' movements. Simply observing each other during these moments in class teaches students to notice how their peers embody the technique in unique and different ways. This enhances their understanding of the technical and artistic concepts explored in class.

Embody what you see! uses these moments of peer observation as inspiration to explore the balletic vocabulary in different ways. As students learn to incorporate some aspect of a peer's performance in their own performance of the exercises, they learn about their movement preferences and how those are different than or similar to their peers. *Embody what you see!* also teaches dancers to move beyond habitual movement patterns and make new artistic choices.

Embody what you see!

Objective:

Dancers use their observations of each other to practice different performance techniques for the class exercises.

Ask your students to work with a partner. The partners will observe each other perform a *centre* combination. Each partner will perform the combination twice.

Step 1: Observe a peer

The observers take note of two to three things the performers excel at during the exercise. The partners then switch roles: observers become performers, and vice versa.

Step 2: Perform what you observed

During the second performance of the combination, each partner embodies the 2–3 qualities they noticed in each other's performance. For example, one partner may have appreciated the use of *glisser* (as a concept) in the other partner's upper body and the use of *elancer* in the lower body.

> ## Step 3: Teach what you embodied
>
> Ask the partners to briefly share how they were inspired by each other's performances. *What did they choose to embody and how did it affect their technique and performance?* Then, ask them to teach each other how they embodied those qualities during the exercise.

#4: Teach movement choices to a peer

Teaching movement choices to a peer was introduced in Step 3 of *Embody what you see!* As students engage in peer-to-peer teaching in this activity, they learn how to observe each other, share ideas, and communicate technical and artistic principles through movement and verbal feedback. This is the value of teaching performance choices to a peer: students have the opportunity to "own" their movement intentions out loud and to observe how their partner translates those movement intentions to their own performance of the exercise.

Class activities: *Embody what you see!* is a great way to initiate this process in your classroom, but also return to previous activities from Chapters 2 and 3 for inspiration. The activities in *Experimenting with movement propensities* from Chapter 3 provide great opportunities for dancers to teach each other how they experimented with their movement preferences and challenges. Similarly, dancers may enjoy teaching each other the movements they created in the Chapter 3 activities from *Creating ballet exercises.* Finally, consider expanding all of the Chapter 2 activities to include opportunities for students to teach each other how they experimented with different physical sensations, expressions, and balletic steps.

As Alterowitz notes, when "students are given the chance to articulate their thoughts and ideas verbally, even if they cannot replicate the material with their bodies, they have a chance to demonstrate more completely what they are learning."[12] In this way, the verbal interaction not only creates a more collaborative classroom, but it also serves as an effective assessment tool for teachers. When you listen to how students teach each other, you gain greater insight into their overall understanding of the balletic vocabulary and concepts.

#5: Provide verbal feedback   Feeling

Depending on the background of your students, providing verbal feedback to peers during the class period may be a new experience. The activities in the previous sections have worked collectively to develop the dancers' observational skills and ability to talk to one another. When your dancers have acquired this level of interaction, they are ready to provide verbal affirmations and suggestions to each other.

Remember, your dancers will experience the same challenges you experienced when first learning how to provide nuanced and directed feedback. So, do not be surprised if the feedback they give each other is simple and succinct in the beginning. Over time, they will learn how to deepen their feedback and provide more substantial suggestions.

Developing the students' ability to provide helpful feedback to each other is a multi-step process. Let's go through it together:

Step 1: The dancers practice giving each other affirmations

I instruct my students to confirm and support what's working in a peer's performance: *What moved them as they watched their peers? What caught their eye? What technical or artistic choices facilitated the quality of the performance?*

As a way to help the students begin this process, I provide them with the following prompts to use with their peers:

I appreciated how you _____. This enhanced your performance because _____.

This moment in the exercise grabbed my attention because _____.

This movement was technically strong. I really noticed how you _____.

After the dancers receive affirmations from their partners, they perform the exercise again. During the second performance, they apply the affirmations they gave to their partners to their own dancing.

Step 2: The dancers provide suggestions to each other

I progress to this step once they demonstrate the ability to provide specific and detailed affirmations to each other (this sometimes takes a while).

I provide them with the following prompts to use with their peers:

What would happen if you explored _____ during this part of the phrase? How does that impact your performance differently?

I noticed that _____ was happening during this part of the exercise. What would happen if you played with _____ instead?

I have an image I would like to share with you for this part of the exercise: _____. How does this image change the movement for you?

After the dancers receive suggestions from their partners, they perform the exercise again, applying both the feedback they provided *and* the feedback they received.

Step 3: Brainstorm about why a suggestion or affirmation was useful

Here are some themes that commonly emerge in my classes:

- Students find it helpful when the person providing feedback physically demonstrates the affirmation or suggestion.
- Students appreciate hearing multiple ways to think about a suggestion: use of verbal feedback, dynamic sounds, and imagery, for example.
- Students enjoy hearing *why* something is being affirmed or suggested.
- What do your students enjoy?

Asking students to use the words "affirmations" and "suggestions" is intentional on my part. I use "affirmation" instead of "positive feedback" because students tend to polarize the feedback when they hear the word positive (i.e. "if this feedback is positive, then the feedback coming next must be negative"). Even though the affirmations come from a place of positivity, semantically the word affirmation encourages them to be more descriptive with their feedback. I use the word "suggestions" instead of the words "critiques" or "corrections" because it encourages greater problem solving and experimentation among both partners, whereas "critiques" tends to cause the students to adopt a "fix-it" approach to their feedback.

Conclusion

Peer education facilitates the creation of a collaborative and interactive classroom environment where students develop their communication skills and learn how to form positive and supportive relationships with one another. When dancers perceive the movements in a technique class as expressive and communicative, they are more apt to bring this understanding into dance rehearsals and performances.

Verbal feedback teaches dancers to articulate out loud the differences and commonalities they observe in each other's performances. According to Palmer, "learning together also offers them [students] a chance to look at reality through the eyes of others, instead of forcing them to process everything through their own limited vision."[13] Similarly, Anttila states, "sharing one's own reflections with others can widen the intersubjective horizon within a dance community, and develop a more caring and compassionate attitude towards one's fellow dancers."[14] Take time to listen to how your students convey their understanding of ballet technique to each another. This will teach you what they do and do not understand, which in turn, will help you plan your classes, provide individualized feedback, and assess your long term curricular planning.

Notes

1   Råman, T. (2009). Collaborative Learning in the Dance Technique Class. *Research in Dance Education*, 10(1): 84.
2   See also: Salosaari, P. (2001). *Multiple Embodiment in Classical Ballet: Educating the Dancer as an Agent of Change in the Cultural Evolution of Ballet*. Helsinki: Theatre Academy. The

idea of multiple perspectives and methods for embodying the classical technique is the subject of Saloosari's dissertation. She states: "It [hearing other dancers' perspectives] freshened and altered the experience of the dance giving multiple views to it rather than one definite one, and thereby deepened the dancers' knowledge of the familiar vocabulary" (p. 79).

3 Fraleigh, S. (1987). *Dance and the Lived Body*. Pittsburgh, PA: University of Pittsburgh Press, pp. 36–37.

4 Many of the peer-education approaches discussed in this chapter were first introduced in the Introduction: see Table I.2 "Simple and complex student-directed activities."

5 Johnston, D. (2006). Private Speech in Ballet. *Research in Dance Education*, 7(1): 7. Additionally, Johnston states:

> The language of ballet is primarily internalised through visualisation. A teacher will demonstrate the prescribed movement to a student, or a student will learn from watching other dancers. Therefore, the intermediate stage in learning ballet is observation rather than articulation through speech. Visual information is internalised by the student, and becomes manifest as the student tries to emulate or embody this visual imagery. However, inhibiting the use of private speech at this point removes the potential for this vital tool to forge a strong alloy with ballet action, in order to help the development of ballet language in the student and strengthen the formation of student cognition (p. 6).

6 Alterowitz, G. (2014). Toward a Feminist Ballet Pedagogy: Teaching Strategies for Ballet Technique Classes in the Twenty-First Century. *Journal of Dance Education*, 14(1): 12.

7 Burnidge, A. (2012). Somatics in the Dance Studio: Embodying Feminist/ Democratic Pedagogy. *Journal of Dance Education*, 12(2): 45.

8 Also reference Chapters 8 and 13.

9 Excess tension is also addressed in Chapters 6, 8, and 10.

10 Chapter 13 expands on these activities from the perspective of Space Effort.

11 Råman, T. (2009), p. 84.

12 Alterowitz, G. (2014), p. 13.

13 Palmer. P. (2010). *The Courage to Teach: Exploring the Inner Landscape of a Teacher's Life,* 2nd ed. San Francisco, CA: John Wiley & Sons, p. 128.

14 Anttila, E. (2007). Mind the Body Unearthing the Affiliation Between the Conscious Body and the Reflective Mind. In L. Rouhiainen (ed.), *Ways of Knowing in Dance and Art*. Helsinki: Theatre Academy, p. 96.

Chapter 5

Laban/Bartenieff Movement Analysis

A tool for facilitating creativity, community, and technique[1]

Many contemporary choreographers and artistic directors are interested in working with dancers who embody a wide range of movement styles. So, one of our tasks as teachers is to facilitate our students' embodiment and understanding of contemporary and classical ballet styles, as well as dance styles beyond the ballet lexicon. Encouraging our students to study other dance styles is one way to help them achieve this versatility. But, as the previous chapters have demonstrated, it is also possible for students to practice both physical and cognitive versatility during ballet class. This deepens their movement literacy and body knowledge, and equally important, it prepares them for the demands of the contemporary dance field.

So, why Laban/Bartenieff Movement Analysis? How does this teaching tool align with these goals?

L/BMA is a comprehensive system for analyzing human movement. Using it in the ballet technique class has broadened my students' movement literacy. This, in turn, has diversified their self-coaching and peer-coaching strategies and helped them analyze their movement experiences in a variety of contexts: when studying other dance technique styles, working with different choreographers, and participating in movement activities outside of dance (i.e. sports, yoga, running, acting, and so on). The L/BMA concepts therefore serve as a unifying "thread" for the diverse embodied experiences my students encounter as dance artists and active human beings.

Both Rudolf Laban and Irmgard Bartenieff worked in a variety of fields and disciplines. Regardless of the population of people they worked with, they used L/BMA movement concepts prescriptively to enhance a person's self-understanding, skill development, and expressive capacity.[2] As a teacher of ballet, you are already familiar with this prescriptive process: you create technique exercises to enhance your students' physical and expressive abilities. L/BMA can serve as a facilitator in this process. As a teaching tool, I use L/BMA prescriptively to:

- teach and plan from movement concepts (Chapter 1);
- develop my students' body knowledge (Chapter 2);
- facilitate peer interaction and education (Chapter 4). *Why?* Because it is an accessible teaching tool for my students to use when providing feedback to one another (Chapter 3).

L/BMA is not the only tool I use in the ballet classroom to achieve the above goals, nor will it be the only one you use. As dance educators, we enter the classroom with a multitude of tools: some we have acquired from our mentors, some from colleagues, some from students, and some from our own research and inquiries. It is my goal to teach you how to integrate the L/BMA concepts with the methodological tools you already use in the classroom. *So, as you explore this chapter and the remaining chapters, ask yourself:*

How do the L/BMA movement concepts . . .

- *align with the teaching tools I already use?*
- *expand my teaching methods and strategies in the ballet classroom?*
- *broaden and deepen my students' and my exploration of ballet technique?*
- *develop my students' artistic and technical skills?*

L/BMA movement categories and concepts

Certified Laban Movement Analysts analyze human movement via four movement categories: Body, Effort, Shape, and Space (BESS).[3] Just as there are multiple routes on a road map for reaching the same destination, it is also possible to use multiple perspectives to approach the same movement. This is the value of the L/BMA theories to contemporary ballet teaching and learning. **The categories of BESS provide a multi-faceted and comprehensive "map" for analyzing ballet technique.**

My dancers and I use different **Body** actions and patterns of connectivity throughout a ballet class as we move from one sequence to another. We also engage in each class exercise energetically, using specific combinations of **Efforts** to add dynamic and expressive variety to the movements. Different ballet sequences require that we **Shape**, or form, our body in unique ways in order to produce coordinated and artistically rich movements. Finally, our intent and pathways in **Space** impact our alignment and the overall efficiency of our movements.

Table 5.1 L/BMA categories of Body, Effort, Shape, and Space

BODY	EFFORT
Dancers focus on alignment, whole body coordination, body part articulation, mobilizing and stabilizing forces in the body, and body phrasing (i.e. how movement is sequenced in the body). Dancers analyze how different body actions invoke different emotions and personal associations (or vice versa).	Dancers analyze the overall energy and dynamic quality of the movement. They analyze how different dynamic choices change the technical and artistic skills needed to perform the movement, and they learn to use Effort to create different moods, characters, and personalities.
SHAPE	**SPACE**
Dancers analyze the form of the body (the constellation of the body parts), how the form of the body changes from one movement to the next, and how external and internal stimuli motivate Shape change.	Dancers explore their Kinesphere, investigate spatial pulls and pathways, use counter-pulls in space to stabilize the body, and analyze the spatial quality of the movement (whether it is 1-D, 2-D, or 3-D in nature).

The categories of BESS provide you and your dancers with both specificity and variety when performing and analyzing classical movements. In order to experience this, first learn Exercise 5.1. Create your own *port de bras* and timing for the exercise.

Exercise 5.1: *Battement degagé* and *temps lié at barre*

Begin in *fifth position*, right leg *devant*, left arm on the *barre*

* Three *battement degagé devant* with the right leg closing *fifth position*
* *Battement degagé devant* a fourth time suspending the leg in the *devant* position
* *Temps lié en avant*, finishing with the left leg in *battement degagé derrière*
* Close the left leg to *fifth position derrière*
* One *battement degagé changé à la seconde* with the right leg
* *Glissé à la seconde* away from the *barre* to left *pointe tendu à la seconde*
* *Temps lié à la seconde* toward the *barre*, right leg closes *fifth derrière*
* Reverse the entire combination starting *derrière*

What if the dancers in your class struggled to move efficiently from the *battement degagé* to the *temps lié en avant* in this exercise? *How might you use each aspect of BESS to analyze this movement phrase?*

Teacher exploration 5.1: Short "romp" through BESS[4]

BODY category

Focus on how the lower body movements sequence from toes to pelvis during the transition from *degagé* to *temps lié*. This helps the dancers fluidly articulate their feet, ankles, knees, and hip joints with greater clarity and coordination. Integrating an exhale (Breath Support) during the movement phrase depresses the rib cage, which in turn, helps the dancers lower their center of gravity thereby accentuating the *plié* during the *temps lié*.

EFFORT category

Ask the dancers to embody a powerful and outpouring (Strong and Free Flowing) movement energy during both movements. The outpouring flow (Free Flow) facilitates greater ease in their movements. The powerful use of force (Strong Weight) enhances their lower body push into and out of the floor during the *temps lié*. This prepares them for the propulsive movement energy needed in jumps.

SHAPE category

Ask the dancers to emphasize the Advancing and Sinking qualities of the pelvis when transitioning from the *degagé* to the *temps lié*, and the Spreading of the thighs during the *plié*. This is especially useful for dancers who restrict the *plié* and/or who initiate forward traveling movements from the ribs (rib leading).

SPACE category

Ask the dancers to "ride" the Forward Spatial Pull throughout the entire movement. This helps them perceive the movements as a connected traveling phrase. Moving further forward into space during this part of the *barre* exercise is especially helpful for dancers who "hold back" during traveling *centre floor* exercises.

Approaching the same movement in different ways helps you provide individualized feedback for your dancers and enhances your dancers' overall movement literacy. *Experiment with this in your own body:*

Embody the above BESS examples and notice how your body awareness shifts as you approach the movement phrase from different perspectives.

- *How does each category enhance your understanding of these steps?*
- *When would you teach the movement phrase from a particular category of BESS? What would your learning goals be for the students?*

Dance educator Jan Erkert notes: "A constant process of doing and undoing is at the core of [dance] training. The smart dancer is not erasing idiosyncratic habits . . . The smart dancer . . . build[s] a broader set of choices."[5] Building a broader set of choices is at the core of the L/BMA approach. As ballet dancers apply the L/BMA theories to their dancing, they develop greater body knowledge and learn how to make a multitude of artistic choices when performing balletic phrases. *Continue to explore this below.*

Teacher exploration 5.2: Exploring a broader set of choices

Use BESS as a "springboard" for exploring different parts of Exercise 5.1

1   *Glissé à la seconde* to left *pointe tendu à la seconde.*
2   *Battement degagé derrière* to *temps lié en arrière.*
3   Upper body *port de bras.*

Body

How would you describe your alignment in each movement?
How do different parts of your body coordinate with each other?
What body parts are stabilizing and what parts are mobilizing?

Effort

How would you describe your overall movement energy for each step?
Forceful? Buoyant? Staccato or legato-like? Controlled or easeful?
How do different movement energies affect the same movement differently?

Shape

How would you describe the form of the step? Is it rounded or wide-spread? Linear or spiral-like?
How is your form changing from one position to the next? Is it opening or closing? Rising or sinking? Advancing or retreating?

Space

Where are your limbs or your entire body traveling to in space? Up? Down? Sideward? Forward? Backward? Or some combination of those directions?

BESS concepts presented in Parts II and III of Creative Ballet Teaching

The categories of BESS house numerous movement concepts applicable to ballet technique. Many, but not all of them, are explored in Parts II and III. Table 5.2 outlines specific L/BMA movement concepts presented in this book.

Similar to the previous chapters, Parts II and III emphasize experiential learning through the use of teacher explorations, journal activities, and class activities. I recommend exploring the BESS concepts and class activities in your body before you introduce them to your students. This will help you decide how to communicate the L/BMA concepts to your students.

Table 5.2 may seem like a lot, but rest assured the following chapters lead you through the BESS categories and concepts easefully. The goal is not to become an expert in L/BMA, but instead to introduce you to the L/BMA concepts as a way to inspire your creativity and use of different teaching tools in the ballet technique classroom.[6] It is my hope that you find ways to use the concepts in your own way. Add the teaching approaches and tools in the following chapters to your ever-growing "handbag" of teaching tools.

Foundational principles in L/BMA inquiry

I recall the first time I was asked to write a "Teaching philosophy statement." Defining my values as an educator and my approach to teaching was a challenging process, but one that proved to be invaluable. Through this process, I discovered foundational principles essential to my teaching identity and practices. These principles continue to influence how I approach the teaching of ballet. I mention this because there are numerous foundational principles that guide L/BMA inquiry and practice. Similarly, these principles influence how

Table 5.2 L/BMA movement categories and supporting movement concepts explored in *Creative Ballet Teaching*

Movement category	Movement concept	Skills explored
BODY (Parts II and III)	Body Connectivity	• Identify distal, mid-limb, and proximal joints • Explore coordination between regions of the body
	Stability and Mobility	• Practice locomotive movements through space • Explore placement, alignment, and balance
SHAPE (Part II)	Shape Flow Support and Shape Qualities (Chapter 6)	• Investigate how the body expands and condenses, and forms three-dimensionally into space
SPACE (Part II)	Spatial Intent and Countertensions (Chapters 7 & 8)	• Clarify the body's intent in space • Explore how oppositional spatial tensions in space enhance balance, alignment, and placement
	Kinesphere and Traceforms (Chapter 8)	• Investigate spatial pathways made by the limbs • Move in different spatial levels and directions
EFFORT (Part III)	Flow (Chapter 10)	• Explore Bound or Free movements
	Weight (Chapter 11)	• Explore Strong or Light movements
	Time (Chapter 12)	• Explore Sudden and Sustained movements
	Space (Chapter 13)	• Explore Direct or Indirect movements

practitioners approach their analysis of human movement and how they use the BESS movement concepts prescriptively with other people.

It is beyond the scope of this book to cover all of the foundational principles that guide L/BMA inquiry.[7] I have chosen instead to discuss three of them (Table 5.3). All three relate to many of the themes and ideas presented in Chapters 1–4.

Table 5.3 Three foundational principles

Parts and Whole	Analyze balletic movement through a study of its parts as well as a study of how the parts relate to the whole
Inner and Outer	Identify how balletic performance is shaped by one's inner experiences (sensing, feeling, and thinking sensibilities) and by one's interactions with the outer world (with other people and the surrounding environment)
Function and Expression	Analyze ballet technique and performance from both functional and expressive perspectives

The foundational principles in Table 5.3, as well as many of the BESS movement concepts presented in Parts II and III, investigate oppositional constructs. This is a theme throughout the L/BMA system, as Certified Movement Analyst Karen Bradley notes: "Laban went out of his way to explore the notion of polar extremes and the need for integration of oppositional concepts."[8] For Laban, "opposites are polar ends along a continuum;"[9] they are not separate, but instead mutually dependent. In L/BMA, analysis of both ends of the continuum is necessary in order to understand the whole continuum. The word "and" is important. Focusing on both the Parts *and* the Whole, the Inner *and* the Outer, the Functional *and* the Expressive is necessary when educating the whole dancer.

Parts and Whole

Parts-to-Whole was indirectly explored in Chapters 1 and 2. If you recall from Chapter 1, when using movement concepts as overarching themes for a technique class, students learn to apply the concepts to multiple steps and exercises, or in other words, to different "parts" of the ballet class. Their comprehension deepens each time they apply the concept to a new experience. In this way, each new application—each "part"—informs their "whole" understanding of the concept (a Whole-Parts-Whole approach). Similarly, in Chapter 2, the development of body knowledge consists of three fundamental parts: body awareness, personal expression, and intent. Even though each category is investigated separately in Chapter 2, it is the collective insight gained from all three categories that defines a holistic understanding of body knowledge.

In the previous section of this chapter, you investigated balletic steps from each category of BESS and then reflected on how each part enriched the whole movement. Here, too, you employed a Parts-to-Whole approach. This type of analysis is common in L/BMA. In her book *Body Movement: Coping with the Environment*, Bartenieff emphasized the importance of "understanding the parts . . . [in order] to recreate the whole, to enliven its mobility and to play harmoniously with a continuously changing environment."[10] Laban, too, emphasized the importance of analyzing both the parts and the whole of any particular movement:

> The body acts like an orchestra in which each section is related to any other and is part of the whole. Its various parts can combine in concerted action, or one part may perform alone as a "soloist" while others accompany. Each action of a particular part of the body has to be understood in relation to the whole.[11]

You likely employ a Parts-to-Whole (or Whole-to-Parts) approach in your ballet technique classes.[12] For example, sometimes it is useful to ask dancers to analyze how a specific part of the body moves in a classical step (i.e. articulating the feet during a *battement tendu*), while other times it is useful for them to analyze how the different parts of the body coordinate together to complete a movement (i.e. how the arms, spine, legs, and feet move together during a *battement tendu*). Similarly, sometimes you focus on one step in an exercise, while other times you analyze how the series of steps connect together in a flowing movement phrase. Ultimately, both perspectives are important: the insights gained from investigating the parts and those gained from analyzing the whole.

When do you ask your dancers to focus on the parts of a movement phrase or specific parts of the body? When do you ask them to focus on the whole movement phrase or the whole body? What are your teaching goals when you make these choices?

Analyze the *glissé à la seconde* to *pointe tendu à la seconde* in Exercise 5.1. When performing this movement phrase, you might choose to focus on certain parts of your body: perhaps the stability of the standing leg during the *battement tendu*, or the shifting of the pelvis during the *glissé*, or the spatial trajectory of the *port de bras*. Focusing on one body part brings clarity to that part and is therefore a useful approach in ballet training.

Take a moment to embody these examples. What do you gain when you focus on one part of the body in Exercise 5.1?

It is also important to analyze how the "parts" impact your understanding of the whole movement. For example, focusing on the pelvic shift during the *glissé* enhances the propulsion of the body during the entire movement phrase. Or, investigating the *port de bras* leads to an understanding of how the arms coordinate with the movements of the lower body.

Embody these two examples. What do you gain when you focus on how the "part" affects the "whole" movement phrase?

Many of the dancers I teach employ a "parts only" approach to performing ballet. They don't initially recognize how "change in any aspect changes the whole configuration."[13] For example, they concentrate on the height of their legs, while simultaneously sacrificing the alignment of the spine and upper body. Or, they focus on one step (i.e. a *grand jeté*), while neglecting the larger movement phrase (i.e. the transition steps before and after the *grand jeté*). When they learn to broaden their focus on the whole body or the whole movement phrase, they learn that many parts (of the body or of the movement phrase) function together to create coordinated and expressive movement.[14]

Learning to perceive wholly is especially important as the steps and sequences increase in difficulty. For example:

Finish the glissé à la seconde with the gesturing leg en l'air at 90 degrees instead of à terre in pointe tendu.

When performing this movement, many dancers initially focus only on the extension of the leg in *à la seconde*. However, if they also focus on the reach of the supporting arm and torso into *second position*, they perform the leg extension with greater ease and stability.

Embody this: as your leg extends to 90 degrees, simultaneously widen your torso and spread your supporting arm further sideward into space. Send the energy of your supporting side beyond the fingertips, like laser beams casting light into space. Is it easier to lift the leg when you establish this side-to-side counter pull between gesturing leg and supporting arm?[15]

Figure 5.1 Send lines of energy from the body into space

Teaching dancers how to analyze both the parts and the whole of any given movement (or series of movements) is a fundamental approach in L/BMA and therefore one that will be returned to in the following chapters. The *Physically sensing!* class activities in Chapter 2 utilized a Parts-to-Whole approach. You may find it helpful to return to those activities when exploring this principle. The following activity is also a fun and simple way to get started.

How the parts affect the whole

Objective:

Dancers explore how changes in one part of the body affect the whole movement.

---

1   Choose two movements from Exercise 5.1.
2   Ask the dancers to change the alignment or muscular engagement in different parts of their body as they perform the movement. I recommend asking them to experiment with the movement in a few ways. In *battement degagé devant*, for example, I might ask them to:

Grip the toes as the foot slides forward and backward.
Press the ribs forward during the movement.
Place the barre arm behind the body.
Look downward during the first degagé, then look upward during the next degagé.
Tightly hold your breath during consecutive degagé.

3   Ask the dancers to reflect on how changes in one part of the body affected the whole body. Some examples include:

How does gripping the toes change the tension level at the knee, hip, and torso?
What do you notice happening at the head and pelvis when you press the ribs forward?
How does the placement of the barre arm affect other parts of the body?
How does head position affect your balance?
How does holding your breath impact your technique and performance?

4   Repeat steps 1–3 with a different step.

Inner and Outer

Clear motivation and intent organizes the body-mind and facilitates the dancer's ability to move in space with greater clarity. Previous chapters have therefore focused on teaching dancers to ask:

What is my motivation as I move?
How do my feelings and sensations affect my movements?
What do I see or hear or feel in the space around me?
Where am I moving and who is moving with me as I dance?

Applying movement concepts to balletic movement (Chapter 1), improvising in class (Chapter 2), and using the teacher's methodological tools (Chapter 3) are Inner-Outer approaches that involve manifesting one's inner impulses and intent externally through movement. Similarly, students engage in an Inner-Outer approach to learning ballet when they attune to their sensations and feelings as they move and reflect on how that impacts their technique and performance (Chapter 2).

The peer interaction and education techniques presented in Chapter 4 also facilitated an Inner-Outer approach to learning ballet. Expressing one's ideas and inquiries to others confirms inner intent, and conversely, listening to a peer's feedback inspires new thoughts, feelings, and sensations. It is a reciprocal relationship, one echoed by Laban Movement Analyst Peggy Hackney: "How I move affects my environment and my outer environment affects my inner experience."[16] Even something as simple as facing a peer at *barre* emphasizes interactive Inner-Outer relationships.

Exploring the relationship between inner impulse and outer form is a reoccurring theme in Laban's writings on dance and movement. Laban understood that movement originated "from an inner excitement of the nerves, caused either by an immediate sense impression, or by a complicated chain of formerly experienced sense impressions stored in the memory," and that this excitement of the brain-body neural networks resulted "in the voluntary or involuntary inner effort or impulse to move."[17] According to Laban, the observable movement that resulted from these inner impulses revealed qualities and patterns unique to that particular person: "each phase of movement, every small transference of weight, every single gesture of any part of the body reveals some feature of our inner life."[18] This is true especially in the dance technique classroom. Dancers interpret and feel the balletic movement differently, and as a result, dancers convey technique concepts and artistic ideas in unique ways; their movements reveal a personal voice—a unique "inner life"—as they dance.

For Hackney, movement not only reveals features of a person's "inner life," but structured movement training, such as dance, also influence how a person's "inner life" develops and evolves:

Movement both initiates and changes emotional feelings and how we think conceptually. It is thus possible to link body training with many areas of life experience . . . This has powerful implications for any kind of education, and particularly for training which is already movement based . . . the movement one does over and over again is influencing the inner life of those doing it.[19]

Ballet dancers learn and practice specific physical and stylistic skills unique to ballet technique. They perceive and assess their movement and their bodies based on these stylistic standards. This causes many of the dancers I teach to fixate on the outer form of their movement (i.e. Did that step (or my body) look "good" or "bad"?). Sometimes this fixation leads to a rather "mechanical" movement affect, one that requires a more conscious integration of personal voice and artistic nuance (e.g. What do I feel when I dance? How is balletic movement more than just a series of steps? How do I imbue the movement with personal meaning?).

In relationship to BESS, different movements engage different parts of the body (Body), travel in different directions and levels (Space), and reveal varying shapes and movement energies (Shape and Effort). These qualitative differences give the balletic steps and exercises different "personalities," and this is something I can explore with my students. We reflect on the unique bodily sensations, feeling-tones, and mental images that arise when performing different movements.

Take a moment to explore this yourself.

Teacher exploration 5.3: How does balletic movement "move" you?

1   Practice the *à la seconde* section from Exercise 5.1. Explore the following:

- Physicality of the movements.
  Examples: How is moving in à la seconde a different experience than devant or derriére or croisé or effacé? How is moving à terre a different experience than en l'air? How is the experience of traveling toward and away from the barre different than staying in one place?
- Imagery that supports the movements.
- Sensations you notice in your body as you perform the movement.

2   Use these images and sensations to teach these movements to your students.

3   Repeat the above process using an exercise you created for technique class.

4   *Reflect: How do these images, sensations, and/or feeling-tones enhance the outer form and quality of the movement?*

Teaching methods that encourage the "inner life" of the dancer to emerge in positive and productive ways certainly influence how dancers perceive themselves. The teaching approaches presented in the previous and remaining chapters seek to accomplish this.

Function and Expression

Laban's teachings and writings analyzed the functional characteristics of movement—body alignment, spatial pathways, movement efficiency—as well as the expressive—mood, psyche, and personal meaning. He wrote in *Choreutics*:

> An observer of a moving person is at once aware, not only of the paths and rhythms of movement, but also of the mood the paths in themselves carry, because the shapes of the movements through space are always more or less coloured by a feeling or an idea.[20]

Bartenieff's methods as a Dance Movement Therapist and Physical Therapist also focused on "patterning connections in the body according to principles of efficient movement *functioning*" and developing "personal *expression* and full psychophysical involvement."[21] Similarly, ballet educators analyze how movements progress efficiently and safely in space *and* how dancers express movements artistically. The interplay of physical action and expressivity are essential principles in L/BMA, and they are also essential principles when studying ballet technique.

Themes of Function and Expression have been explored throughout Part I. In Chapter 2, the development of body knowledge included a focus on strengthening a dancer's body awareness *and* expressive skills. Chapter 3 explored how teaching tools, such as imagery, movement experimentation, and designing exercises, impacted both the dancers' technical *and* artistic development. And, in this chapter, L/BMA is presented as one of many tools to use in the classroom to help your students strengthen their coordination, artistry, and understanding of the balletic vocabulary.

Take a moment to explore the distinction between Function and Expression below.

Teacher exploration 5.4: Function and Expression

1   Observe the *glissé à la second* to *pointe tendu à la second* in Exercise 5.1 from a functional perspective.

Example: Focus on seamlessly shifting your weight from one leg to the other, or assessing your lower body alignment, or performing a fluid and lifted *port de bras* throughout the entirety of the movement.

Create a list of functional/technical characteristics you focus on when teaching these movements to your students.

2   Analyze the *glissé à la second* to *pointe tendu* from an expressive perspective.

Example: Focus on the dynamic quality of the movement, performing it with a forceful attitude and then a gentle attitude. Or, create an image for the movement: *"my port de bras moves like a calm breeze on a warm summer day."* Or, think about something you desire as you perform the movement: *"As I initiate the glissé à la second I gather what I desire in my arms. As I push from the ground to the pointe tendu, I send those desires into the space around me."*

Create a list of expressive/artistic approaches you use when teaching this movement to your students.

Both functional and expressive approaches to teaching ballet are necessary when developing a dancer's technical and artistic skills. Emphasizing artistic choice and self-expression during ballet technique class teaches dancers how to uniquely perform and interpret the balletic vocabulary. This, in turn, enhances their body awareness and technical skills. Recall from Chapter 2: "Moving expressively provides different technical challenges and leads to the development of more refined technique skills."[22] Conversely, working on technical development during class teaches dancers how to perform the movement with precision and clarity, which in turn, enhances their capacity for self-expression and artistry.

The following two class activities present step-by-step processes for exploring the relationship between function and expression in technique class. *Function to expression* challenges dancers to analyze how a technique concept enhances their performance and overall expressive potential.[23] *Expression to function* applies the reverse approach.[24]

I tend to approach movement expressively with my students before I focus on the functional details. Some of my colleagues prefer to do the opposite. Either approach is valid; I suggest choosing the approach that parallels your teaching preferences. Regardless of the approach used, "the slightest change in any movement element (Body/Effort/Shape/Space) affects the functional as well as the expressive content."[25] When function and expression are integrated, the culture of the dance classroom promotes the development of skilled dancers who understand that expression and meaning are integral in every stage of technique training.[26]

Function to expression

Objective:

Dancers explore how increased technical proficiency improves expressive potential.

Step 1: Identify and define the functional (technical) concept

Use the below list or create your own list of technique concepts. Then, choose one concept from the list to explore in class.

> *stability in the lower body   core support   propulsion through space*
> *any of the seven traditional movements*
> *articulation of the arms and legs   alignment   spatial clarity*

Step 2: Apply the functional quality to balletic steps and exercises

a   Create a warm-up and a few technique exercises that highlight the concept (see also: *Developing a concept* in Chapter 1).
b   Once the dancers achieve an understanding of the concept (a process that may take a few classes), ask them to work on the concept in two or three additional classroom exercises.
c   Ask the dancers to show and teach a peer how they applied the functional concept to one of their exercises.

Step 3: Reflection

Ask the dancers to reflect on the functional/technique concept. *What did they discover or feel in their bodies? How did the concept enhance their performance?*

Expression to function

Objective:

Dancers explore how expressive approaches improve technical proficiency.

Step 1: Identify and define the expressive approach

Use the below list or create your own list of expressive approaches. Then, choose one approach from the list to explore in class.

> *imagery   embody characters or moods   props*
> *use music with dynamic variety   use visual art or poetry as inspiration*
> *create stories for the exercises   any of the seven traditional movements*
> (See also: Expressing skills, skillfully expressing! in Chapter 2)

Step 2: Use the expressive approach to explore a technique/functional concept

a   Identify a technique concept to work on during class. Reference the list in the *Function to expression* activity or your own list. Then, use one or two of the above expressive approaches to teach the technique concept to your students.

b   Challenge the dancers to apply the expressive approach in their own way during an exercise. For example, if you are using visual imagery, ask them to create their own images.

c   Instruct the dancers to show and teach a peer the expressive approach they used.

Step 3: Reflection

Ask the dancers to reflect on the expressive approach. *What did they discover or feel in their bodies? How did the expressive approach enhance their technical execution of the movements?*

Conclusion

The explorations and class activities presented in this chapter and in Parts II and III use L/BMA movement concepts in the classroom to enhance your students' body awareness, inner intent, and ability to make diverse artistic choices when dancing. L/BMA provides "a means to equip students with an understanding of movement such that they are in greater control of their own development and versatility."[27] It is one of many tools to use in the classroom to help students acquire increased understanding of the balletic vocabulary.

Practice using the L/BMA movement concepts as a way to broaden your feedback approach. Sometimes providing feedback from one perspective—Body, perhaps—works better for one dancer, while providing feedback from a different perspective—Space, perhaps—works better for another dancer. This also teaches dancers to approach balletic movement from multiple perspectives. There are, in fact, many ways a codified movement sequence can be performed and interpreted. Using LMA/BF as a navigational tool helps dancers nurture, strengthen, and experiment with the many possibilities. This process teaches them to interpret and "color" the balletic steps in personal ways and to make conscious decisions about how to execute the technique phrases.

Notes

1   Parts of this chapter were first presented in: Whittier, C. (2013). Transforming Tradition: The Integration of Laban Movement Analysis and Classical Ballet. *NOFOD/SDHS Conference Proceedings*, pp. 399–405.

2   Bradley, K. (2009). *Rudolf Laban*. Oxford: Routledge. Karen Bradley highlights this point stating: "Laban's approach shows us that we can develop a greater repertoire of possible [movement] configurations, clarify the baseline of movement patterns with which we are already comfortable, and observe and embody other patterns that convey different qualities and configurations" (p. 89).

3   The Bartenieff Fundamentals are located in the "Body" category of LMA theory.

4   L/BMA terminology is capitalized. This distinguishes L/BMA movement concepts (i.e. Light in the context of L/BMA Weight Effort) from standard language (i.e. "That is a light weighted box").

5   Erkert, J. (2003). *Harnessing the Wind: The Art of Teaching Modern Dance*. Champaign, IL: Human Kinetics, p. 12.

6   If gaining greater expertise is something you are interested in, there are different L/BMA Certification Programs around the globe. I certified with *Integrated Movement Studies* and now serve as Director for that Program.

7   Other principles include, but are not limited to: Exertion-Recuperation, Stability-Mobility, Simple-Complex, Conscious-Unconscious, Relationship (Self-Self, Self-Other, etc.), Connectivity, and Intent.

8   Bradley, K. (2009), p. 41.

9   Ibid., 41.
10   Bartenieff, I. (1980, 2002). *Body Movement: Coping with the Environment.* New York: Rout-
     ledge, p. x.
11   Laban, R. (2011b). Revised and enlarged by Ullman, L. *Mastery of Movement* (4th edn),
     Alton, UK: Dance Books, p. 37.
12   The process moves in any direction. I often employ a cyclical approach: Parts to Whole
     to Parts and so on. The two points of analysis—parts or whole—inform each other.
13   Bartenieff, I. (1980, 2002), p. x.
14   Laban, R. (2011b). Laban noted: "The movements of each part of body are related to
     those of any other part or parts through temporal, spatial and tensional properties" (p.
     50).
15   This movement exploration is investigated further in Chapter 7.
16   Hackney, P. (2000). *Making Connections: Total Body Integration Through Bartenieff Fundamen-
     tals.* New York: Routledge, p. 37.
17   Laban, R. (2011b), p. 19.
18   Ibid., 19.
19   Hackney, P. (2000), p. 45.
20   Laban, R. (2011a). *Choreutics*, 4th edn (L. Ullman, ed.), Alton, Hampshire: UK, p. 48.
21   Hackney, P. (2000), p. 31.
22   Reference Chapter 2: "Personal expression."
23   A similar teaching table was first presented in: Whittier, C. (2006). Laban Movement
     Analysis to Classical Ballet Pedagogy. *Journal of Dance Education,* 6(4): 124–132.
24   Both activities are designed for the adolescent/adult dancer. If using these activities with
     younger dancers, alter the reflective questions so that they are more developmentally
     appropriate. Regardless of age, it is important that students participate in the learning
     process cognitively, reflectively, and interactively. They need time to experiment with
     movement and physically and/or verbally articulate what's happening.
25   Hackney, P. (2000), p. 45.
26   Whittier, C. (2006), p. 128.
27   Groff, E. (1990). Laban Movement Analysis: A Historical, Philosophical and Theoretical
     Perspective. Unpublished Masters Thesis, Connecticut College, New London, CT,
     USA, p. 61.

Part II

Improving balance and motion

Chapter 6

Discovering the three-dimensional body

Shape Flow Support and Shape Qualities[1]

A forceful exhale. She sinks and advances into a sharp plié with one arm spreading and rising with command. Her left knee and elbow bend as her fingers flare creating a jagged angularity. Her body twists with controlled intensity. A sustained inhale fills her torso and expands her body upward into space. Her arms spread wide creating an image of an impenetrable wall. She twists and rises into sous-sus; her shoulders and ribs expand outward and upward. Her spine lengthens. Her core hollows. She quickly bends and inclines her torso to the right while her arms forcefully sweep through the air in smooth arc-like motions. She advances through her upper body as one arm pierces the space in front of her; her pelvis and legs lengthen strongly toward the floor. She is soaring, yet rooted.[2]

Many times, after I have viewed a live or recorded ballet performance, I close my eyes and recall the dramatic "snap shots" that flooded my senses during the performance. Often, I see the form of the movement first: images of legs and arms unfolding into the space and bodily shapes that are angular, twisting, linear, or rounded. Both classical and contemporary balletic movement is sculptural in nature. Dancers inhabit clear forms in space, and as viewers, we capture those images in our memories.

Balletic movement is not static sculpture, however. Images of bodies bending and elongating, expanding and condensing, descending and ascending also race into my memory after a performance. Dancers pass into and out of still shapes, their bodies pouring from one place to the next like water flowing into different containers. Sometimes dancers flow smoothly from one position to the next and other times the transitions are choppy or abrupt. The rhythm of one's breath, the spatial trajectory of the movement, the choreographic intent, and the dancers' artistic choices all influence the flow and phrasing of movement.

Many upper level ballet students fall into physical patterns of "making shapes." While their balletic positions are clear and consistent, their transitions between the shapes are elusive. "Transitions," in this case, do not refer to connecting steps in ballet technique, such as *pas de bourrée, temps lié,* or *tombé.* Instead, "transitions" refer to the process of shape change that happens as the body moves from one position to the next. This way of thinking about transitions challenges dancers to focus on the more subtle movement qualities in an exercise.

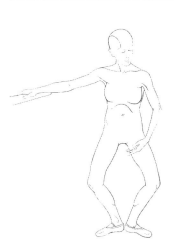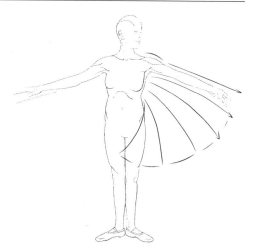

Figure 6.1 The still shape, and the Shaping from between balletic positions

Balletic positions provide clarity for the body—they are the "containers" for the body to flow into and out of. When ballet dancers emphasize only the static shape of the balletic positions, they miss out on a vital part of the balletic style: the actual process of moving—changes in breathing patterns, subtle changes in the limbs and torso, and the three-dimensional process of moving through space. Similarly, dance educator Pam Musil cautions:

> If students see only the external shaping of the movement . . . they often miss subtle qualitative nuances that imbue the movement with flavor and meaning. Or, if they focus too heavily on the periphery . . . and ignore what is happening in the core of the body, they can miss the essence behind the movement.[3]

So, *how do we teach and describe the forming process of the body to ballet dancers?* Chapter 6 explores this question by applying two Laban/Bartenieff Movement Analysis (L/BMA) concepts to ballet technique: Shape Flow Support and Shape Qualities. Collectively, these concepts teach dancers to focus on how shape changes in the torso support the movement of the limbs in space, and how the form of the movements flow from one position to the next.

Teachers first: embodying Shape Flow Support and Shape Qualities

Breathing initiates three-dimensional shape changes in the torso during the process of inhalation and exhalation. During inhalation, the diaphragm pulls downward as the ribs expand and rise. As the ribs move away from the pelvis, the abdominal wall lengthens and widens. The downward motion of the diaphragm compresses the organs against the expanded abdominal wall and allows

Table 6.1 Breathing is three-dimensional

Inhalation	Exhalation
Diaphragm pulls *downward*	Diaphragm *ascends upward*
Ribs expand *upward and outward*	Ribs depress *downward and inward*
Abdominal wall *lengthens and widens*	Abdominal wall *shortens and narrows*

the lungs to fill with oxygen. During exhalation, this process reverses: the ribs depress and narrow as the diaphragm tendon ascends and relaxes its contraction. As the distance between the ribs and pelvis shortens, the abdominals increase their contractile pull towards the body's midline, pressing the organs inward and upward.[4] *To breathe is to experience oppositional directional forces in the torso; the ribs, diaphragm, abdominals, and organs all interact in an interrelated dance.*[5]

Teaching dancers to use breath rhythmically, expressively, and directionally in dance technique training supports their movement phrasing and the flow of the body's form in space. Shape Flow Support (SFS) provides an ideal conceptual tool for such learning.

SFS accentuates the body's inner volume by providing directionality to the flowing and forming process of breath. *Lengthening* and *Shortening* emphasizes Growing and Shrinking along the vertical dimension, *Widening* and *Narrowing* along the horizontal dimension, and *Bulging* and *Hollowing* along the sagittal dimension. This three-dimensional shape change supports the body's changing and flowing form, hence the term Shape Flow Support.

Table 6.2 Shape Flow Support

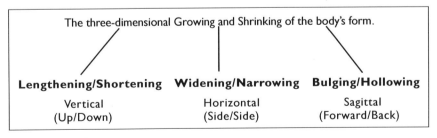

The three-dimensional Growing and Shrinking of the body's form.		
Lengthening/Shortening	**Widening/Narrowing**	**Bulging/Hollowing**
Vertical (Up/Down)	Horizontal (Side/Side)	Sagittal (Forward/Back)

Teacher exploration 6.1 explores SFS through a series of breathing activities. Attend to the three-dimensionality of the ribs in these activities. The ribs traverse the torso like hula-hoops, connecting the spine to the sternum.[6]

Trace the pathway of each set of ribs from lower to upper, and from back to front.

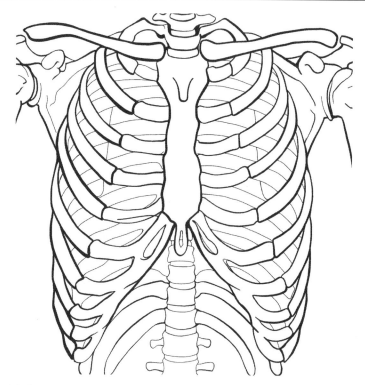

Figure 6.2 The ribs traverse the torso from vertebrae to sternum

During Teacher exploration 6.1, notice how the back surfaces of the rib cage (thorax) participate in the form change. Perhaps, it is useful to imagine the ribs as arms gently embracing you from back to front. As you breathe, feel your body yield into that embrace.

Teacher exploration 6.1: Shape Flow Support and three-dimensional breathing

Preparation

- *Begin sitting.* If in a chair, place your "sitz" bones at the edge of the chair to firmly ground your feet against the floor. If it is difficult to feel the back surfaces of your body Growing and Shrinking during these exercises, sit on the floor with your back against a wall or place an exercise ball between your torso and the back of the chair to enhance the tactile feedback.
- *Attend to your breathing patterns:* Which is more pronounced—inhalation or exhalation? Where do you feel your breath most active in

your body? Establish an easeful breathing rhythm. Do not force your inhales and exhales beyond what you can support. This causes excess tension in the abdominals and upper back. If this happens, simply stop and wiggle your spine, stretch, laugh out loud, or sing along to your favorite song before returning to the activities.

1   **Lengthening and Shortening**: Imagine your spine is a long, elastic band. As you inhale and exhale, **Lengthen** the band upward and downward at the same time. The "sitz" bones and tail reach downward, grounding your pelvis into the floor, as your head and neck float upward toward the sky. On your next exhale, **Shorten** the elastic band, softening the two ends of the spine back toward the center of the torso. This rhythm of Lengthening and Shortening is common during *plié* (see Figure 6.4).

Place your hands on your sternum and your lower back (lumbar spine)—feel those two points moving toward and away from each other as you breathe. What about the back of the neck (cervical spine) and belly?

2   **Widening and Narrowing**: Breathe into your width. Imagine your midline is a closed fan or peacock feathers. As you inhale and exhale, feel the fan or feathers opening sideward, causing the ribcage to **Widen**, similar to the sensation you feel when you expand your arms and legs into a wide *à la seconde* position. Avoid pushing your ribs forward into space as you Widen—emphasize the horizontal expansion from the back and front surfaces of the ribs simultaneously.

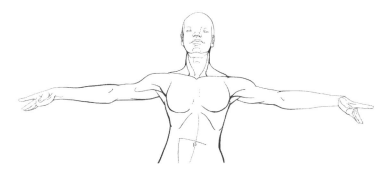

Figure 6.3 Widen the torso into *à la seconde*

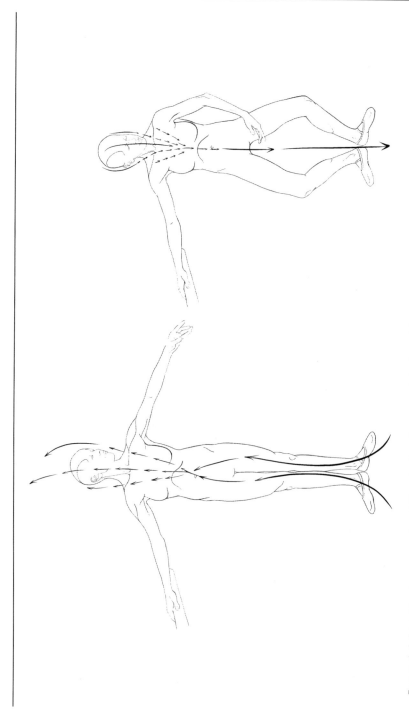

Figure 6.4 Lengthening upward and Shortening downward during *plié*

On your next exhale, imagine the fan or feathers folding inward, **Narrowing** the ribs toward your midline, similar to the sensation of closing your arms and legs inward from *à la seconde* to *first position*. Apply this breath pattern in the shoulder girdle, and then in the pelvis/hip joints. *What does it feel like to imagine peacock feathers Widening and Narrowing these body regions?* (see Figure 6.9).

3   **Bulging and Hollowing**: Breathe into your depth. Imagine your heart and lungs are balloons lining the inside of your rib cage. Feel the balloons inflating the front surfaces of the ribs and belly, as if you were **Bulging** forward into *attitude derrière*. Deflate the balloons feeling the front surfaces **Hollowing** inward toward your center, similar to moving backward in a *temps lié en arrière*.

Figure 6.5 Upper body Bulges forward in *attitude derrière*

Bulge forward and backward at the same time, "inflating" all at once. Then, feel the simultaneous Hollowing of the front and back surfaces, similar to the feeling of being zipped into a tightly fit costume.

So, how do the explorations in Teacher exploration 6.1 apply to balletic movement? In order to address this question, first learn the *port de bras* exercise in Exercise 6.1. Move through the exercise at your own pace and rhythm.

Exercise 6.1 *Port de bras* with *battement fondu developpé* (at *barre*)

Begin in *fifth position*: left leg *devant*, left arm *bras bas*, right hand on the *barre*.

Part I

* Move the left arm to *demi-second* with a slight *cambré* to the left, and then back to *bras bas*.
* Repeat this three more times: moving from *bras bas* to *second position*, then to *fifth position allongé*, and finally to *fifth position* passing through the previous arm positions.

Part II

* Extend the left arm forward into *arabesque port de bras*, twisting the spine and shoulder girdle slightly to the right. The *épaulment* in the torso causes the right arm to slide backwards along the *barre*.
* Perform the *arabesque port de bras* to the other side, reversing the arms, spinal rotation, and *épaulment* (the right arm releases the *barre*).
* Relevé *sous-sus*, lifting both arms to *allongé fifth position* returning the torso to *en face*.
* Maintaining *sous-sus, port de corps* downward and forward toward the floor. Raise the body back to vertical, rolling through the vertebrae from lower to upper. End in *sous-sus* with the left arm in *second position*, right arm on the *barre*.

Part III

* Left *fondu developpé devant*; left arm moves from *first* to *fifth*.
* *Tombé devant* on the left (in *plié*), right leg to *pointe tendu derrière*, left arm extending forward in an *arabesque* line. Close the right leg to *fifth position*.
* Left *fondu developpé à la seconde*; left arm moves through *first* to *second position*.
* Left *fondu developpé derrière* to *arabesque*; left arm moves through *first* and reaches into *arabesque* line.
* *Plié relevé* in *arabesque*. Balance; and lower to *fifth position plié*.

Explore Exercise 6.1 using SFS and conscious breathing in Teacher exploration 6.2. There is no one-to-one correlation between inhaling and expansive SFS qualities and exhaling and condensing SFS qualities (i.e. Lengthening can occur during both the inhalation and exhalation). Experiment with your breath in ways that facilitate functional and expressive SFS in Exercise 6.1.

If you become too cerebral in the below explorations, stop! Instead, begin moving through the exercise in any way you want. It is important to return to the feeling-tone of the exercise, and to experience the natural, kinesthetic intelligence of your body moving in space.

Teacher exploration 6.2: Shape Flow Support and Exercise 6.1

1   **Expansive, Growing SFS—Lengthening, Widening, and Bulging.**

- **Lengthening**. *When is Exercise 6.1 supported by Lengthening upward toward the head or downward toward the pelvis? When is it useful to Lengthen upward and downward simultaneously?*
- **Widening**. *When is it helpful to Widen to the right or left, or both sides simultaneously?* For example, Widening the *barre* side of the torso when executing the *fondu developpé à la second* keeps my supporting side active and stable.
- **Bulging**. *When is it useful to expand the torso or pelvis to the front (Bulging forward) or to the back (Bulging backward)?* For example, *Bulging* in the backspace (with Lengthening of the spine) realigns the shoulders with the pelvis as the leg lowers from *arabesque* to *fifth position* in the last movement of the exercise.

2   **Condensing, Shrinking SFS—Shortening, Narrowing, and Hollowing.**

- As you embody each of the condensing qualities, ask: *When is it useful to allow the head and neck to soften downward (Shorten) from a Lengthened position? When is it useful to allow the ribs to Narrow in toward the midline? When does Hollowing through the navel center or chest support your technique?*

3   **Explore phrasing between Expansive and Condensing SFS qualities**.

- *How do you follow rhythms of Growing and Shrinking throughout the exercise? What rhythms support your technical or expressive execution of the movement?*
- *Do you ever expand and condense simultaneously?* For example: Widening and Lengthening the upper spine as the navel center Hollows.

Shape Qualities—an outward expression of Shape Flow Support

Similar to SFS, Shape Qualities (SQs) describe how the body changes its form three dimensionally. SQs provide ballet dancers with an outer shaping pathway in space. There are six SQs: *Rising, Sinking, Spreading, Enclosing, Advancing,* and *Retreating*. The names indicate the actions.

Table 6.3 Shape Qualities

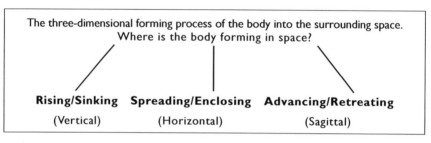

The three-dimensional forming process of the body into the surrounding space.
Where is the body forming in space?

Rising/Sinking   **Spreading/Enclosing**   **Advancing/Retreating**

(Vertical)   (Horizontal)   (Sagittal)

Even though you did not focus on SQs in Teacher exploration 6.2, you used them to perform Exercise 6.1. For example:

*   *Fifth position allongé* involved Rising and Spreading in the arms.
*   Each *fondu* involved Sinking and Spreading in the lower body.
*   *Tombé en avant* involved Advancing through the whole body.

Instead of exploring SQs in isolation, Teacher exploration 6.3 investigates how SFS phrases into SQs. Moving from SFS to SQs is especially useful in ballet, but it is difficult to teach until you have fully experimented with it in your body. As you explore Exercise 6.1 again, notice how SFS underpins Rising and Sinking, Spreading and Enclosing, Retreating and Advancing.

Teacher exploration 6.3: Phrasing from Shape Flow Support to Shape Qualities

1   Experiment with Part I of Exercise 6.1.

*   Inhale, filling your body with air. Exhale, depressing the ribs and **Widening** through the left side of the torso as the left arm **Spreads** into *demi-second* (see Figure 6.1).

    ○   **Enclose** the arm to *bras bas* as your spine **Lengthens** upwards and downwards.

- Repeat this three more times, **Rising** a little higher through the left arm each time you leave *bras bas*. **Lengthen** and **Widen** your torso in *fifth position*.

Figure 6.6 Lengthening and Widening the torso

2   Experiment with Part II.

- Exhale and **Shorten** slightly through the upper spine as the left arm **Advances** into an *arabesque port de bras*. As this happens, **Retreat** the right arm along the *barre*, **Widening** the rib cage.
   - Pause. Inhale in this *port de bras*, **Bulging** slightly through the upper chest accentuating the **Advancing** left arm.
- Switch the *arabesque port de bras*, **Advancing** the right arm and **Retreating** the left arm in space. Emphasize the moment of **Spreading** through both arms in the middle.
- During an exhale or inhale, **Lengthen** and **Widen** the torso as the arms **Rise** and **Spread** into *sous-sus* with *allongé fifth port de bras*.

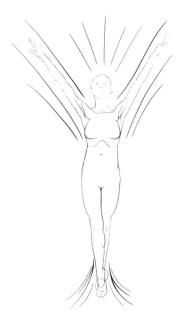

Figure 6.7 Rising and Spreading into *sous-sus*

- **Advance** and **Sink** the upper body as you dive downward in the *port de corps*. **Hollow** through the core to initiate the **Rising** of the upper body back to *sous-sus*.
- **Widen** the torso and **Spread** both arms into *second position*.

3   Experiment with Part III in your own way.

- *How does SFS assist your movement when the legs Advance or Spread or Retreat into space during the battement fondu developpé?*
- *How do SQs assist your level changes and movements through space?*

I made specific Shape choices as I led you through the above exploration, but you could have made different choices. For example, you might:

- Choose different SFS elements for certain movements, e.g. *Narrowing instead of Widening as the arm Spreads to 2nd position.*
- Embody more than one SFS or SQs element at a time, e.g. *Hollowing during some of the Lengthening moments.*
- Cluster SFS and SQs in different ways, e.g. *Rising the body and arms into sous-sus while Shortening the torso.*

There are many possibilities to explore! Move through Teacher exploration 6.3 again. This time experiment with SFS and SQs in your own way, making any choices you want.

Teaching students to "shape" into space

When dancers apply SFS and SQs to their movement, they learn to invest in the subtle and dynamic nuances of shape change. Active participation in the forming process becomes a primary goal. According to dance educator and Movement Analyst Peggy Hackney, applying this process of shape change to movement is "particularly important for dancers who seem to get stuck in trying to 'make the right shape,' but are not connecting internally to enjoy the forming process itself."[7] SFS initiates internal, subtle shape changes in the body, which are lived out externally in space via SQs. Both offer increased awareness about how the whole body moves from one position to the next, and when supported by conscious and active breathing patterns, "heightens awareness of the center of the body around which the process revolves."[8]

Dancers will experience different artistic and technical benefits from using SFS and SQs in class. Reflect on your own experience for a moment: **What technical and artistic benefits did you experience as you explored SFS and SQs?** Based on those challenges:

When would you focus on SFS and SQs with your students? What technical or artistic goals are you trying to achieve?

How would you explain SFS and SQs to your students? What seems important to communicate or emphasize?

Technically, SFS and SQs help ballet dancers discover how to initiate and support movement in the torso and pelvis, access three-dimensionally supported movement, and stabilize the body in dynamic rather than static ways.

Artistically, learning to enjoy the forming process supports an *inner to outer* approach to ballet technique, one that works *through* the body. Somatic educator Richard Strozzi Heckler notes,

[T]o work through the body is to work with our internal experience, and not simply to strive for a better posture, alleviate a physical symptom, elicit a certain emotional response, or be able to move more gracefully, although all of that may happen.[9]

As dancers discover more internally motivated reasons for arriving in and transitioning between the various classical positions, they begin to reveal unique dancing styles. They learn to make different choices depending on what they want to feel technically and artistically.

When first teaching SFS to your students, I suggest starting with an activity similar to Teacher exploration 6.1. This gives your students the opportunity to physically sense the connection between active breathing and shape change at the torso.

Table 6.4 Technical and artistic benefits for Shape Flow Support and Shape Qualities

Shape Flow Support and **Shape Qualities** are practical concepts to use when teaching students how to:

1. *Accentuate the form change that accompanies breath.* For example, a dancer may exhale as they Advance and Sink the pelvis and leg into a *chassé en avant* and then inhale as they Lengthen the spine upward into a *sauté arabesque*.
2. *Initiate and support movements from the torso*, such as Lengthening the spine in two directions to initiate the Rising of the body into a *relevé sous-sus*.
3. *Dance with three-dimensional volume*, such as Rising, Spreading, and Advancing the upper body in a *croisé attitude derrière* (Figure 6.8).
4. *Stabilize dynamically in balances*, such as reinvesting in the Lengthening of the spine as during each exhale in a *relevé retiré* balance; or, accentuating the oppositional forces of the Retreating leg and the Advancing arm during a balance in *arabesque*.
5. *Make different qualitative choices about shape change*. For example, during a *piqué first arabesque*, one dancer may emphasize Rising, while another emphasizes Advancing, and another emphasizes both Rising and Advancing with Widening in the chest and back.

Figure 6.8 Advancing the upper body into *croisé attitude derrière*

My students initially resist breathing audibly in ballet technique class. This may be true for your students too. This is why I like using SFS to introduce breath support. Many of my ballet students are skilled at thinking about movement spatially because ballet technique trains for spatial clarity. SFS capitalizes on this intelligence by teaching students how to direct their breath along internal spatial pathways. When they think about breath as a spatial process, they begin to discover purpose and intent for their breath—how Lengthening upward with an inhale supports a *relevé sous-sus*, for example.

As another approach for promoting conscious breathing in class, I instruct my students to restrict their breath during technique exercises. This builds kinesthetic understanding of what restricted breath patterns feel like and how it impacts their dancing. Most notably, they experience excess tension in the skeletal joints and increased difficulty coordinating the movements of their limbs with each other. As Bartenieff notes, "movement rides on the flow of breath," and when students hold their breath during particular movements "they forego the many subtle inner shape changes in the cavities (mouth, chest, abdomen) of the body and fine gradations of changes that occur in different configurations of limbs, trunk, head."[10]

Sometimes students restrict their breath because they are overly focused on "sucking in their stomachs" or "pulling up." This is a common pattern in ballet technique, in part because of the stylistic emphasis on verticality. But, as Eric Franklin cautions:

> Vehemently pulling in your stomach muscles prevent the organs from moving forward, impeding the diaphragm's downward motion . . . Constant gripping of the abdominals creates compensatory actions such as lifting the shoulder girdle in an effort to increase the space within the lungs ... making the body less stable and hindering balance and turns.[11]

This is why it is important to cue students to feel their belly center changing as they move through the activities from Teacher exploration 6.1. Allowing the abdominals to change in tone increases the effectiveness of the diaphragm as it moves downward and upward, and it teaches students to sustain abdominal support *and* breathe fully at the same time!

The following activities, *Grow and expand; shrink and condense!*, apply SFS and SQs to *barre* and *centre* exercises. The expansive SFS and SQs elements are emphasized much more frequently in ballet technique classes. So, both activities also highlight the condensing SFS and SQs elements; students develop body awareness for movements that descend, retreat, and move toward the core of the body. When these qualities are phrased with the elements that ascend, advance, and travel away from the core, the dancers access greater three-dimensional volume in their bodies.

Grow and expand; shrink and condense!

Objective:

Dancers transition into and out of balletic positions with three-dimensional awareness.

Shape Flow Support

1   Create a *demi/grand plié* exercise performed in a circle, dancers facing the inside of the circle.
2   Ask the dancers to: *Imagine each joint in your body as tiny balloons. There are even balloons between each vertebrae in the spine and in the knuckles of your fingers and toes. Each balloon in your body breathes as you breathe, growing and shrinking your whole body.*
3   Cue the dancers to notice the expansiveness of their shape change during the exercise:

   • *Feel the balloons* **Lengthening** *upward or downward as you descend and ascend in the pliés.*
   • *Feel the balloons* **Widening** *your torso to the dancers standing next to you in the circle.*
   • *Notice how you* **Bulge** *through your front surfaces or through your back surfaces, expanding your body toward or away from dancers standing across the circle from you.*

4   As they perform the exercise a second time, cue them to pay attention to the shrinking and condensing of their body balloons:

   • **Shortening** *as the balloons between each vertebrae deflate smoothly from Lengthening.*
   • **Narrowing** *as the balloons in the shoulders, pelvis, and ribs deflate from Widening.*
   • **Hollowing** *as the balloons in the belly, lungs, and ribs deflate from Bulging.*

5   *How did SFS affect your technique? How are expansive and condensing SFS elements expressively different?*

Shape Qualities

1   Create a series of *barre* and *centre* exercises that incorporate steps that travel *en avant, en arrière,* and *en côte,* as well as steps that change level vertically (i.e. *relevé/plié* and *sauté*).

2   Ask the dancers to focus on the Condensing SQs in the exercise. For example:

- **Retreating** when traveling backwards or when a dancer must move the torso, legs, or arms backwards in space. Retreating the upper body *with* the lower body during steps that travel *en arrière* teaches dancers to keep their shoulders over the pelvis.

- **Enclosing** during any *port de bras* that passes through *first position.* This helps dancers release tension through the sternum and ribs when moving the arms from more expansive movements. *Enclosing* is also helpful to emphasize during lower body movements that close into *fifth position* or cross the midline of the body.

Figure 6.9 Enclosing the arms and legs

- **Sinking** when teaching dancers to work on *ballon* during *petite* or *grand allegro* combinations. *Sinking* helps them emphasize the creasing of the ankles, knees, and hips when landing from jumps. This facilitates a buoyant rebound because they don't lift their heels or grip the hip flexors when they land.

3   Repeat Step #2, but focus on the Expansive SQs: **Rising, Spreading,** and **Advancing.**

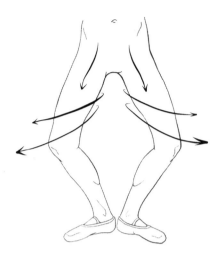

Figure 6.10 Spreading (and Sinking) the lower body during *plié*

4   *How did SQs affect your technique? How are the expansive and condensing SQs expressively different?*

Once your dancers establish familiarity with singular SFS and SQs elements, begin to explore how to use them in clusters: Rising with Spreading, or Lengthening downward with Sinking, for example. As Teacher exploration 6.3 revealed, balletic movements rarely reveal only one SFS or SQs element at a time. There are multiple shape elements happening simultaneously. It would be difficult (and unrealistic) for dancers to focus on all of them at once. Since movement is three-dimensional, dancers can make different choices about what to work on in any given movement(s). Shape change, therefore, becomes a meaningful process that supports their technical and artistic goals. For example, they might emphasize Rising out of a *temps lié en avant* which would be kinesthetically and visually different than emphasizing Advancing in this same movement.

Try that example in your body. What technical and artistic differences do you feel?

The next activity, *"Ballooning" in shape clusters!*, explores how SFS and SQs cluster together when performing balletic movement. This activity extends over six technique classes to give the dancers an opportunity to explore the movement from different Shape perspectives. This is a complex activity. I use it in class once my students have demonstrated a firm understanding of each individual SFS and SQs element.

"Ballooning" in shape clusters!

Objective:

Dancers learn to transition into and out of classical positions with greater three-dimensional complexity.

Port de bras with battement fondu developpé

Preparation: Teach Exercise 6.1 to your students and explore it with them in six consecutive classes.

1   **Classes 1–3**: Choose which SFS and SQs elements to highlight in Exercise 6.1. *How do your choices achieve specific technical or artistic goals you have for your students?* Here are some examples I explored with my students:

- **Retreating** the leg while the arm **Advances** enhances the process of getting into the *arabesque*. **Retreating and Widening** the upper body realigns the shoulders with the pelvis when lowering the leg from *arabesque* to *fifth position*.
- **Spreading with Sinking** during *plié* widens the students' base of support and engages the muscles that support outward rotation (See Figure 6.10). **Rising with Spreading** in the arms and torso expands the upper body into the *fifth allongé* (See Figure 6.7).
- **Advancing with Sinking** in the lower body during the *tombé en avant* activates the propulsion of the pelvis in space. **Bulging and Advancing** in the upper body enhances the dynamism of moving forward.
- **Hollowing with Lengthening** upward during the *battement fondu developpé* counteracts the idea of sucking in the belly (navel to spine) and instead gives the core engagement spatial intentionality up and back (navel to upper spine).

Figure 6.11 Hollowing and Lengthening from navel to upper spine

2   **Classes 4–5**: Ask the dancers to make different SFS and SQs choices in four places in the exercise. Similar to your process, ask them: *How do your choices support what you want to feel technically or expressively in the exercise?* After they have performed the exercise, ask them: *How did your choices facilitate your technique and performance?*

3   **Class 6**: Ask the dancers to teach their Shape choices to a peer. Encourage them to share why they made those choices. Then, ask them: *What did you learn by experiencing the choices your peers made? How would you apply those choices to your own dancing?*

In general, anytime I notice my dancers performing with a disjointed movement phrasing—moving from position to position like a series of photographs—I know it's time to play with Shape Flow Support and Shape Qualities. Exercise 6.1 is ideal for initiating this exploration. Once your dancers have gained deeper understanding of SFS and SQs, however, begin to apply the Shape concepts to other technique exercises. For example, exploring Shape concepts during *petite allegro* helps my dancers discover greater fluidity in their upper body *port de bras* while their legs move quickly, and in *grand allegro* accessing clear Shaping choices helps them propel their bodies into the air with greater support from their core.

Providing the dancers with opportunities to make their own Shaping choices is also important. This teaches them about their individual preferences and develops their understanding of ballet technique. If you notice them making the same choices from class to class, ask them to work with a peer who makes different choices. This is true for you too! If you are stuck in a rut, find inspiration in your students' Shape choices and incorporate some of those ideas into your technique exercises.

Notes

1 Parts of this chapter first appeared in: Whittier, C. (2006). Laban Movement Analysis to Classical Ballet Pedagogy. *Journal of Dance Education*, 6(4): 124–132; and in Whittier, C. (2010). Classical Ballet Pedagogy. In V. Preston-Dunlop and L. Sawyers, (eds), *The Dynamic Body in Space: Exploring and Developing Rudolf Laban's Ideas for the 21st Century*. Alton, UK: Dance Books, pp. 235–246.

2 I wrote this description as I watched a video recording of Misty Copeland performing *Desparatos*, choreographed by Marcelo Gomes: www.youtube.com/watch?v=T-n9Ti0V8mI. Misty Copeland is a member of the American Ballet Theatre in New York City (USA). Gomez, a former dancer with ABT, now choreographs professionally.

3 Musil, P.S. (2001). Chaos Theory and Dance Technique. *Journal of Dance Education*, 1(4): 150.

4 See also: Hackney, P. (2000). *Making Connections*. New York: Routledge, Chapter 6. Breath Connectivity is the first pattern of six Total Patterns of Body Connectivity in the Bartenieff Fundamentals.

5 See also: Franklin, E. (1996b). *Dynamic Alignment through Imagery*. Champaign, IL: Human Kinetics, Chapter 16. Franklin discusses the relationship between the diaphragm, lung, ribs, abdominals, and internal organs during breathing.

6 The 12 sets of ribs connect to the 12 thoracic vertebrae. The ten upper sets of ribs connect to the sternum. Reference Chapter 6 in *Creative Ballet Learning* for an active exploration of the thorax and spine.

7 Hackney, P. (2000), p. 223.

8 Bartenieff, I. (1980, 2002). *Body Movement: Coping with the Environment*. New York: Routledge, p. 232.

9 Heckler, R.S. (1993). *The Anatomy of Change: East/West Approaches to Body/Mind Therapy*. Berkley, CA: North Atlantic Books, p. 16.

10 Bartenieff, I. 1980, p. 232.

11 Franklin, E. (1996b), pp. 262–263. See also: Hackney, P. (2000): "In fact, holding the abdominals keeps them from participating in their natural ongoing reciprocal action with the diaphragm and will lessen the sense of internal connectivity" (p. 64).

Chapter 7

Balancing three-dimensionally
Spatial Intent and Countertensions

Stillness, balance, and stability occur throughout a ballet technique class. Teachers consistently ask dancers to:

embody elongated spinal postures;
maintain one *port de bras* throughout an entire exercise;
suspend balances *en relevé*;
stand on one leg for prolonged periods of time;
maintain *epaulment* positioning throughout *centre* floor work.

Often times, these moments of stillness seem static, but in reality, every minor shift in a body part during a sustained balance or a maintained posture creates muscular adjustments throughout the dancer's entire body. In speaking about Laban, Irmgard Bartenieff wrote: "The dynamic image of 'upright posture' is described by Laban as an ongoing, cohesive, three-dimensional process that creates and recreates a series of relationships of Up/Down, Right/Left, and Forward/Backward."[1]

Learning how to stabilize the body effectively requires dancers to continually reinvest in changing spatial relationships. In this way, "balance . . . is a dynamic process, not a steady state."[2] As the balletic position shifts, the spatial integrity of the whole body shifts.

In my experience, however, pre-professional dancers do not always perceive balance, posture, or placement as dynamic. They are often preoccupied with the parts of the body that are moving and do not recognize the important role the stationary body parts play in stabilizing their movement and facilitating whole body coordination. Ballet educator, Rory Foster, makes similar observations. Perhaps these descriptive accounts are familiar to you too:

Many students . . . go into positions where they look posed and static ... the head being cocked at a prescribed angle with the eyes glued to the outstretched arm or hand, or they just stare out into space, devoid of . . . how their *epaulment* and upper body contribute to the entire shape and the dynamic breadth of the position . . . They grip their muscles in order to hold their placement.[3]

When we dance, we experience "changes in muscular activation and sensation related to shifts in . . . [our] the plumb line of gravity,"[4] and those shifts occur in both small and large movements. Even when only one limb is moving, the entire body accommodates spatially. For example, when the leg moves from *devant* to *derrière* in a *balançoire* at *barre*, the top of the pelvis moves forward slightly, as the bottom of the pelvis moves backwards. As this happens, the upper body shifts slightly forward and upward and the *barre* arm slides forward along the *barre*. This subtle upper body weight shift serves as a counterbalance to the backward and downward movement of the leg into *derrière*.

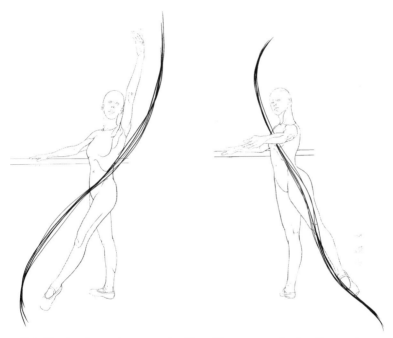

Figure 7.1 Moving from *devant* to *derrière* affects upper body alignment

When dancers grip the *barre* or their torso muscles during the *balançoire* (a pattern I often observe), they overlook these subtle weight shifts and changing intentions in space.

So, how do ballet dancers develop sensitivity to these subtle weight shifts and oppositional tensions in the body?

And, how does that knowledge facilitate three-dimensional, dynamic stability?

The Shape concepts from the previous chapter provide some answers to these questions. When dancers physically and cognitively understand how bodily form expands and condenses three-dimensionally, they begin to perceive balance and stability as a three-dimensional, dynamic process. The Shape Flow Support and Shape Qualities terminology are therefore referenced throughout this chapter. In addition to this, two new movement concepts from Laban/Bartenieff Movement Analysis (L/BMA) are introduced: **Spatial Intent** and **Countertensions**.

Teachers first: embodying countertensions with intent

Intent, as it was explored in Chapter 2, involves making conscious decisions about what to focus on and experiment with during technique class. **Spatial Intent**, therefore, involves the decisions dancers make about their use of space. Consciously investing in the spatial pathways of the limbs and torso strengthens a dancer's technique and facilitates overall movement clarity.

Countertensions describe the oppositional (*counter*) spatial *tensions* that support human movement. Since movement is three-dimensional, oppositional spatial tensions occur in all three dimensions.

Countertensional forces are always active in the body whether or not we are conscious of them. When standing, for example, my muscles produce a contractile force that resists the downward pull of gravity. The resulting effect is that

Table 7.1 Countertensional pulls occur in three dimensions

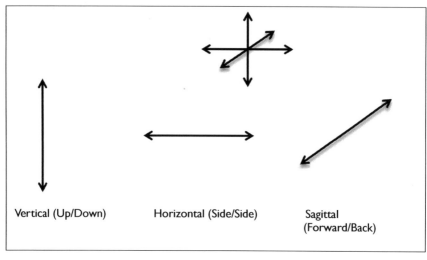

Vertical (Up/Down)   Horizontal (Side/Side)   Sagittal (Forward/Back)

I maintain my uprightness and vertical axis. If I release the contraction of my muscles, gravity will pull me downward.

When I dance, I embody Countertensions consciously. I actively engage the oppositional pulls within my body and use my limbs and torso to project those "lines of energy" into space. Take a moment to experience this yourself.

Embody the examples in Table 7.2. As you do so, imagine the spatial lines as laser beams radiating from the center of your body, through the limbs, and finally into space. What technical benefits do you experience as you investigate this type of Spatial Intent?

Table 7.2 What are Countertensions?

• Oppositional spatial pulls of Upward and Downward (Vertical)	*Plié relevé sous-sus*: press your legs downward as your body Rises upward from the *plié*; then engage the upward and downward pulls in space in equal proportion to stabilize (Figure 7.2)
• Oppositional spatial pulls of Rightward and Leftward (Horizontal)	*Developpé à la seconde*: as the left leg develops sideward into space, Spread the supporting arm and shoulder complex rightward, thereby expanding the shape and "anchoring" the movement of the gesturing leg (Figure 7.3)
• Oppositional spatial pulls of Forward and Backward (Sagittal)	*First arabesque*: the leg Retreats backward in space from the core as the opposite arm and scapula Advance forward, like a rubber band being stretched in opposite directions (Figure 7.7)
	Temps lié en arrière: a directional reach forward and downward into a *pointe tendu devant* controls and stabilizes the backwards movement of the *temps lié* (Figure 7.1)
• Oppositional spatial pulls combine in complex ways	*Croisé attitude derrière*: the use of *épaulment* creates complex pulls of forward, upward, and sideward through the upper body and arms, while the standing leg Lengthens downward and the *attitude* leg extends backward (Figure 7.4)

Figure 7.2 Explore vertical Countertensions in *sous-sus*

Figure 7.3 Explore horizontal Countertensions in *developpé à la seconde*

The experience of moving in a three-dimensional world with a three-dimensional body means Countertensions exist between different body parts and between the body and space. **I therefore like to think of Countertensions as lines of *oppositional connection* that extend through my body and into my surrounding space.** In this way, the forms you make with your body and the spatial forces impacting your body are in relationship with one another. Reflect on this:

Did you feel how the different balletic positions in Table 7.2 created different spatial lines of connection in your body? And, did you feel how you could continue the intent of those lines out into space beyond your body?

Figure 7.4 Explore vertical, horizontal, and sagittal Countertensions in *croisé attitude*

Spatial concepts sometimes feel abstract and intangible to work with in class. So, it's important to use tangible, sensate methods when introducing these concepts to your students. My favorite tool to use: long elastic Exercise Bands (a.k.a. physical therapy bands or therabands). When dancers pull the ends of the Exercise Bands apart, they kinesthetically feel and visually observe the concepts of Spatial Intent and Countertensions. Their arms produce a clear directional force in space (Spatial Intent) and the force is produced in opposite directions (Countertensions). The Exercise Bands also reveal a visual line that stretches from one part of the body to another part passing through the center of the body.

Figure 7.5 Exercise Bands reveal Countertensions

My students experience "Ah-hah!" moments about their placement when they use Exercise Bands. The Exercise Bands provide them with a visual tool for understanding the spatial qualities of alignment. If any body part along the line of the Exercise Band "grips" or disengages, it becomes increasingly difficult for the dancers to maintain oppositional tension in the Band (Figure 7.6). The dancers quickly discover that the spatial tensions necessary for stability "must constantly renew themselves . . . [and] attempting to 'hold' or 'fix' [the] tensions results in tenseness which is static."[5] This is where the Bands are helpful. Every body part along the line of the Band must participate in producing the elastic countertensions. As this happens, the dancers begin to engage multiple parts of the body collaboratively in order to achieve elongated, dynamic stability.

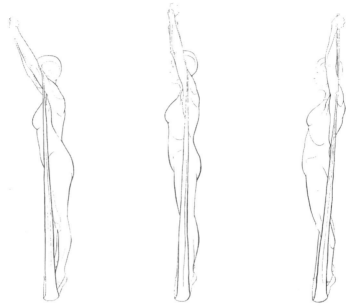

Figure 7.6 Exercise Bands reveal alignment differences

Teacher exploration 7.1 takes you through a series of activities I often use in my classes. There are multiple ways to experiment with holding and using the Exercise Bands; what is efficient for one person may not be efficient for another. It is therefore important to experiment with the Exercise Bands before using them with your dancers. The below exploration provides introductory ideas and activities. Once you become familiar with using the bands, however, experiment with other ways to use them in class.

Teacher exploration 7.1: Playing with Exercise Bands

Materials: one 6- or 7-foot long Exercise Band.[6]

Relevé in *first position*

1   Stand in *first position* with your metatarsals resting on the middle of the Exercise Band. Hold the two ends of the Band with your hands.

---

2   *Relevé* in *first position*, pressing your metatarsals and toes into the band so that your feet are firmly rooted into the floor. As you *relevé*, raise both arms to *fifth position* passing through *first position*.

3   Organize your whole body along the Countertensional through-line. Instead of only reaching the feet downward and the arms upward, also feel how the front surfaces of the ribs and the lower pelvis Lengthen downward toward the feet, while the front surfaces of the pelvis and upper spine Lengthen upward toward the arms. Exhale, and invest in the Lengthening of the *whole* body into space (see Figure 7.6)

First arabesque

1   Attach one end of the Exercise Band to the right foot and hold the other end with the left hand. (I typically wrap the Band around my foot twice before tying the knot on the topside of the foot.)

2   Stand in *fifth position* with the right foot *derrière* and the arms in *first bras bas*. Glide the right leg and left arm away from each other as you reach into *first arabesque*. The Band should cross along the front surfaces of your body. Lengthen and Widen your torso along the diagonal line of the Band. Advance and Widen the left scapula as the right thigh reaches backward.

Figure 7.7 Explore sagittal Countertensions during *arabesque*

3   Experiment with moving the right leg from *arabesque* to *attitude* while simultaneously moving the left arm from the *arabesque port de bras* to *first position*.

4   Keep the Band attached to the same limbs and perform the *arabesque* on the other side so that the right leg is now your standing leg. I suggest allowing the Band to pass along the back side of the right leg and torso toward the left arm. Spread and Widen the left arm and the left side of the torso in space to resist the backward pull of the Band. Exhale, and ground the right leg into the floor.

Developpé à la Seconde

1   Keep the Band attached to the right leg and left arm (as in the previous example). Begin in *fifth position* with the arms in *second position*.
2   Pass through *retiré* as you *developpé* the right leg to *à la seconde*. Continually reinvest in the sideward reach of the left arm in *second position* as the right leg develops into space. Explore this movement: first with the Band passing along the front surfaces of the body and second with it passing along the back surfaces. *Do you have a preference?*
3   Expand your body along the whole line of the band and not just at the distal ends. In order to feel this, "grip" one of the skeletal joints along the band line. For example, tighten the muscles in your left shoulder joint. Then, lessen that tension and Widen the left shoulder toward the left hand. Repeat this process with other body parts: the right foot or hip joint, the left side of the ribs or scapula. Each time, release the tension directionally into space along the line of pull of the Band (either right or leftward). Widening and Spreading are useful Shape elements to embody in this example (Figure 7.3).

Port de bras

1   Place the middle of the Band along the back of the torso so that it touches the bottom of the scapulae (inferior angles). Pull the Band underneath the armpits and wrap it over the top of the upper arms and underneath the lower arms. Hold each end of the Band firmly in each hand.

Figure 7.8 How to hold the Exercise Band

2   Reach your arms into *second position*. There should be some effort involved in maintaining this position. If your arms don't feel as though they will be pulled inwards and slightly backwards in space, increase the Band tension.
3   Place the right hand on the *barre* (with the palm of the hand over the Band). Reach the left arm into *second position*. Begin to perform *battement tendu* or *degagé* with the left leg, maintaining the *second position port de bras*. *What Spatial Intent helps you maintain an active and stable upper body as the lower body moves through space?*
4   Step away from the *barre* and experiment with a *centre floor tendu* exercise. Instead of maintaining *second position port de bras*, move the arms into *croisé, effacé*, and *écharté port de bras*. *What Countertensional pulls do you notice between each arm and between each arm and the other parts of the body?*

Now that you have acquired a basic kinesthetic understanding of Countertensions and Spatial Intent, let's apply these two concepts to a *grand adagio*. As you learn the following *adagio* (Exercise 7.1), take note of the places where these spatial concepts assist your dancing. Create your own counts and timing for the movement.

Exercise 7.1: *Grand adagio* in centre (one side)

Begin in *fifth position en face*, left leg *devant*, arms *bras bas*.

1   *Glissé* to the left passing through *second position plié* and extend the right leg to *à la seconde en l'air* (both arms open to *second position*).

   Enveloppé the right leg into *retiré* as the left arm Rises to *fifth position* and the right Encloses to *first position*.

Figure 7.9 Retiré position

(*Transition*: right leg closes *fifth position derrière* to initiate the next movement)

2   Initiate with the same *glissé*, but progress into left *relevé soutenu* ending in *sous-sus* (left leg *devant*). Repeat the same *port de bras* as above.

3   Left *glissé effacé en avant*, ending with left in *demi-plié* and the right in *pointe tendu derrière*. Left arm reaches low; right arm *allongé fifth position* (Figure 7.17).

   Extend the left leg and *rond de jambe en dedans* the right leg to *pointe tendu effacé devant* (rotate ¼ turn right); left arm Rises to *fifth* and right arm Spreads into *second* (Figure 7.18).

4   *Temps lié en avant* to *first arabesque* and balance on the right leg.

5   Slowly lower the left leg to *fifth position derrière* as the right arm Rises above the head (Figure 7.11).

6 Right *degagé effacé devant* to 90 degrees (or higher) with corresponding arms.

7 Right *grand rond de jambe en dehors* to *croisé attitude derrière*; arms finish in *croisé port de bras*. (Figure 7.4).

8 Left *promenade en dedans* in *attitude derrière*, ending in *effacé attitude derrière* (complete 1¼ revolutions).

9 Right *passé developpé* into *croisé devant* with corresponding arms.

10 *Relevé sous-sus*, and repeat *adagio* on the other side.

Countertensional through-lines support and stabilize numerous steps in the above *grand adagio*. Here are some of the categories of movement that stood out to me.

Moments of stillness, when a position crystallizes in space

Some examples include: *retiré* at the beginning of the exercise, *first arabesque*, *effacé devant* at 90°, and *effacé attitude derrière*.

There is typically more than one Countertension supporting these movements. For example, in the *retiré*, you might engage the:

° *Up/Down Countertension* from the standing leg to the raised arm.
° *Side/Side Countertension* from the *retiré* thigh to the opposite ribs.
° *Both Countertensions simultaneously*, or other Countertensions.

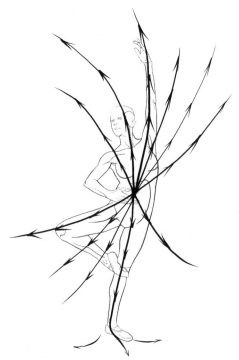

Figure 7.10 Explore different Countertensions during *retiré*

My technical and expressive goals guide my choices. When I feel "ungrounded," for example, I typically emphasize the Up/Down Countertension. When I need to clarify the relationship between the supporting and gesturing sides, I enjoy the Side/Side Countertension. When I want my performance to be richer in volume, I emphasize both Countertensions.

Embody the retiré. How do your choices support your technical and expressive goals? Then, investigate two more crystallized positions from the grand adagio. How does your intent in space and your embodiment of counter-pulls support your movement?

Movements that revolve in space

The *promenade en dedans* in *attitude derrière* is the clearest example. Use the Exercise Band to experiment with this movement in Teacher exploration 7.2.

Teacher exploration 7.2: *Promenade en dedans* in *attitude derrière*

1 **First Countertension:** *fifth position* **arm (right) to the standing leg (left)**

   Attach the Band to your left foot and right hand, passing along the front or back surface of the torso (your preference). Begin the *promenade* and notice how this Countertension serves as an elongated axis for the body.
   Also notice how the right shoulder pushes forward in space as the left side of the pelvis moves backward. This line of connection provides a stabilizing force for the *promenade*. Rotate your head to the left as you *promenade* to accentuate this.

2 **Second Countertension: right thigh in** *attitude* **to the left arm in** *second position*

   Attach the Band to your right foot and left hand, passing along the front surface of your torso. As you promenade, Advance (slightly) the left arm in *second position* while you simultaneously Retreat the right leg in *attitude*. My dancers typically perform this *promenade* with the *second position* arm behind their torsos. This placement "pinches" the left scapula and flares the ribs, which increases tension in the torso. When they Spread and Advance the *second position* arm, they achieve greater stability.

Balances with a changing vertical axis

Some examples include: *first arabesque* to *fifth position* (Figure 7.11, shown with Exercise Band) and *grand rond de jambe en dehors*.

Figure 7.11 Explore how the vertical axis changes from *arabesque* to *fifth position*

Similar to the Figure 7.11, the *grand rond de jambe en dehors* also "rides" changing vertical Countertensions as the leg moves from *effacé* to *écharté* to *croisé*. Even though the Spatial Intent changes during the *grand rond de jambe*, the overall concept of oppositional stability is constant. This is because "spatial tensions develop in constantly changing degrees throughout the whole path [of the movement], not just between the beginning and end of it."[7] Consequently, every time the vertical axis shifts, the Countertensions shift; and as the Countertensions shift, the Spatial Intent of the limbs and torso shift. As Foster writes:

> Whenever the torso changes positions or there is a weight transfer from one leg to the other, the vertical axis changes correspondingly. Placement is the continual redistribution of weight between the head, torso, pelvis, arms, and legs in relation to the vertical axis.[8]

As Foster highlights, placement is not a fixed posture, but instead a dynamic, spatial coordination of multiple body parts. The oppositional lines from the supporting arm to the gesturing leg in the *grand rond de jambe* facilitate torso stability and greater ease of motion in the gesturing leg. Experiment with this in Teacher exploration 7.3.

Teacher exploration 7.3: Changing vertical axes

1 *First arabesque* **to the** *fifth position*: Attach the Exercise Band to the left hand and right foot to investigate the *first arabesque* to the *fifth position* (see Figure 7.11).

- Notice how the Band reveals the changing Countertensional Axes. Pay attention to how the:
  a Ribs, pelvis, and head change in relationship to each other.
  b Arms and legs change in relationship to each other and to the torso.

2 *Grand rond de jambe en dehors*: Practice this without the Band.

- Notice how vertical axis changes its inclination as your right leg moves from *devant* to *derrière*.

  What is the spatial relationship between the head, torso, and pelvis when your leg is devant? How does this relationship shift spatially as you move to écharté, and then from écharté to croisé attitude?

- Focus on the relationship between arms and the right leg. As the right leg Spreads to *écharté*, the left arm Spreads in equal proportion to *second position*. As the right leg Retreats to *attitude derrière*, the right arm Advances and Rises to *fifth position*.

  Do you feel how the arms move in **spatial** *coordination with the left leg?*

Teaching students to embody spatial concepts

Reflect on the explorations from the *Teachers first* section. **What technical and artistic benefits did you experience as you explored Countertensions and Spatial Intent in the** *grand adagio* **exercise?** Based on those challenges:

When would you focus on these spatial concepts with your students? What technical or artistic goals are you trying to achieve?

How would you explain these spatial concepts to your students? What seems important to communicate or emphasize?

In general, when I observe dancers "gripping" their muscles or moving with excess tension, what I am often observing is an underutilized engagement of Countertensional pulls and Spatial Intent. Not surprisingly, as dancers learn to apply these spatial concepts to their dancing, they often experience profound changes in their ability to access dynamic stability. This is because "working with the concept of opposition encourages a lengthened musculature, allowing the dancer to be aware of subtle changes in gravitational pulls."[9] As multiple parts of the body organize around Countertensional through–lines, the tension needed to perform the movement is diffused throughout the torso and limbs.[10] This is in contrast to a focus on "pulling up" or "sucking in" or "standing up straight," which encourages a static relationship to posture and placement.

This difference is significant for pre–professional ballet dancers. Approaching alignment and placement with a "fix it" mentality promotes quick and over-simplified bodily changes that prove difficult to sustain. For example, dancers may push the bottom of the pelvis forward to prevent forward tilt of the pelvis. If they fail to notice how the movement of the pelvis affects the placement of other parts of the body (upper back, ribs, knees, for example), the dancers will practice forced positions and body postures. Countertensions teach dancers to perceive the body relationally.

Artistically, Countertensions and Spatial Intent aid in the development of a spatially expansive and grounded movement style. According to Body–Mind Centering practitioner Linda Hartley, "without grounding and a clear spatial sense we easily become lost as we move."[11] So, at a very basic level, these two LMA concepts help to prevent dancers from becoming "lost in space" as they move.

When first teaching Countertensions and Spatial Intent to your students, I suggest starting with an activity similar to Teacher exploration 7.1. The Bands are easy to incorporate into the regular structure of your class. Often, my dancers tie one end of the Bands to the *barre* and hold the other end with the outside arm. They then use the Bands during select *barre* exercises. This teaches them to consistently reinvest in the spatial reach of the outside arm, especially when the arm maintains the same *port de bras* for an extended period of time. This is a significant realization. They discover that the outside arm (and torso) serves a purpose beyond mere aesthetic decoration; it is a consistent source of stability (See Table 7.3).

It is also easy to incorporate the Bands into simple *centre* exercises, especially if the dancers hold both ends of the Bands with their hands. For more complex *centre* exercises, I typically ask the dancers to use the Bands after the exercise is over as a way to practice singular movements or short movement phrases.

Table 7.3 Technical and artistic benefits of Countertensions and Spatial Intent

Countertensions and **Spatial Intent** are practical concepts to use when teaching students how to:

1. *Align the body in different movements.* These concepts provide a "whole picture" approach for understanding how alignment and placement shift in different movements: a fifth position *grand plié versus* a balance in *attitude derrière,* for example.
2. *Perceive the body relationally.* Feeling the spatial connections between different body parts aids both mobility and stability.
3. *Stabilize dynamically in balances.* Engaging oppositional lines of pull elongate the dancer's musculature, which promotes greater adaptability during balances.
4. *Decrease muscular tension.* When multiple parts of the body organize around Countertensional through-lines, the tension needed for balance and stability is diffused throughout the body.
5. *Make different spatial choices.* In a *piqué first arabesque,* for example, one dancer may emphasize the Countertension from the supporting leg to the top of the head while another emphasizes the Countertension from the forward arm to the *arabesque* leg.

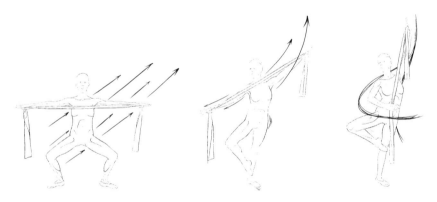

Figure 7.12 Explore *glissé* to *retiré* with the Exercise Band

In order to embody the oppositional tensions needed for balance and stability, students must acquire deeper knowledge about the body and how the different parts of the body coordinate with one another. The Bands provide a tangible and visual starting point, but ultimately, the students need to learn how to access these concepts without the Bands. I use touch, imagery, and basic anatomical information as a way to deepen their understanding.

What basic anatomical information do I teach? I keep it simple. We identify different joints in the body and explore how those joints coordinate with each other. First, I organize the major skeletal joints of the body into four categories:

1   *Distal joints*: hands/wrists, feet/ankles, and head.
2   *Mid-limbs joints*: elbows and knees.
3   *Proximal joints*: shoulder girdle (shoulders/scapulae/clavicles) and hip joints.
4   *Torso*: pelvis, spine, and ribs.

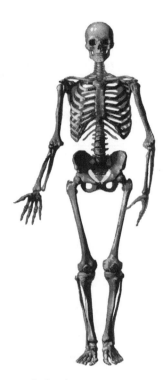

Figure 7.13 Identify different skeletal joints

Next, the dancers use self-touch to locate each of the joints on their bodies. We typically locate our distal joints first and then move inward toward the center of the body. We explore the movements and volume of each joint with our hands. We then repeat this in the opposite direction, moving from core outward to the distal joints. I often ask the dancers to help each other locate the scapulae since it is difficult for them to do this on their own. Many dancers are surprised at the size of the scapulae and how far down the tips of the scapulae are located. Finally, we explore how moving one joint through space affects how the adjacent joints move and feel: for example, moving the shoulder joints creates motion in the scapulae; moving the pelvis creates motion in the lower spine and hip joints.[12]

Explore some of these possibilities on your own for a moment. Move any of the distal, mid-limb, proximal, or core joints through space and notice how the other joints accommodate.

Why do I teach my students to locate these four categories of skeletal joints? My dancers are less aware of how the mid-limb and proximal joints support their body during balances and moments of stability. They tend to reach into space from the hands, feet, and head while simultaneously "gripping" their muscles around the mid-limb and proximal joints (easily observed when they lock their elbow and knee joints or become excessively tense in the shoulders and pelvis). This has a profound effect on their ability to access whole-body Countertensional stability. The mid-limb and proximal joints serve as intermediaries between the core and the distal joints. So, when dancers grip those joints, they lessen the responsiveness between the core and the limbs. Developing kinesthetic awareness in the mid-limbs and proximal joints therefore facilitates stronger coordination between the core and the limbs and greater Countertensional stability.[13]

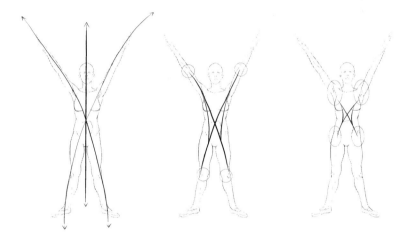

Figure 7.14 Lines of connection between the a) distal, b) mid-limb, and c) proximal joints

The imagery/touch activity, *Body connections!*, is great for teaching dancers to sense and feel 1) the different bodily joints, and 2) the relationship between different parts of the body. Touch and imagery are the primary teaching tools used in this activity. Touch is particularly important because when "combined with the other senses, much more of the brain is activated, thus . . . tapping into more learning potential."[14] This is why I enjoy using *Body connections!* as a warm-up activity; the use of touch warms up their body–mind connections and the dancers continue to reference the pathways they traced throughout technique class.

Body connections! presents just one of many scripts to use. Make this activity your own by exploring your own script! Similarly, feel free to explore different body pathways than those presented below. Perhaps your dancers need to increase awareness of the pathways that connect the pelvis to the feet or one arm to the other arm. There are many possibilities, so follow your instincts!

Body connections!

Objective:

Dancers develop kinesthetic awareness of different body parts relationships.

The students may choose imagery that supports the line of connections you are emphasizing in the body. My students have imagined these lines as:

Ribbons/streamers	*Starfish*	*Rubber bands*
Paint strokes	*Rivers*	*Sunrays*

The image of Sunrays is used below.

Imagine your body is the sun with rays of light shooting out in all directions. The light travels through your body from the core, where it is hottest, through each of the limbs, cooling as it travels from the distal edges of the body into space. These rays of light connect different parts of your body together bringing them into relationship with one another. Some rays connect the opposite shoulders and hips, elbows and knees, and hands and feet.

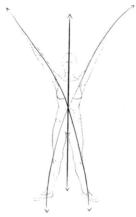

Figure 7.15 Rays of light emanating in all directions

Tracing the pathways from the arms to the pelvis

1   *Locate the tips of the left fingers and trace a pathway from your fingers to your sternum, passing along the left elbow, shoulder joint, and clavicle. Keep the right hand on the top of the sternum as you move your left arm through space. Imagine*

the sunray emanating from the sternum, through the arm, and out through the fingertips into space. Where are you sending the light?

2 *Trace the pathway from the sternum to the pubic bone, passing along the navel. Maintain the locating touch at the pubic bone as you again move your arm through space. Imagine sending the warmth of the sunray from your core to your arm. Feel how your belly center and ribs expand and condense or twist and untwist as the arm moves through various port de bras, and as the torso moves in and out of épaulment. Notice how the pelvis and core anchor the movement of the arm.*

3 Ask the students to repeat the tracing touch along the backside of the torso from the arms to the scapulae. This is best accomplished with a partner, but this activity also works without a partner if you have a student who prefers to work solo.

Trace the pathway from the fingers to the scapula. Trace along the periphery of the scapula to feel the location of inner edges and the bottom tips of the scapula. Maintain this touch as the arm moves through space. Continue the touch to the sacrum/tail location. With one hand touching the sacrum, move the arm through space, noticing again how the pelvis anchors the movements of the arm.

Tracing the pathways from the feet to the head ("figure eight")[15]

1 *Place your hands on the first three toes of your foot. Trace upward to the navel, passing along the knees, inner thighs, and hip joints. From the navel, sweep along the lower ribs to the back of the spine. Continue upward along the upper spine and neck until you reach the top of the head. Extend your arms upward in space. Inhale and exhale imagining the sunrays along the whole pathway from feet to head.*

2 *Reverse this pathway. Begin at the top of the head. Trace along the face all the way down to the navel, passing along the upper ribs and sternum. From the navel, sweep along the lower ribs to the sacrum and tail (coccyx). Continue downward along the hamstrings to the heel bones and finally along the side of the feet to the last two toes.*

3 Ask the students to perform a different balletic movements, experimenting with these upward and downward feet to head sensations (see Figure 7.16).

Tracing other pathways

Explore other pathways of connection in the body:

- *Trace from one arm to the other arm passing along the clavicles.*
- *Trace from right leg to right arm passing through the core.*
- *What about proximal joint connections? For example, from the left shoulder to the right hip joint.*
- *Or, mid-limb connections? For example, from the left knee to the left elbow.*
- *What other connections can you trace in your body?*

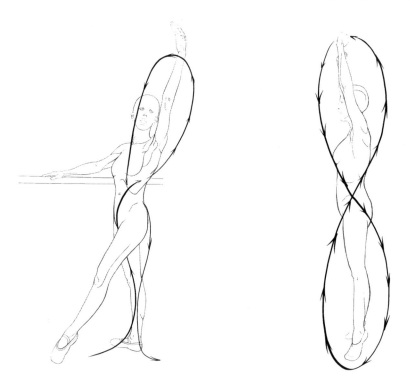

Figure 7.16 Figure eight image during *tendu* and *relevé*

Body connections! develops the body awareness needed for strengthening the dancers' core-to-limb and limb-to-limb relationships. In order for this to lead to positive changes in their technique skills, however, they need opportunities to apply this awareness directly to balletic movement. *Barre* is a great place to start. My dancers trace specific pathways in their body between each *barre* exercise. For example:

- Tracing feet-to-head pathways prior to a *demi/grand plié* exercise develops awareness of how the push from the lower body travels upward through the body as they extend their legs, engaging the up/down Countertension.

- Activating arms-to-pelvis connections enliven the *barre* arm and activate the use of the scapulae and spine during *port de bras*.

My verbal and touch cueing during the exercises also reinforces these connections.

How would you explore these connections during barre? How would you cue the dancers to attend to these connections while they dance?

Body connections! ends with the dancers exploring other relationships in their bodies. When my dancers do this, they discover relationships that seem particularly relevant to their technique goals. For example, a dancer exploring the pathway from the *barre* arm to the gesturing arm will experience the same exercise quite differently than a dancer exploring the connection between the standing leg and the outside arm. There are multiple oppositional relationships in the body for any given movement: those that connect oppositional pulls from one limb to another limb via the core of the body; those that connect the proximal joints of one limb to the distal joints of the same limb; those that travel from up to down, or side to side, or back to front; and so on. This variability gives you and your dancers the freedom to explore numerous Countertensional relationships throughout class.

As dancers sense and feel the relationship between different parts of the body, they improve their ability to access the Countertensional pulls during balletic steps. *Opposition creates connection!* explores the *grand adagio* from the *Teachers first* section, focusing specifically on oppositional relationships between the supporting and gesturing sides of the body and between the upper and lower body. Remind the dancers to extend the Countertensional pulls from their bodies into space. **In this way, they embody both spatial through-lines and spatial trajectories!**

Opposition creates connection!

Objective:

Dancers learn how to engage oppositional lines of connection in their bodies and extend those lines into space during balletic movements.

Preparation: Teach the *grand adagio* to your students.

Note: If, at any point, these activities start to feel too introspective or cerebral, ask the dancers to explore the activities with the Exercise Bands. Or, ask them to work in pairs and apply locating touches in the opposite limbs while each partner moves.

Practice different Countertensions in the *adagio*

Ask the dancers to trace the pathways from the left arm to the right leg, and vice versa. Focus on these connections during:

1   ***Glissé second position* to *à la seconde*.** *Widen the left side of the torso as you glissé left into second position plié. Spread the left arm away from the right leg as it lifts and Spreads into à la seconde. Engage the side/side Countertension.*

2   ***Glissé effacé en avant* to left *pointe tendu derrière*.** *Sink and Spread into demi-plié as the left arm Rises and Spreads into allongé second position. Notice the Countertensions between the arms, and between the right thigh and left arm.*

Figure 7.17 Explore the Countertensions in *pointe tendu derrière*

3   **Left *pointe tendu effacé devant*.** *Notice two "cross" Countertensions: 1) lengthen the right side of the torso upward and slightly backward in opposition to the forward and downward reach of the left leg into pointe tendu devant. 2) feel the left shoulder and right side of the pelvis Widen away from each other.*

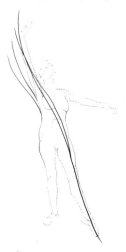

Figure 7.18 Explore the Countertensions in *pointe tendu devant*

4   *Temps lié* into *left first arabesque*: Ask the dancers to work with a partner. One partner places a hand on the left side of the other partner's pelvis and the other hand on the right shoulder joint. The partners should maintain this locating touch as the dancers move from *temps lié* to *first arabesque*—this means that both partners need to actively shift their weight through space. *Attend to the relationship between these two points of contact. Notice the Countertension between the right shoulder and the left hip joint. How does it support your movement during both the temps lié and the lift of the leg into arabesque?*

5   **Explore three other movements from the *grand adagio*.**

Extension activities

- **Teacher's or dancer's choice!** Trace other pathways of connection in the body and apply those pathways to the *Adagio*: arm to arm, feet to head, right lower to right upper, and so on.
- **Shift your weight!** Ask the dancers to attend to the relationships between the head, shoulder girdle, ribs, and pelvis in *grand rond de jambe* and *first arabesque* to *fifth position* (similar to Teacher exploration 7.3).
- **Just the legs!** Focus on the Countertensions that exist between lower body joints. For example, in the *pointe tendu effacé devant*, the pelvis has a slightly backward Spatial Intent (even though the pelvis is not actually moving backward) in order to counteract the leg moving forward in the *tendu*. Ask the dancers to allow the pelvis to move forward with the leg in the *tendu devant*. Then, ask them to stabilize the pelvis as the leg moves forward. *Do they feel the slightly backward (and sideward) intent of the pelvis in space?*
- **Barre exercises**: Focus on pathways between the *barre* arm and the outside leg. For example: Sliding the *barre* arm forward when lifting the leg into *arabesque* and then sliding it backwards when lowering the leg to *fifth position*. Widening the shoulder girdle and arm closest to the *barre* during a *developpé à la seconde*. Over time, dancers learn to use the *barre* dynamically in the same way that they would use a partner's hand in a *pas de deux*.

Notes

1 Bartenieff, I. (1980). *Body Movement: Coping with the Environment*. New York: Routledge, p. 21.
2 Moore, C.L. (2009). *The Harmonic Structure of Movement, Music, and Dance According to Rudolf Laban*. Lewiston, NY: The Edwin Mellen Press, p. 196.
3 Foster, R. (2010). *Ballet Pedagogy: the Art of Teaching*. Gainesville, FL: University Press of Florida, p. 2.

4   Moore, C.L. (2009), p. 121.
5   Bartenieff, I. (1980, 2002), p. 108.
6   I purchase large rolls of Exercise Bands online. I then use scissors to cut the roll into multiple 6- to 7-foot long strips.
7   Bartenieff, I. (1980, 2002), p. 105.
8   Foster, R. (2010), p. 61.
9   Paskevska, A. (2005). *Ballet Beyond Tradition.* New York: Routledge, p. 56.
10 See also: Bartenieff, I. (1980, 2002): "Recognition of kinetic muscular chains—the sequence of muscles used in a movement—diminishes the exclusive dependence on individual muscle strength for movement power" (p. 21).
11 Hartley, L. (1995). *Wisdom of the Body Moving: An Introduction to Body-Mind Centering,* 2nd edn. Berkeley, CA: North Atlantic Books, p. 146.
12 See also: The Guided Explorations in Chapter 6 of *Creative Ballet Learning* (student manual).
13 See also: Hackney, P. (2000). *Making Connections: Total Body Integration Through Bartenieff Fundamentals.* New York: Routledge, Chapter 7. Core-Distal Connectivity is one of the six Patterns of Total Body Connectivity in the Bartenieff Fundamentals. In Core-Distal Connectivity the body is "organized by a pattern of connectivity that begins in the center core of the body and radiates out through the torso to the proximal joints, the mid-limbs and all the way to the distal ends of the extremities" (p. 68).
14 Hannaford, C. (1995). *Smart Moves: Why Learning is not all in your Head.* Arlington, VA: Great Ocean Publishers, p. 41.
15 See also: Hackney, P. (2000), p. 101. Hackney explores some of these pathways in chapter 8: Head–Tail Connectivity.

Chapter 8

Moving three-dimensionally
Traceforms and Kinesphere

Have you ever played with glow sticks or sparklers or laser pointers in the dark? Have you performed balletic movement holding streamers in your hands? If so, you have likely discovered the joy of using these objects to create fleeting pictures in the air. Perhaps you drew zigzags or spirals that traveled from high to low, or maybe you wrote your name in cursive. These objects made it possible for you to see the impressions your movement left in the space. Every time you move, you "design" the space around your body—your Kinesphere—with a landscape of varied lines and pathways. Some are linear and laser-like, others curve through the space, and some twist in spiral-like pathways. Laban referred to this aspect of movement as "living architecture ... made up of pathways tracing shapes in space."[1] He called these pathways Traceforms, and was fascinated with how humans "traced" and "formed" the space around their bodies. He wrote: "[A]n urge was borne, the urge to contact space that is invisible. This urge which tends into space is the pleasure to move. All movement tends into space, both the space around us and the space within us."[2]

I am equally as fascinated with this. When I take ballet class, I sometimes imagine that my body is covered in paint and that the air around my body is an artist's canvas. I wonder:

> *What will this canvas look like by the end of ballet class? What lines and pathways will I have painted with my limbs and torso?*
> *What spatial zones around my body will have the most paint? Those in front or behind me? Above me or low to the floor? To the right or left?*
> *Will the paint be close to my body's center, or will it be located far away from me?*
> *What parts of my canvas will have no paint at all?*

Dancers enliven the three-dimensional sphere of space around their bodies in different ways throughout a technique class. At the advanced levels, ballet dancers often use both their arms and legs to "paint" the middle and high areas of their Kinespheres, and while the upper body does, at times, move at a low level, ballet dancers typically paint the low areas with their legs and feet. They also "paint" the areas behind and in front of the body as they move *derrière* and *devant* and travel *en arrière* and *en avant*. "Painting" the right and left areas in equal proportions is a goal in ballet classes, but depending on a dancer's (or a teacher's) preferences for demonstrating and marking exercises, one side may have many more "paint strokes" than the other.

Figure 8.1 "Painting" the space with the limbs

The pathways dancers "paint" in their Kinespheres are just as interesting. Some pathways move from the center of their bodies outward, like the linear, unfolding of the leg forward from *retiré* during a *developpé devant*. Some of these pathways trace a border at the edge of their Kinespheres like the curving pathway traced by the leg during a *rond de jambe en dehors* or by the arm as it moves from *second* to *fifth position*. And, some of these pathways are far more complex and three-dimensional, like gradual spiraling of the upper and lower body into *épaulment* when moving from *fifth position* to *croisé attitude derrière*.

How do ballet dancers develop sensitivity to the different ways they "trace" and "form" the space around their bodies?

How do they learn to access clear directionality of the body and limbs during locomotive upper and lower body movements?

And, how does this knowledge facilitate three-dimensional, dynamic mobility?

You have already begun to address these questions in the previous chapters. The movement concepts from Chapters 6 and 7 underpin the dynamic exploration of one's Kinesphere. Shape Flow Support and Shape Qualities teach dancers how to shape and form the torso and limbs from one position to the next, and Spatial Intent and Countertensions provide dancers with clear spatial trajectories for this forming process.

Instead of focusing on balance and stability, Chapter 8 shifts the focus to mobility and propulsion through space. In addition to revisiting the movement concepts from the previous two chapters, Chapter 8 introduces two new Laban/Bartenieff Movement Analysis (L/BMA) movement concepts: **Kinesphere** and **Traceforms**. Collectively, these concepts facilitate full-bodied, three-dimensional movement through space.

Teachers first: exploring Traceforms in your Kinesphere

Holding markers in both hands, begin to draw imaginary lines in the empty space nearest to your body. Create lines in space that almost touch your torso, head, legs, and feet. Imagine you are tracing the location of a blanket that once enveloped you. Next, extend your arms further into space and repeat the same process, drawing the space above, below, in front and behind you. Finally, lunge onto one leg in varying directions reaching your arms further into space while keeping your other leg rooted to where you were just standing. Create a large "bubble" the color of your markers in the spaces that exist far away from your body. When you are finished, stand in the middle of your bubble, and notice all of the places you visited in your Kinesphere: those near and far, high and low, in front and behind, and to the sides . . . and . . . all of the places in between.

Your **Kinesphere** is the space directly around your body; it is your personal space. When moving with large reaching gestures, your Kinesphere size grows as you discover its outer edges with the distal joints of your body. When moving with small reaching gestures, it shrinks as you explore its inner landscapes. Any part of your body can move to any region of your Kinesphere depending on your movement preferences and on the capacities and limitations of your body. For example, I have always enjoyed exploring my Kinesphere with my lower body, but it was much easier for me to reach into the high zones of my Kinesphere with my feet when I was younger.

You colored many different spatial regions with your markers in the above exploration. In L/BMA, these are referred to as the Zones of your Kinesphere. Since the human body is three-dimensional, the Zones of the Kinesphere are also three-dimensional. And, since humans complete tasks that are both near and far away from the body (sewing a pointe shoe verses executing a *grand jeté*), the Kinesphere grows and shrinks with your actions (Table 8.1).

Table 8.1 Kinesphere Zones and Size

Zones	Size
High	
Middle	Small-Reach
Low	Mid-Reach
Front	Large-Reach
Back	
Right	
Left	

It is possible to combine Kinesphere Zones and Size in varied ways. *Explore moving the following examples in a non-balletic way.*

1   Large-Reach movements directed to the Forward Low Zones.
2   Large-Reach movements directed to the Back Right High Zones.
3   Small-Reach movements directed to the Low Zones on your Right and Left.
4   Small-Reach movements directed to the Left High Zones.
5   Mid-Reach movements directed to the Back Low Zones.
6   Mid-Reach movements directed to Forward Middle Zones.

Explore these examples again. This time, identify balletic movements that take place in these zones. For example, in #1, I performed a *battement degagé devant* to a lunge in *fourth position* followed by an expansive forward and downward reaching *port de corps*. In #3, I performed a *petite second position échappé* emphasizing the side low zones with my legs at the top of the jump. In #5, I performed a *battement tendu derrière*, but I could have just as easily performed a *battement frappé derrière*. **What balletic movements did you discover?**

As you explored the above movements, you not only traveled to different Zones but you also created different pathways, or **Traceforms**, in your Kinesphere. It is easy to identify the Traceforms when moving your limbs largely, but you create Traceforms in your Kinesphere even when your arms and legs, or any other part of your body, moves with a small range of motion. Recall again your experience playing with sparklers or streamers. The spatial pathways you create when you make small circles with a sparkler or a streamer are just as observable as when you make large circles. Both leave visible impressions in the space.

Similarly, any part of the body can create pathways in the Kinesphere. Imagine I placed sparklers on the major joints of your body—from core to distal—and then asked you to perform a *plié* exercise at *barre*. (If sparklers seem too intense an image, perhaps imagine little motion capture technology sensors placed in the same locations.) As you perform the *plié* exercise, the sparklers or motion sensors reveal numerous Traceforms created by different parts of your body. For example, your:

- Knees create linear Traceforms that descend and ascend while moving toward and away from your body.
- Elbow creates a triangular Traceform as your arm moves from *second*, to *bras bas*, to *first*, and back to *second position*.
- Head creates an elliptical Traceform as it follows your gesturing arm.

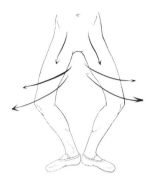

Figure 8.2 The knees create linear Traceforms during *plié*

Exploring how different parts of the body travel through different Zones of the Kinesphere is a great way to deepen Spatial Intent and body awareness. As dancers practice attending to the trajectory of their bodies in space, they learn to ask: *How does this movement travel through my Kinesphere?*

Knowing where to go (the Zone) and how to get there (the Traceform) are crucial steps in actually getting there. *Take a moment to embody some of these ideas in* Teacher exploration 8.1.

Teacher exploration 8.1: Creating Traceforms in your Kinesphere

Choose an image that works for you in the following exploration. Some possibilities might be:

glow stickers   *sparklers*   *motion sensors*   *lasers*   *paint brushes*

I chose to use the image of "Glow Stickers" for the following activity.
Imagine you are in a dark room with glow stickers attached to each of your proximal, mid-limbs, and distal joints. Even imagine you have glow stickers attached to each of the 24 vertebrae in the movable spine. Take a moment and touch each of these locations on your body.

Upper body

1   *Explore the space around your body with your arms.* Play freely with both contemporary and classical *port de bras*, imagining how the glow stickers on each upper body joint illuminate different pathways in space. Eventually, choose one *port de bras* to repeat:

  • ***Where is this port de bras moving in your Kinesphere?*** *Up to down? Side to side? Forward to back? Or, some combination of all these directions?*
  • ***How small or large is the port de bras?*** *Does it change in size?*
  • ***What is the design of the Traceform?*** *Are the glow stickers revealing pathways that are curved? Linear? Triangular? Circular? Spiral-like?*

2   *Notice one part of the upper body at a time.*

  • ***How does each joint in the upper body, from distal to core, create a unique Traceform?*** Attend to the spatial pathway of the hands, then the elbows, the shoulders, and finally the scapula. Notice differences in the size and design of the Traceforms.

Change your *port de bras* at any time you feel compelled to explore a new possibility in space.

Lower body

Repeat the above process with the lower body. As you move your lower body through various contemporary and classical ballet movements, notice the size and design of the Traceforms your feet, knees, and hips leave in space.

The primary purpose of the above exploration was to deepen your kines-thetic understanding of Traceforms and Kinesphere Zones, and to experience how different parts of the body create unique spatial pathways in space. Explor-ing the Traceforms of each joint in isolation is a great method for increasing intentionality and awareness in different body parts during balletic movement. It may be useful, for example, to attend to the spatial pathway of the upper thighs during a *rond de jambe*, especially when working on elongation and mobility of the legs in space. Or, you may investigate the spatial pathways of the elbows during *port de bras* in order to activate the upper arms.

Practice those two examples in your own body.

Teacher exploration 8.2 continues the above investigations. Instead of focus-ing on the Traceforms of different joints in isolation, Teacher exploration 8.2 focuses on how Traceforms in one part of the body relate to Traceforms in another part of the body. The purpose here is to investigate core–to–limb relationships and whole body coordination (similar to the Countertension explorations in the last chapter).

Teacher exploration 8.2: Traceforms in relationship

Upper body and spine

1   *Notice more than one part of the upper body at a time as you explore contemporary or classical port de bras.*

• **How do the Traceforms in different parts of the upper body relate to each other?** Attend to the Traceforms in two parts of the upper body simultaneously: the pathways of the hands and elbows, or shoulders and hands, or the scapula and elbows, and so on.

How do the two parts coordinate with each other to produce spatially active port de bras?

2   *Follow the movements of your arms with your head and upper spine.*

• **How is the spine moving in relationship to the arms?**

What parts of your spine are moving the most—the neck (cervical), the upper and middle spine (thoracic), the lower spine (lumbar)? Are the glow stickers on your vertebrae curving to the right or left? Are they changing levels? Are they spiraling—one part of the spine twisting to the right as another part twists to the left, for example?

Lower body and spine

1   *Repeat the above process with your lower body.* Explore how the Traceforms of the feet, knees, and hips relate to each other.

2   When you feel ready, *allow your spine to respond to the movements of your legs.* In particular, notice how the pelvis moves in relationship to the legs and how the spine moves in relationship to the pelvis.

Initiating movements from different body parts is another way to explore how the Traceforms in different joints affect each other. *For example, perform the following port de bras:*
Bras bas to first position to second position and back to bras bas.
Do this port de bras four times. Initiate the movement from the fingertips the first time. Then initiate from the elbows, then the shoulders, and finally the scapulae.

Each initiation, whether distal or proximal, caused the other joints to move: the fingertips and elbows always lifted and glided through the space, the shoulders rotated, and the scapulae glided along the rib cage. But, if your experience was similar to mine, you likely felt a different kinesthetic journey with each initiation point. For example, I loved the feeling of initiating with my elbows. This initiation accentuated the Traceforms of my upper arm, especially the Traceform from *second position* to *bras bas*.[3] I enjoyed how the elbows created a tiny curved Traceform that retreated and rose slightly as the arms lifted and turned over before lowering to *bras bas*. Sometimes initiating with my elbows in other parts of the *port de bras* caused unnecessary elevation in my shoulder girdle, however. Attending to the scapulae in these moments helped. As I moved my arms upward from *bras bas* to *first position*, for example, I actively depressed and widened the scapulae along the rib cage, which provided a natural up/down Countertension to the movement.[4]

What body part or parts did you enjoy initiating with in the above port de bras?
Did some initiation points feel more stylistically accurate to you?
Did some seem to lead to interesting contemporary explorations?

Focusing on Traceforms and Kinesphere in technique class helps me approach balletic movement differently for different dancers. I may cue one dancer to attend to the front zones of the Kinesphere while I cue another dancer to attend to the zones behind the body. One dancer may receive touch feedback at the proximal joints while another receives touch at the distal joints. Making these determinations broadens my ability to provide helpful and appropriate hands on and verbal feedback throughout class.

Let's continue to explore the versatility of these two spatial concepts in the next section.

Teaching students to trace the space

As the below list indicates, balletic terminology and movement is spatially oriented. By the time dancers reach the pre-professional level, they have learned this vocabulary, and they understand that most steps—such as *glissade* or *temps lié* or *pas de bourrée*—can be performed in a variety of directions in space. The adaptability of how and where steps travel in space is an essential skill needed at the advanced levels of ballet technique.

en arrière (backward)
en avant (forward)
en l'air (in the air)
à terre (on the ground)
dessous (under)
dessus (over)

devant (in front)
derrière (behind)
de côté (sideways)
en dedans (inward)
en dehors (outward)

When I teach Traceforms and Kinesphere to my students, I do so with relative ease. *Why?* Traceforms and Kinesphere align with their basic kinesthetic understanding of ballet technique by reinforcing the importance of moving in clear spatial directions. These two concepts broaden the students' conception of space. Instead of focusing solely on directions and locations, Traceforms and Kinesphere teach dancers to also attend to the spatial *pathways* that connect their movement from one location to another. In my experience, ballet dancers are less practiced at attending to this. This is similar to some of the issues presented in Chapter 6: ballet dancers are quite familiar with Shape as a position, as a static form, and much less familiar with the concept of Shape as a forming process, as a dynamic unfolding of many forms over time. I often find that deepening the dancers' understanding of Traceforms and Kinesphere deepens their understanding of Shape Qualities and Shape Flow Support (and vice versa).

Reflect on the explorations from the *Teachers first* section. **What technical and artistic benefits did you experience as you explored Traceforms and Kinesphere?** Based on those challenges:

When would you focus on these spatial concepts with your students? What technical or artistic goals are you trying to achieve?

How would you explain these spatial concepts to your students? What seems important to communicate or emphasize?

As students explore the concepts of Traceforms and Kinesphere, they embody greater spatial clarity at the beginning, middle, and end of a movement. They learn to focus on where movement originates, how it travels through space, and where it concludes. Focusing on Kinesphere size also teaches students to analyze how movements increase and decrease in size throughout a movement phrase; embodying these differences adds artistic variety to their dancing. Similarly, students gain a variety of methods for increasing spatial awareness in underutilized parts of their bodies when they investigate how different parts of the body create unique Traceforms in space.

Table 8.2 Technical and artistic benefits of Kinesphere and Traceforms

Kinesphere and **Traceforms** are useful concepts to focus on when teaching dancers how to:

1. *Emphasize the size of their movements in space.* Phrasing from subtle, petite movements to expansive, grand movements, and vice versa.
2. *Clarify the Spatial Intent of the movement,* such as moving to the Forward Upward Zone—direction of flight for the body in *sauté first arabesque (Figure 8.3)*—or to the Rightward Middle Zone—reaching one leg to *à la second* at 90 degrees—or to the Backward Low Zone—reaching one leg to fourth position lunge at the end of an *en dehors pirouette.*
3. *Clarify the spatial pathway traced by the limbs and torso,* such as moving the lower body from Place Middle to Forward Middle—*développé devant* at 90 degrees from *retiré* —or from Upward to Backward High to Backward Middle Zones—*cambré derrière.*
4. *Enliven spatial awareness in different parts of the body,* such as the pathway of the head during *grand port de corps,* or the elbows and knees in *pas de basque,* or the fingers and toes in *penché arabesque.*
5. *Strengthen core-to-limb coordination,* such as attending to how the pathway of the head moves in relationship to the pathway of the lower spine in *grand port de corps,* or how the pathway of the fingers and toes move in relationship to the elbows and knees in *pas de basque,* or how the pathway of the pelvis and ribs move in relationship to the fingers and toes in *penché arabesque.*

When first teaching these spatial concepts to your dancers, I suggest a simple to complex progression, similar to Teacher explorations 8.1 and 8.2. In those explorations, you first attended to Kinesphere Zone and Size. Then, you analyzed the general Traceform of your movements. Next, you focused on the Traceforms created by individual body parts, and finally you focused on the relationship between different Traceforms in different parts of the body. The following five-class activity, *Painting the space!* follows this progression in a fun and playful way.

Painting the space! teaches dancers to attend to the three-dimensional Traceforms around their bodies. Through improvisational play, they explore movements in multiple directions, and they experiment with making different pictures and designs in the space around their bodies. As Dance Educator Lorin Johnson notes, "when students explore how their bodies can envelope, carve, penetrate, shape, and interact with the space around them, they

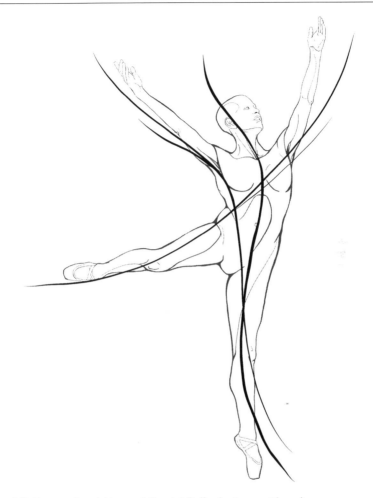

Figure 8.3 Forward and Upward Spatial Pulls during *sauté arabesque*

immediately fill each movement with the immediacy of their own discoveries."[5] This facilitates a more animated and joyful exploration of the space around their bodies.

Similar to Chapter 7, I suggest using props when first teaching the spatial concepts to your dancers. Streamers or long strips of fabric are tangible and accessible tools for visualizing the concepts. Dancers may hold them in their hands or tie them on different parts of their bodies. This helps them feel and see, quite literally, the spatial pathways for different joints.

Painting the space!

(Five-class activity)

Objective:

Dancers accentuate the spatial pathways traced by the body, and deepen their spatial awareness in different parts of the body.

Preparation: Give each dancer a 3–4 foot fabric streamer, scarf, strip of fabric, leg warmers.

Part I: Up, down, and all around!

Warm-up for the first class: *Hold the fabric in one hand. Improvise with the fabric, moving it through the space in any way you want. Move the fabric up and down, forward and back, side to side, near to and far away from your body. Where in space can you move the fabric?*

How many different pictures can you "paint" in the space? Notice the pathways of those pictures: paint circles or zigzags, straight lines or spirals. How would you describe the pictures you are creating?

Ask the dancers to tie the props to another body part: the head, knees, shoulders, waist/pelvis, and so on. Repeat the above exploration with the new body part, cueing them to notice the Traceforms created by this part of the body. Experiment with two more body parts before moving to Part II.

Part II: Painting at *Barre*

Class 1: Distal joints

1   Bring the fabric props to *barre*. During select exercises, ask the dancers to tie the scarves to the gesturing wrists or ankles, or to the head (around the forehead or around the hair). I suggest doing this for at least six exercises at *barre*: two with the wrists, two with the ankles, and two with the head.

2   Make sure the exercises you select include a wide range of movement for each of those body parts (for example, for the wrists any exercise with mobile *port de bras*; for the head an exercise that includes full-bodied *port de corps*; for the ankles a *battement fondu* or *rond de jambe*). Note: you may find the scarves cumbersome to use on the lower body. It is important for the dancers to use a tactile "prop" they can see and feel. A leg warmer around the ankle is a simple alternative to the scarves.

3   During the exercises, cue the dancers to: *Imagine your hands (or feet or head) are paintbrushes covered in the color of your fabric. Are you painting the space close to your body or far away? Are the paint strokes small or large? Is the fabric traveling toward or away from your body?*

4   When they repeat the exercise on the other side, ask them: *What direction is the fabric moving in your Kinesphere? Do your hands (or feet or head) paint the space up High or down Low? Backwards or Forwards? Right or Left?*

Classes 2 and 3: Mid-limb and proximal joints

1   Repeat the above exploration in the next two classes. In Class 2, ask the dancers to tie the scarves (or leg warmers) around their elbows and knees, and in Class 3 around their shoulders and upper thighs/ hip joints.

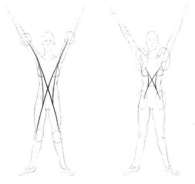

Figure 8.4 "Paint" the space with the mid-limb and proximal joints

2   **Class 2: Mid-limbs**. *What lines in space are the elbows and knees painting? Are they straight or curved? Circular or triangular? Spiral-like?*
As you progress through *barre*, ask them:
What Zones in your Kinesphere are you painting with the color of your fabric? Are the mid-limbs moving the fabric in more than one direction simultaneously—Backward and Downward or Upward and Sideward, for example?

3   **Class 3: Proximal joints**. *Imagine the entire upper arm (or upper thigh) as a giant paint sponge. Similar to the previous explorations, notice how the "sponges" move through your Kinesphere, scattering the space with the color of your fabric. Also explore how the Traceforms change level and locations in your Kinesphere. For example, do the paint strokes move from Low to High, Back to Front, or Side to Side? Perhaps they move from Back and Down to Forward and Down (a balançoire, for example).*

Part III: Choose the parts that paint!

Classes 4 and 5: Dancer's choice

1   Ask the dancers to choose two different parts of the body to focus on at *barre*. Encourage them to make different choices in Classes 4 and 5. *What parts of your body need more spatial awareness today? Your distal joints? Your mid-limbs joints, or possibly your proximal joints? Or, maybe some combination of these different joints, your elbows and hip joints, or your knees and hips, or your shoulders and fingers, for example.*

2   Continue using the scarves (or leg warmers). Or, if you prefer, discard the props and simply ask the dancers to give a massaging self-touch to those parts of their bodies. For some *barre* exercises, cue them to: *Focus on only one part at a time. How is that part painting the space? How is the movement of that part of your body facilitating your execution of the balletic steps?*

3   Allow the exploration to become more complex in some of the *barre* exercises. *Focus on both parts simultaneously. First, trace the connection from one part to the other part. For example, if you focused on the hands and the hips, trace the pathways on your body from the hands to the hips. You can cross sides—right hand to left hip—or stay on the same side—right hand to right hip. As you perform the barre exercises, notice how those parts of your body are working together to facilitate your movement. How do both parts Trace and Form the space? How do the pathways of both parts relate to each other? How does that facilitate your technical execution of the barre exercises?*

In *Painting the space!* the dancers chose freely the parts of the body they wanted to focus on during Classes 4 and 5. When I observe the choices my dancers make, I discover how they use the movement concepts to achieve their technical goals. This enhances my ability to work positively with their individual differences as I provide them with verbal and hands on feedback.

You may, however, decide to limit the exploration in Classes 4 and 5 to particular regions of the body—only the lower or only the upper, for example. This approach is useful when you need to work on the technique of a specific body region during *barre*. Similarly, I often ask my dancers to choose one part in the upper body and one part in the lower body—the shoulders and hips, for example. This is a good approach when dancers need to enhance the coordination between the upper and lower body: noticing when the upper is stable, while the lower is mobile (and vice versa), or how Traceforms in the lower relate to or support the Traceforms in the upper (and vice versa). In general, there are many options to explore in *Painting the space!*.[6] **Trust your instincts, and as you navigate the activity, make it your own!**

Moving the Kinesphere through space

Dancers move from place to place in the dance studio while simultaneously moving from place to place in their Kinespheres. For example, as I *chassé en avant* from corner to corner in the dance studio, I gradually move my arms through my Kinesphere from *second position*, to *bras bas*, to *first position* and finally to *fifth position*. The spatial pathways my arms trace in my Kinesphere are just as important as my spatial pathway across the dance studio.

Sometimes dancers forget to invest in *how* their torso and limbs move in their Kinespheres as they travel across the studio floor. They tend to place their limbs (arms and head, especially) in fixed positions as they move through the space. Or, they move their arms and legs choppily from one position to the next because they focus on the position instead of the pathway. In either case, attending to how they are moving in their Kinespheres typically improves their ability to travel through space. Let's analyze the above *chassé en avant* to illustrate this point.

As you chassé across the floor, slide your leading leg to the Forward Low Zone of your Kinesphere as you initiate each chassé. Also accentuate the forwardness of the upper body Traceform from bras bas to fifth position. Then, open the arms in a slightly forward path along the edge of your Kinesphere as you move from fifth to second position.

In the above example, pushing and reaching into the Forward Zones of the Kinesphere with both the upper and lower body enhances the forward path across the studio floor.

Students maximize their locomotive potential when they learn how to "push" and "reach" their upper and lower limbs past the edge of their Kinespheres into clear spatial directions. The Exercise Bands (also used in Chapter 7) are effective in teaching them how to activate these connections. The Bands provide a spatial resistance for dancers to push against. This helps them feel how the Spatial Intent of the body both initiates and guides their locomotion. Imagery is also helpful here. Imagining laser beams emanating from the body enhances the feeling of moving one's Kinesphere through space along clear spatial directions.

The following activities explore locomotive movement from these perspectives. I suggest experimenting with these activities in your body before using them in class with your dancers. This will assist your verbal clarity as you teach the activities to your students. You will also discover a variety of ways to apply the ideas from these activities to other movements and exercises in class. Similar to *Painting the space!*, adapt *Move into space at barre!* to fit your educational objectives.

Move into space at *barre*!

Objective:

Dancers clarify the Spatial Intent of movements that locomote through the general space.

The below activities explore *balancé* at *barre*, but you could also explore *pas de bourée, temps lié, glissé, glissade,* and so on.

Preparation: Give each dancer a 6- or 7-foot long Exercise Band. Ask the dancers to tie one end of the Bands to the *barre* and hold the other end with the outside arm. Begin to explore a series of traveling steps at *barre*.

Balancé à la seconde to piqué sous-sus

1   Begin in *fifth position* with the right leg *devant*, the left arm holding the *barre*, and the right arm holding the Band with the Band crossing in front of the torso.

2   *Balancé à la seconde* to the right. The Band should become stretched and extended. If the dancers really push the Band into the sideward Zone of the Kinesphere, they will experience how the spatial intent continues throughout the entire traveling movement. Cue them to:

   Spread the body rightward as the right arm reaches into the Side Middle Zone and the right leg extends into the Side Low Zone of the Kinesphere. Imagine your right arm and leg are casting laser beams into the space. Follow the line of those laser beams past the edge of your Kinesphere as you then travel sideward in the balancé.

3   *Piqué sous-sus* left back to the *barre*. *The laser beams reverse as you execute the piqué sous-sus toward the barre. Allow your body to follow the free flowing momentum of the Band as it pulls you Sideward toward the barre. Do not try to establish a perfect balance in piqué sous-sus. Instead, enjoy the momentum and excitement of being pulled past the extended leg and arm toward the barre. Do you notice how your body travels along a sideward spatial pathway through space and in your Kinesphere?*

   Extension: Turn the *piqué sous-sus* into a *piqué detourné* to the other side. My students love doing this because the Band forcefully pulls the right side of the body sideward and around to the other side. This is technically useful because when turning to the left, the right side of the body provides the push and force for the turn.

Balancé en avant to piqué sous-sus en arrière

Follow the above process, but this time the students begin facing away from the *barre*.

As you perform the balancé, reach the leading arm into the Forward High Zones and the leading leg into the Forward Low Zones. Cast the laser beams outward as you travel your Kinesphere forward through space. As you perform the piqué sous-sus en arrière, allow the Exercise Band to pull you beyond the downward and backward reach of the leg (see Figure 8.5).

Extension: Reverse this movement. Ask the dancers to begin facing the *barre* and then perform a *balancé en arrière* and a *piqué sous-sus en avant*.

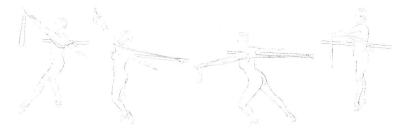

Figure 8.5 Use Exercise Bands during *balancé en avant* to *piqué sous-sus en arrière*

Explore the movements from *Move into space at barre!* in *centre*. For example, if you explored *balancé* (as I did in the above activities), create a *balancé* exercise in *centre*, and instead of using Exercise Bands, ask the dancers to dance toward and away from a partner as they perform the exercise. I often divide my dancers into Stage Left and Right groups with both groups facing Center Stage. Each dancer stands directly across from a partner. The Stage Left group performs the exercise to the left while the Stage Right group performs it to the right, so that the two groups mirror each other (see the "Facing a partner in *centre*" diagram). I then teach them an exercise that includes traveling movements in all directions: *en avant, arrière*, and *en côté*. Sometimes they learn a *petite* or *medium allegro*, a *balancé* exercise with turns, or a slow traveling *grand adagio*. There are many possibilities.

Diagram: Facing a partner in *centre*

O...O
    O...O
O...O
    O...O
O...O
    O...O
O...O

My dancers enjoy facing a partner during *centre* exercises for many reasons. They love the feeling of challenging their partners to propel into the Forward, Backward, and Sideward Zones of their Kinespheres. This teaches them how to reach beyond the extension of their legs and arms during *balancé*, or *piqué*, or *chassé* (and, of course, many other steps), and they practice projecting their energy into space beyond the edges of their Kinespheres. Similarly, they become aware of how their Traceforms change in levels, size, and directions, which facilitates greater spatial clarity of their body during locomotion. Finally, they enjoy relating to and moving with each other, and often remark that the experience is similar to dancing with each other on stage in ensemble choreography.

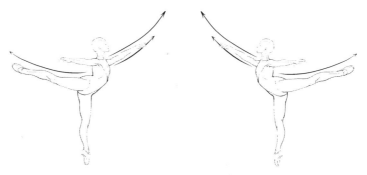

Figure 8.6 Face a partner during *barre* and *centre*

As you introduce Traceforms and Kinesphere to your students, continue to explore the many ways your dancers relate spatially to each other during *centre* exercises. Create exercises "in the round" where they "chase" people along the circle both behind and in front of them, or exercises that travel toward a partner from corner to corner. You might also teach them basic *pas de deux* partnering skills and ask them to partner each other during simple *adagios* or traveling movements. This is something I do in my class quite often, regardless of the gender of my students. They practice partnering each other during exercises where receiving spatial guidance at the arms or torso facilitates clearer directionality in their Kinespheres and propulsion through space.

Similar to the concepts explored in the previous two chapters, there are numerous ways you and your dancers can apply the concepts of Traceforms and Kinesphere to ballet technique. Sometimes it is important to be highly specific and restrictive as you explore these concepts, and other times it is more productive to create open-ended explorations that allow for multiple discoveries. Ultimately, it is important your dancers understand the decisions they make in the technique classroom and how those decisions impact their technical and artistic development.

Notes

1 Laban, R.; Ullman, L. (ed.). (2011a). *Choreutics*, 4th edn. Alton, UK: Dance Books, p. 5.
2 Laban, R. (1984). *A Vision of Dynamic Space* (L. Ullman, ed.). London: Laban Archives in Association with Flamer Press, p. 54.
3 It also enhanced the inward rotation of the shoulder joint needed for the first two movements of the *port de bras*: *bras bas* to *first* and *first* to *second position*.
4 For the reader familiar with kinesiology: I accentuated the actions of depression, upward rotation, and abduction of the scapulae as the arms lifted.
5 Johnson, L. (2011a). More than Skin Deep: the Enduring Practice of Ballet in Universities. *Theatre, Dance and Performance Training*, 2(2): 187.
6 Other options might be: regions on the right or left side of the body only, upper left regions and lower right regions (and vice versa), the head and the pelvis.

Part III

Deeping dynamism

Chapter 9

The dynamic palette
Introduction to Effort

Energy and dynamism is felt every time a dancer jumps, turns, and balances. A dancer's use of dynamics impacts the energy of the movement, the mood of the audience, and the overall message of the choreography.

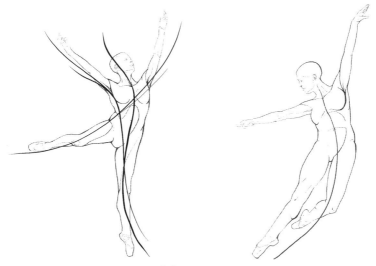

Figure 9.1 Dancing is energetic and dynamic

Performing the same series of steps with a different set of dynamics will change the feeling tone of the movement. A dancer may choose to perform a *grand adagio* with delicate fluidity, conveying perhaps a gentle and serene attitude, or that dancer may perform the same *adagio* with a controlled and firm quality in order to convey a feeling of boldness or determination.

Use of dynamic cueing in the technique classroom is commonplace among ballet educators. Verbal cues, such as, "*Float like a feather at the top of the pique arabesque*," invokes a feeling of weightless suspension, whereas "*Feel the light and sprightly rhythm of the petite allegro*" encourages buoyant speed and delicacy.

Teachers also regularly use dynamic sounding and dynamic verbs and adverbs, such as those listed below, when demonstrating exercises or providing students with critical feedback.

Do you ever whisper, shout, or suspend your words when presenting exercises?
Or, sing songs or rhythms with your voice?
Or, make gasps and sweeping sounds with your breath?

Imagine the dynamics you would use with your voice as you say the following words:

Press	Burst	Float	Skitter	Elongate
Billow	Pierce	Timidly	Smoothly	
Quickly	Leisurely	Forcefully	Gently	Glide

There are many tools teachers use to teach movement dynamics to their students. Part III: Deepening dynamism explores one of them: **Effort**. Ballet teachers spend a lot of time in class teaching the "ABCs" of ballet technique. The intent of Chapters 9–14 is to build on that knowledge by exploring the "ABCs" of movement dynamics. If you have ever experienced difficulty getting your students to "perform more fully," "dance with a more engaged and alert attitude," or "do more than just the steps," these are the chapters for you. Learning the "ABCs" of dynamics facilitates your ability to create dynamically rich and challenging classes and it gives your students the tools for performing more artistically and proficiently in technique class.

Effort: general definition

Effort is a primary area of study within Laban/Bartenieff Movement Analysis (L/BMA). We are in the realm of Effort when we consider the overall energy and dynamic quality of any given movement. There are four main categories within the Effort framework and each category is broken down into two polar parts:

- *Flow Effort*—*Bound and Free Flow*, describes the fluid quality of the dancers' movements. Are they contained or outpouring? (Chapter 10)
- *Weight Effort*—*Strong and Light Weight*, describes how dancers engage their mass as they move. Do they move powerfully or delicately? (Chapter 11)
- *Time Effort*—*Sudden and Sustained Time*, describes how the dancers' intuitive sense of time causes them to move. Are they urgent? Or, do they linger? (Chapter 12)
- *Space Effort*—*Direct and Indirect Space*, describes how dancers attend to their environment. Are they single-focused or multi-focused? (Chapter 13)

A journey through Effort reveals numerous dynamic possibilities. You and your dancers might practice and perform each Effort quality in isolation—Strong Weight during a *plié*, for example—or in combination with other Effort qualities—Strong Weight with Bound Flow and Direct Space, a grouping often seen during a *piqué arabesque en pointe*. **Effort is a comprehensive "map" for movement dynamics.**

Figure 9.2 Explore a Strong, Bound, and Direct *piqué arabesque*

Use of a particular Effort or combination of Efforts affects how your students execute balletic movements. For example, a *sauté arabesque* performed with out-pouring power (Free Flow and Strong Weight) looks and feels quite different than a *sauté arabesque* performed with controlled delicacy (Bound Flow and Light Weight). The first teaches your dancers how to execute the movement with force and momentum, while the second teaches them how to execute it with lifted control.

Since there are many possible Effort permutations to explore, navigating through LMA Effort provides you and your dancers with both flexibility and specificity.

Why study Effort in ballet class?

Dancers enter the technique classroom as dynamic, expressive individuals. Similarly, the movement phrases teachers present in ballet class are dynamic even when movement dynamics are not the focus in class. One does not have to concentrate on dynamics in order to be dynamic; Effort is present whether we are conscious of it or not. **So, if this is true, why is useful for you and your dancers to be conscious of Effort during class?**

1   Ballet dancers perform dances of differing dynamics and qualities.

Ask dancers to identify their favorite part of ballet class and the answers will certainly vary. Some love large, flowing waltzes, others enjoy sharp, fast *petite allegros*, and others prefer the slow, controlled qualities of an *adagio*. Ultimately, however, dancers must prepare to work with different choreographers and to perform different roles on stage. It is therefore important for both teachers and dancers to acquire breadth in their movement preferences.

L/BMA Effort is a broad and multifaceted tool for expanding a dancer's and teacher's dynamic range and preferences.

2   **Ballet dancers respond to and analyze the dynamic nuances within the musical accompaniment, technique class phrases, and balletic choreography.**

In advanced and intermediate classes, teachers ask dancers to personify the music through their movement. They are expected to skillfully express the musical textures, tones, accents, and rhythms. They must also analyze how the instructor or choreographer performed the movement phrases: was it executed smoothly or sharply? Delicately or with force? Evenly or with syncopated timing?

Explorations in L/BMA Effort teach dancers and teachers about dynamic variety. This strengthens their ability to identify and analyze the dynamic nuances in the musical accompaniment and balletic movement.

3   **Ballet dancers express differing moods and emotions when dancing.**

In a story ballet, the dancers portray characters and tell stories through their movements. When there is no story or character, the dancers must still convey the overall feeling-tone of the choreography. Dancers need opportunities in class to embody the balletic vocabulary with particular moods, emotions, or characters in mind. A *grand jeté devant*, for example, is simply a step until the dancer animates it with a particular dynamic energy: is it solemn or uplifting, demure or bold, cautious or unrestrained? What dynamic qualities does the dancer embody in order to convey those moods?

Studies in L/BMA Effort increase a dancer's capacity to interpret and embody the emotional content and expressive nature of the balletic movement.

Figure 9.3 Explore different dynamic choices during *grand jeté devant*

4   **Ballet dancers perform as soloists and dance with others.**

All dancers must eventually develop a unique dancing style and artistic identity. Challenging dancers to make conscious performance choices about their use of movement dynamics in the technique classroom is one way to develop artistry. Additionally, ballet dancers must learn how to adjust their dynamic preferences in order to move successfully as a member of the *corps de ballet* or an ensemble.

Dancers develop their artistic attitudes and sensibilities as soloists and as members of an ensemble when they learn to experiment with L/BMA Effort in class.

5   **Ballet dancers contribute to the choreographic process.**

In today's contemporary ballet culture, dancers interpret the choreographer's ideas, create movement phrases collaboratively and on their own, and improvise with the thematic content of the choreography. When ballet dancers are given the freedom to improvise and experiment with their own dynamic choices during technique class, they practice the skills needed for working with contemporary choreographers.

As your students learn to navigate through the vast landscape of Effort qualities, they will expand their expressive range and strengthen their ability to make conscious choices about their performance energy when executing balletic sequences and choreography.

Effort, artistry, and technique

Conscious use of Effort in class positively impacts technical and artistic development. Artistically, experimenting with Effort teaches dancers how to use their energy specifically and variedly in order to create different moods and qualities when dancing. This is a similar artistic process to those employed by musicians; even though a musical score typically includes annotations that reveal the composer's intentions, a musical score is simply a series of notes until the musician or conductor interprets the score and brings specific qualitative nuances to the surface. Similarly, even though a choreographer or teacher indicates the intention of a movement phrase to the dancers, the dancers must decide how to actualize those intentions, a process that typically involves interpretation and artistic choice.

Technically, embodying different Efforts will change the physical organization of the body: muscle tone, proprioceptive responses, neuromuscular connections, breath support, and body sequencing shift and change as the dancers' Effort-life changes. Use of a particular Effort quality therefore changes how the dancers execute the classical steps: for example, they will access greater force in a *battement dégagé* using Strong Weight, more buoyancy using Light Weight, more immediacy using Sudden Time, more control using Bound Flow, and so on. As the Effort qualities change, the technical skills required to achieve the movement also change.

Take a moment to experience this in your own body in Teacher exploration 9.1.

Teacher exploration 9.1: How does Effort impact my technique and artistry?

1 Recall a *battement dégagé* exercise you taught in class recently.
2 Embody different Efforts as you perform the *battement dégagé* exercise.

   a Perform some steps with Light Weight (delicate use of force) and others with Strong Weight (powerful or commanding use of your force).
   b Move on to Time Effort, performing some steps with Sudden Time (urgency) and some with Sustained Time (lingering).
   c Explore Space Effort. Perform the exercise with a Direct (channeled or pinpointed awareness) and then with an Indirect (all-encompassing and expansive awareness).
   d Explore Flow Effort, alternating between Bound Flow (a contained and controlled attitude) and Free Flow (an easeful and outpouring attitude).

3 Notice how the technical and artistic challenges change as the Effort qualities change.

   • How does each Effort quality affect your muscular engagement and your body connectivity differently? For example, does a particular Effort help you stabilize your standing leg, or find greater ease in your upper body or more clarity in your gesturing leg?
   • What are the technical benefits to a Strong Weighted *battement dégagé*? How is this different than a Light Weighted *battement dégagé*? What about a Sustained versus a Sudden *battement dégagé*? Or, a Direct verses an Indirect *battement dégagé*? Or, a Free versus a Bound Flowing *battement dégagé*?
   • How does each Effort quality promote a different artistic attitude? Do you notice any characters or feeling tones emerge as you play with each Effort quality?

Any Effort quality can be performed in combination with other Efforts. For example, embodying Strong Weight and Free Flow teaches dancers how to perform powerful movements with greater ease, and depending on the context of the movement, this combination is useful for conveying a variety of artistic attitudes: abandoned fury, outpouring confidence, or joyous celebration, to name a few. As another example, embodying Direct Space with Bound Flow and Light Weight teaches dancers how to channel their movements directly in space with delicacy and control. This combination of artistic qualities often appears in Classical and Romantic Ballets.

Table 9.1 presents the technical and artistic benefits for each Effort quality. These will be explored in greater detail in the next five chapters. Add to the benefits in Table 9.1 as you and your students experiment with Effort during class.

Table 9.1 Artistic and technical benefits for the eight Effort qualities

Effort	Technical benefits	Artistic benefits
	Moving with . . .	*Performing with an attitude of . . .*
Sudden Time	Speed and agility	Urgency
Sustained Time	Prolonged suspension	Lingering indulgence
Direct Space	Channeled attention	Pinpointed awareness
Indirect Space	Multiple points of focus	Expansive awareness
Strong Weight	Power and force	Firm command
Light Weight	Delicacy and buoyancy	Gentle softness
Bound Flow	Controlled fluidity	Measured containment
Free Flow	Outpouring fluidity	Easefulness

Using Effort to enliven the class atmosphere

Most dance educators have experienced teaching students with low energy or motivation. Of course, sometimes this is unavoidable in the classroom. Busy school schedules, distractions outside of class, fear about looking awkward or "wrong" in class, and poor body image are all factors that may result in low energy, inhibited movement patterns, or lack of initiative in class. Dancers enter our classes as "full vessels" and this certainly impacts their performance in class. It is therefore important for dance educators to maintain dialogue with their students inside and outside of class, demonstrate positive support for their development as human beings, and take into consideration their lives beyond the walls of the dance studio.

I have met many teachers who find positive ways to promote greater motivation and energy among their students: some use upbeat music, others give students props to use while dancing, and many give students the opportunity to observe and work with each other during class. These are just some of the many ways teachers enliven the class atmosphere.

Teacher exploration 9.2: Journal about your teaching

In what ways do you already promote an active and engaged classroom atmosphere? When addressing this question, consider your verbal cueing and physical demonstrations, your feedback style, and the many other ways you activate students during class.

Effort is energy. It is not surprising then that Effort is an ideal tool for creating an alert and engaged in-class atmosphere. **Effortful verbal cueing, movement phrases, and class activities will energize students.**

Changing the "Effort-life" of the classroom atmosphere is a positive way to affect student behavior and energy. Table 9.2 presents Effort solutions I use when my students demonstrate low energy, loss of focus, or lack of initiative. These approaches are explored in greater depth in the following chapters.

Table 9.2 Using Effort to enliven the class atmosphere

Common observations	Possible Effort solutions
• The students demonstrate a loss of focus; they are staring blankly into space	*Incorporate Direct or Indirect Space into your class exercises and activities.* Use of Space Effort requires dancers to be aware of their environment with their eyes, heads, and generally their whole bodies.
• The students have fatigued looking postures	*Incorporate Light or Strong Weight into your class exercises and activities.* Use of Weight Effort combats passive postures by activating the mass of the body, either with buoyant lift (Light Weight) or with driving power (Strong Weight).
• The students seem to be "going through the motions" at *barre*	*Incorporate Sustained and Sudden Time into your class exercises and activities.* Use of Time Effort requires your dancers to experiment with variations in rhythm and timing, creating a more present attitude and a conscious connection to the musical rhythms.
• The students move cautiously through the space; they "hold back" when they perform the movements	*Incorporate Free Flow or Strong Weight into your class exercises and activities.* Use of Free Flow requires dancers to perform with an unconstrained energy and a "go with the flow" attitude. Strong Weight requires a powerful energy; they learn how to "put their weight into it".
• The students are rushing through the movement, causing them to move with less specificity	*Incorporate Bound Flow into your class exercises and activities.* Use of Bound Flow requires dancers to perform with a controlled movement energy. This will help them focus on the details of the movement.

Using Effort in class: some first steps

Rudolf Laban recognized that a "conscious prompting of movement expression was what made the act of movement performance possible."[1] There are many tools teachers use to evoke self-expression in dance students. Effort is one of them. Conscious use of Effort in the technique classroom awakens your students' energetic and emotional sensibilities, fostering more dynamic and expressive movement during class. Part III: Deepening dynamism asks you and your dancers to consider the following questions:

- *What is the expressive/dynamic "life" of my movement?*
- *How do I convey specific moods, feelings, or ideas through my dancing?*
- *How is the overall mood of my movement effected when I perform the same steps with different dynamics?*
- *How do different Efforts help me execute the balletic phrases with greater technical proficiency?*

In addition to the below suggestions, the next five chapters present numerous activities for addressing these questions and teaching the "ABCs" of Effort to your students.

Using specific terminology

When you use balletic terminology in class, you create a common reference point with your students. You will experience the same benefits when you teach your students Effort terminology. If the Effort words become a part of your daily verbal cueing (similar to your use of ballet terminology), it will also become a part of your students' vocabulary. If your dancers are able to verbally "call out" and then physically perform your Effort choices after a demonstration, they are well on their way to understanding movement dynamics. This is also an important perceptive skill to develop for dance auditions and when working with different choreographers. **Remember: ballet dancers are used to learning and using terminology in class. They are good at it!**

Variety in verbal cueing

When you teach an exercise to your students for the first time, how do you use your voice?

- Do you speak the counts for each step as you physically demonstrate the movement?
- Do you say the names of the balletic steps as you are performing the movement?
- Do you use rhythmical sounds with your voice?
- Do you sing a melody that corresponds to the movements?
- Do you use evocative imagery or words to describe the movements?
- Do you use some combination of the above methods?

There are many ways to integrate Effort qualities into your voice and words when teaching an exercise to your students. It is important to use an approach that is most natural for you when you first demonstrate an exercise. During your second demonstration, however, begin to incorporate a more varied approach to your verbal cueing, one that gives students more qualitative information about the Effort-life of the movement.

Chapters 10–13 present numerous Effort images and synonyms to use when describing movement and coaching your dancers. Singing or sounding the dynamic phrasing of your in–class exercises is another Effort approach for adding variety to your verbal cueing. For example, teach your students to analyze whether a step needs a powerful "Pop!," a softly sounded "Wwwhhhishhhhh," a gentle and quick "Tap!," or a "Hhhmmmmmnn" that slowly rises in inflection. This is an approach used in Creative Movement classes, and it is especially useful at the pre-professional level when the exercises become increasingly complex in terms of rhythm and sequencing. Students will learn the exercises more quickly when they sing or sound out the Effort rhythms, and it will challenge them to be more creative with their dynamic choices.

Making choices

Give students opportunities to make individual choices about their use of Effort during their performance of the class exercises. Challenge them to create Effort-focused *barre* or *centre* exercises or choreograph their own Effort choices for a structured class combination that you created. Chapter 14, in particular, focuses on methods you can employ in order to strengthen your students' ability to make conscious choices about their use of dynamics during class.

Peer interaction

Provide time in class for students to work on movement dynamics with each other. Ask them to:

- Perform their dynamic choices from a class phrase for a partner.
- Give each other feedback about their use of Effort.
- Teach each other the dynamic choices they made during an exercise.
- Share Effort imagery with a peer.
- Create Effort-focused *barre* or *centre* exercises together.

Effort variation

Design classes that promote Effort variety:

- Use dynamically varied music in class.
- Create dynamically varied in–class exercises.
- Give students the opportunity to perform the same steps with different Efforts.

The next five chapters include exploration exercises that promote Effort variation in class. To get started now, however, reference *Using effortful music!*. In my experience, intermediate and advanced students are skilled at responding to changes in tempo and meter, but have more difficulty embodying complex musical phrasing, syncopated rhythms, and changes in musical intensity (a powerful piece versus delicate piece, for example). So, begin your exploration of Effort by consciously choosing musical selections that vary in dynamics. Play a Strong and bold piece of music for a *plié* combination, a Light and Sudden piece for a *battement tendu*, a syncopated piece of music for a *battement frappé*, and so on. This develops the dancers' ability to respond to music of differing tones and textures, and they learn to perform the balletic steps with different energies and personalities.

Using Effortful music!

Objective:

Dancers strengthen their ability to respond to the dynamic nuances in the musical accompaniment.

Musical romp!

1 When listening to recorded music designed specifically for a ballet class, notice the dynamic variety from one song to the next: Is the piece of music fast and light? Slow and gentle? Powerful? Syncopated?
2 Consciously incorporate the dynamic qualities from the music into your exercises, verbal cueing, and physical demonstrations.

Note: Also use contemporary and popular musical selections in class, and invite your dancers to bring music into class too.

Romp around the classics!

If you're looking for music that inspires dynamic variety and interesting movement phrasing, look at the musical selections from the Romantic and Classical ballets of the 19th and 20th centuries. Designing in-class exercises to the music from popular ballets, such as *Sleeping Beauty*, *Giselle*, *La Slyphide*, *Don Quixote*, *Petroushka*, and *Firebird*, will increase your dancers dynamic range and improve their understanding of the ballet classics.

Note

1 Groff, E. (1990). Laban Movement Analysis: A Historical, Philosophical and Theoretical Perspective. Unpublished Masters Thesis, Connecticut College, New London, CT, USA, p. 96.

Chapter 10

Fluidity

Free and Bound Flow

Balletic movement has a rhythm of tension and release, inflow and outflow. Sometimes the steady flow of energy is unhindered, or **Free**, and sometimes it is controlled, or **Bound**. A *grand battement* typically initiates with an unhindered (Free Flow) toss of the leg upward in space followed immediately by a controlled (Bound Flow) descent of the leg back to *fifth position*. A *balancé à la seconde* is often performed with outpouring fluidity (Free) and a *promenade* in *first arabesque* with contained fluidity (Bound).

Bound Flow animates ballet characters, such as the noble and dignified Apollo in George Balanchine's ballet *Apollo*, as well as onstage scenarios, such as Swanhilda's cautious and sneaky investigation of Dr. Coppelius's doll shop in *Coppelia*. The use of Bound Flow also creates a regal onstage atmosphere in the opening scene of Balanchine's *Serenade*: the ensemble of dancers stand calmly in parallel position, arms gliding toward their faces with controlled elegance.

Free Flow animates familiar ballet characters, such as the excited, uninhibited demeanor of the Petrushka Doll in in Act I of *Petrushka*. Free Flow is also a common quality in the celebratory finales, codas, and national dances in popular classical ballets. Even in contemporary or neoclassical ballets, such as George Balanchine's *Who Cares?* Free Flow is essential in conveying an outpouring and carefree atmosphere.

Table 10.1 presents a list of synonyms, images, and musical suggestions for teaching Flow Effort. Add to each list as you and your dancers explore Effort.

Table 10.1 Synonyms, imagery, and musical suggestions for Flow Effort

Bound Flow	Free Flow
Synonyms	*Synonyms*
Controlled	Unhindered
Contained	Sweeping
Restrained	Outpouring
Careful	Unconstrained
Withheld	Carefree
Crystallize	Unimpeded
Imagery	*Imagery*
Water pooling in an eddy	Water flowing over a cliff
Stoic gait of a lion	Streamers freely blowing in the breeze
Cautious creeping in a haunted house	Carefree monkey swinging through the trees

Album: *Uncommon Disturbances*, Edgar Meyer with Béla Fleck and Mike Marshall

   Free: "Barnyard Disturbance"

Album: *Foreign Legion*, Tin Hat

   Bound: "Sunrise at Independence"

Album: *Divenire*, Ludovico Einaudi

   Free: "Fly"

Album: *Kronos Quartet*, Released 1985–1995
   Free: "Mai Nozipo"

Album: *Astor in Paris*, 3 Leg Torso

   Bound (mostly): Bill's Last Adventure and The Cat and the Rooster

Album: *Possessed*, Balanescu Quartet

   Free: "Hanging Upside Down"

Album: *The 50 Most Essential Pieces of Classical Music*

   Free: Concerto for Violin in E Major, RV 269, Op. 8:1, "Spring": I. Allegro, The Four Seasons, Vivaldi
   Bound: Troi Gymnopédies: Gymnopédie No. 1, Satie
   Bound: Cello Concerto No. 1 in C Major, Hob VIIb/1: II. Adagio, Haydn
   Free: Cavatina, Stanley Meyers

Teachers first: embodying and using Flow Effort

Teacher exploration 10.1: Exploring Flow Effort through breath

Take a moment to notice your breath, and its ongoing rhythms of inflowing and outflowing. Allow your limbs to begin flowing inward and outward with each inhalation and exhalation. Continue this natural rhythm for a few cycles.

   Bound Flow: *Begin to restrict slightly the flow of your breath and limbs, as if you were containing your inner feelings and energy at the edges of your skin.*

Allow the flowing energy in your body to travel outward to the boundaries of your body and back inward with measured control. Continue this manner of breathing for a few cycles, allowing your breath to gradually become more Bound each time.

Free Flow: *Begin to free up the flow of your breath and limbs. Allow the edges of your skin to become more permeable, so that your energy flows outward beyond the boundaries of your skin, and then back inward from the surrounding space. Feelings and thoughts pour outward and inward with unrestricted release. Continue this manner of breathing for a few cycles, allowing your breath to gradually become more Free each time.*

In Chapter 6 we explored breath support as a way to experience the Growing and Shrinking of the body's form—Shape Flow Support. In this chapter, we return to breath. Breath is one of the many ways to experience and access Flow Effort. As we breathe, oxygen and carbon dioxide flow through our respiratory networks and into our fluid circulatory system. Respiration supports the body's fluidity, and "links our inner and outer environment in a continuous stream of breath."[1] Our breath patterns are "influenced by and . . . reflective of changes in consciousness, feelings, and thoughts."[2] Those feelings may cause us to contain our breath and energy at the edges of our skin (Bound Flow), or they might cause those edges to become permeable, allowing the energy and breath to pour outward (Free Flow).[3] Even though the process of breathing is automatic, *consciously* Freeing and Binding our "continuous stream" of breath facilitates the ongoing, energetic flow of our bodies through space.

Let's apply these ideas to ballet class. First, learn the *centre floor waltz* exercise shown in Exercise 10.1. Create your own *port de bras* for the movement.

Exercise 10.1: *Centre* floor waltz

Music: moderate ¾ meter

Begin in *fifth position en face*, right leg *devant*
  1 & a Right *balancé à la seconde*
  2 & a Left *balancé à la seconde*
  3 & a Right *balancé à la seconde* to the right
  4 & a Left *chassé effacé en avant, pas de bourée.* End in *sous-sus croisé* with right leg *devant*
  5 & a *Plié fifth* into *chassé croisé en avant* to *relevé croisé attitude derrière*
  6 & a Lower the *derrière* leg (left leg) to *croisé* fourth position
  7 & a Double *pirouette en dehors*
  8 & a Land in *croisé* fourth position lunge

Focus on Free and Bound Flow as you perform the *centre floor waltz* exercise. As you do so, allow the quality of your breath to parallel your Flow Effort.

Teacher exploration 10.2: Embodying Free and Bound Flow

1   **Focus on Free Flow as you perform the *centre floor waltz*.** Execute the *balancé à la seconde* with a sweeping and easeful quality. Allow your breath to unreservedly pour out from the core of your body, through your arms and legs, and into space. Imagine your limbs are streamers Freely flowing in a breeze.

    Embody this energy and breathing quality during the *pirouette*, the *relevé* into *croisé attitude derrière*, and the *chassé effacé pas de bourée*. *How does Free Flowing breath and movement support your technique?*

2   **Focus on Bound Flow as you perform the *centre floor waltz*.** Execute the *chassé effacé en avant* and *pas de bourée dessous* with control, emphasizing each movement of the legs with clarity and form, and perhaps conjuring feelings of regal elegance. Control the flow of your breath and contain your body's energy at the edge of your skin.

    Embody this energy during the *pirouette*, the *croisé attitude derrière*, or the *balancé à la seconde*. *How does Bound Flowing breath and movement support your technique?*

3   **Alternate between Free and Bound Flow.** Execute the preparation before the *pirouette* with Bound Flow and use Free Flow during the pirouette and the landing. Adopt a carefree attitude during the first and third *balancé* and a restrained and controlled attitude during the second *balancé*. *How does each influence your breathing patterns and rhythm?*

    Experiment with alternating from Free to Bound Flow in other parts of the exercise. *How does the centre floor waltz follow rhythms of Freeing and Binding in both breath and movement?*

How did Free and Bound Flow affect your use of breath and your performance of the *centre floor waltz*?

You may have noticed that Bound Flow was effective when you needed to control your breath, crystallize a balance, or decrease your momentum, whereas Free Flow was effective when you needed to release your breath, travel through space, or increase your momentum. This is not to say that Free and Bound Flow are only useful in these instances. Any step in ballet may be performed with either quality. Performing a balance with Free Flow instead of Bound Flow, for example, may help you embody the balance with less tension. Similarly, performing an easily flowing step, such as a *balancé*, with Bound Flow instead of Free Flow may help you clarify the form of the movement. Take a moment to experiment with this idea:

Choose three steps or phrases from the centre floor waltz and perform them first with Free Flow and then with Bound Flow. How does each Effort quality assist your technical performance of the exercise differently?

How do you know when to use Free or Bound Flow when cueing your students and creating exercises for class? Free Flow is likely important if you are using words or sounds such as *sweeping, flying, tossing, whoosh,* or *swish* to describe the energy quality of the movement. Bound Flow is likely important if you are using words such as *contain, control, pull together, carefully,* or *crystallize* to describe the movement. Also take note of the sound of your voice or the quality of your breath when teaching class phrases. *Is your voice or breath binding or outpouring in quality?*

It is easy for either Free or Bound Flow to become predominant in your movement style and consequently your class exercises. Perhaps you have recognized this in your students. *Do some of your students dance with a loose or sweeping movement style while some perform with a measured and controlled movement style?* While your movement patterns are likely more balanced than your students, you, too, have established Flow Effort preferences. Diversifying your preferences will impact your teaching when demonstrating movement or creating exercises.

The emphasis on teaching shapes, line, positions, and steps in ballet technique provides ample experiences for ballet dancers to embody and experience Bound Flow, so pay particular attention to how Free Flow enhances your class exercises. Many movements in ballet have an outpouring, sweeping energy. When ballet dancers perform these movements with *excessive* Bound Flow, it restricts their ability to perform the movement fully. This is addressed in the next section.

Teaching Flow Effort to your students

Bound Flow is effective to access when practicing movements that require control or when conveying a restrained performance energy. Free Flow is effective to access when practicing movements that require ease of motion or when conveying an unhindered performance energy. Reflect on your own experience for a moment: **What technical and artistic challenges did you experience as you explored Free and Bound Flow?** Based on those challenges:

When would you focus on Bound or Free Flow with your students? What technical or artistic goals are you trying to achieve?

How would you explain Bound or Free Flow to your students? What seems important to communicate or emphasize?

Reference Table 10.2 for suggestions of when to use Bound and Free Flow Effort in ballet class. Add to these suggestions as you explore the above questions.

Table 10.2 Technical and artistic benefits for Flow Effort

Bound Flow is a practical movement quality to use when teaching students how to:

1. *Articulate each part of a complex movement.* For example, *pas de basque* can be broken down into four distinct parts: the *tendu devant*, the *demi-ronde to à la seconde*, the transfer of weight to the initial gesturing leg, and the closing of the trailing leg to *fifth position plié*. Embodying these four parts with controlled flow helps dancers achieve greater clarity.
2. *Perform controlled movement transitions*, especially during the landings of complex jumps, or when the dancer generally needs more control and clarity between larger movements.
3. *Crystallize a balance*, such as when dancers contain their flow for a final, prolonged balance after completing a series of large, traveling jumps.
4. *Dance with an artistic attitude that emphasizes a controlled emotional state*: nervous, proud, restrained, noble, sneaky, tense, contained aggression, and so on.[+]

Free Flow is a practical movement quality to use when teaching students how to:

1. *Focus on the mobility, momentum, or trajectory of the movement.* During a *pas de basque*, for example, the dancers might connect the *devant* and *à la seconde* movements in one Freely Flowing phrase or to use the momentum of *demi-ronde* in order to travel more during the weight transfer through *à la seconde*.
2. *Practice Free and flowing movement transitions*, especially when the dancers are too controlled and restrained in their movements.
3. *Move the upper body easefully during fast footwork*, a quality often needed in *petite allegro*.
4. *Dance with an artistic attitude that emphasizes an unconstrained emotional state*: carefree, playful, uninhibited, celebratory, excited, reckless, out of control, and so on.[+]

[+] Artistically, the use of Bound and Free Flow may convey a large range of emotional states depending on the mood or context of the choreography or class phrases.

Since any movement in ballet can be performed with Bound or Free Flow, determining which quality to use is highly dependent on the technical and artistic criteria you are working on in your classes. Consider the following phrases from the Exercise 10.1:

• Left *chassé effacé en avant*, *pas de bourée dessous* ending in *croisé sous-sus*
• *Plié* fifth, *chassé croisé en avant* to *relevé croisé attitude derrière*

Many of my students bypass the *sous-sus* and the *fifth position* in between the *pas de bourée dessous* and the *chassé croisé en avant*. We therefore practice the *pas de bourée* with Bound Flow in order to accentuate:

1 The high *relevé* of the feet.
2 Directionality of each step. The *pas de bourée* initiates as the right leg moves into *sous-sus derrière*, continues as the left leg moves into *second position demi-pointe*, and ends as the right leg moves into *sous-sus devant*.
3 Descent from *sous-sus* to *plié fifth* before the second *chassé croisé en avant*. This also helps them maintain the outward rotation of the *devant* leg as they move into *relevé attitude*, which increases the stability of the balance.

The use of Bound Flow helps the dancers practice classical form and placement, controlled movement transitions, and stable balances.

On the other hand, when analyzing Exercise 10.1 from the perspective of Free Flow, many of my students have difficulty actually moving and traveling through the space. Steps that should travel, such as *chassé en avant* and *balancé à la seconde*, remain in one spot, and upper body movements that should be sweeping and fluid are rigid and stiff. In these instances, using Free Flow helps them "release" their momentum in order to:

1 Travel beyond the reach of the leg during each *balancé* and *chassé en avant*.
2 Experience more fluidity and freedom of motion in the upper body *port de bras*.
3 Transition smoothly from the *balance à la seconde* to the *chassé*.

The use of Free Flow helps the dancers access greater mobility in the upper and lower body and practice smooth movement transitions from *en face* to *effacé* positions.

Excessive Bound Flow in ballet technique classes

Excess tension in the body is caused by many factors—tight fascia and muscles, constricted breathing patterns, overreliance on singular body parts or joints when dancing, excessive Bound Flow, and so on. Additionally, psychological factors, such as fear, insecurity, or cautiousness, also cause excess tension in a dancer's body. This is something I often observe when dancers work on *pirouettes en pointe*; their fear of falling or spraining their ankles causes them to constrict their muscles and hold their breath. *Have you observed this?*

Since excess bodily tension has many causes, there are also many ways to address it in the ballet technique classroom. In Part II, we explored how Shape Flow Support (Chapter 6) and Countertensions (Chapter 7) lessen excess tension. Accessing greater Free Flow Effort in ballet technique classes is another way to do this.

Precise and controlled movement is emphasized in ballet training. Not surprisingly, it is easy for dancers to become *excessively* Bound in their performance of balletic movements. The increased muscular tension that results from excessive use of Bound Flow is counterproductive and tends to cause restricted body postures (especially in the proximal joints and torso), less adaptability and mobility in the spine, and decreased range of motion of the lower body joints (see Table 10.3). Ultimately, excess tension in these highly mobile joints causes the dancers' movements to become rigid and stiff and reduces their ability to travel fully through space during across-the-floor sequences.

Table 10.3 Possible signs of excessive Bound Flow

When Bound Flow is excessive, dancers usually exhibit more than one of these while dancing:

1. Tense spinal postures and clenched jaws
2. Restricted breathing patterns
3. Stiffness in the hip joints and shoulders
4. Pinched shoulder blades
5. Unmoving or fixed rib cages
6. Rigidity in the fingers, wrists, and toes
7. Reduced range of motion in lower body
8. Restricted ability to travel through space

It is common for ballet dancers to restrict their breathing when they attempt difficult balances, perform complex or fast sequences, or execute muscularly taxing movements, such as those found in *grand adagios*. Restricted breathing patterns may cause high intensity Bound Flow. *Do your dancers emit loud, breathy exhales after they finish performing a difficult exercise?* Incorporating conscious, Free Flowing breathing during class is one of the simplest ways to reduce excessive Bound Flow.

Freely flowing, breathing, and releasing! presents two activities intended to promote Free Flow breathing patterns during class.

Freely flowing, breathing, and releasing!

Objective:

Dancers embody Free Flow and Breath Support to reduce movement rigidity and stiffness.

Enjoy the exhale!

Choreograph Free Flowing exhales into your class exercises. Natural places to do this are during:

1   *Steps that are naturally Free Flowing.* Examples include: *grand relevés* performed in *grand waltz* or *allegro* sequences; forceful jumps, such as *sauté arabesque* or *jeté en tournant*; and steps that are generally Free Flowing in nature, such as *balancé, pas de basque, chassé, grand jeté,* and *fouetté.* Free Flowing exhales during these steps will promote outpouring flow.

2   *Movements that require momentum* require dancers to lower their centers of gravity and push down into the ground through their lower bodies. A Free Flowing exhale, along with an inner artistic attitude of outpouring one's energy into the space, will facilitate a more easeful execution of these steps.

3   *Balances.* Typically when dancers initiate one or two-legged balances, they excessively Bind their energy as if some imagined object is suddenly pressing them downward in space. *Is this image familiar to you?* If so, ask your dancers to Freely exhale during their balances. Start with two-legged balances, such as a *sous-sus* or first position *relevé.* Invite them to:

Send an outpouring exhale upward and outward as you release the barre and initiate the balance. While in the balance, Freely and Lightly exhale again and send your energy past the edges of your body, flowing outward from your center to your limbs and out into the space around you. Imagine your body as warm rays of the sun with heat flowing outward from your breath center. Feel the energy Freely expanding in all directions with each exhale.

Apply this approach to one-legged balances on and off of *relevé.*

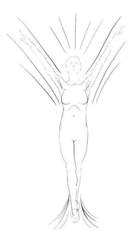

Figure 10.1 Use a Free Flowing, outpouring exhale during *sous-sus*

Ballooning!

Ballooning was first explored in Chapter 6 from the perspective of Shape Flow Support and Shape Qualities. This activity explores Ballooning again from the perspective of Flow Effort.

1   *Teach your students the following Battement Fondu en croix at barre*:

   Battement fondu devant (counts 1–4); *à la seconde* (counts 5–8); *derrière* (counts 1–4); *à la seconde* (counts 5–8)

2   *Perform the exercise with Free Flow.* Imagine your body is a balloon Freely emptying and filling. The air in the balloon flows easefully outward and inward as you move through each battement fondu. Hear the air making a "whooshing" sound as it courses in and out.

Figure 10.2 Imagine air Freely Flowing from the body into space

3   *Perform the exercise again with excessive Bound Flow.* Tightly restrict the flow of air leaving and entering your body balloon. Hear the air making a constricted squeaking sound as it fills and empties the balloon.

4   Ask the dancers to reflect on these two experiences.

Expansion: Ask the dancers to imagine the balloons in different joints of their body (similar to the explorations in Chapter 6).

Incorporating Free Flow into upper body movements is explored in the next series of activities: *Unlock the upper!*. For many dancers, learning how to move the upper body Freely in space will help them breathe more actively. Do not be surprised if your dancers lose their core support as they perform the *Unlock the upper!* activities. Sometimes dancers get a little "loose" when they practice embodying Free Flow attitudinally and physically. This is okay. Your dancers need to physically experience "Freeing up their Flow" as an energetic contrast to excessive Binding. Over time, they will learn how to modulate their Flow Effort: Binding when they need more control and Freeing their Flow when they need greater ease of motion.

Unlock the upper!

Objective:

Dancers use Free Flow to move their upper bodies with greater ease.

Get flowing!

Preparation: Give each dancer a 3–4 foot fabric streamer, scarf, or strip of fabric. These props were also used in Chapter 8 to investigate Traceforms. This activity uses the same props to explore the concept of Flow.

Ask the dancers to hold the props while executing Exercise 10.1. As they are moving, provide verbal cueing that encourages Free Flow manipulation of the props: *Imagine fabric is streaming Freely from the core of your body out through the arms and fingers and the neck and head. What if your legs were streamers? How would they flow in the space?*

Use flowing props in a wide variety of exercises during class: *barre* exercises, across-the-floor waltzes, variations, and *grand allegros*.

Expansion activity: Toss it out!: During repeating traveling jumps with active upper body *port de bras* (i.e. a series of *sauté arabesques*, *chassés*, traveling *soubresauts* and *changements*), give your dancers something tangible to toss into the space, such as tennis balls, medium weighted fabric, or their own ballet slippers. If they are not allowing their energy to Flow Freely, it will be difficult to toss the props into space.

Port de bras!

This is a relatively simple activity. After teaching a *barre* or *centre* exercise, instruct the dancers to perform only the upper body *port de bras* when the music starts. Use imagery and words that promote Free Flowing upper bodies. Provide a variety of images for them to choose from, or ask them to create their own images.

Imagine that a soft ocean breeze is carrying the upper body and arms through space.

Imagine that your arms and torso are the water currents in an easily moving river.

Imagine your chest and arms are windsocks. Feel the warm breeze flow through the windsock and into space.

Flow with a friend!

Dancers typically take their class experiences quite seriously, which is good, but it is also important for them to Freely emanate outpouring joy through their bodies while dancing highly technical movements. Simply facing a partner while performing any *barre* or *centre* floor ballet sequences is a quick and simple way to encourage an outpouring attitude while dancing (not to mention a little laughter).

Move the arms in any direction!

Do your dancers stiffen their upper bodies when performing *petite allegro* and fast footwork at the *barre*? Does this create a "robotic" and choppy upper body *port de bras*? This is common. In order to address this, ask your dancers to move their arms Freely in any direction when performing fast footwork at *barre*, preparatory jumps, *petite allegro*, and repetitive across-the-floor movements, such as a series of *chassés* or *chaîné turns*. For example, teach them the following preparatory jump exercise:

Eight sautés *in parallel, eight in* first, *eight in* second, *and eight* changements

Cue the dancers to move their arms continuously through classical *port de bras* during each set of eight or if they really need to loosen up, ask them to create non-classical arm movements. For example, they might toss the arms in random directions during each set of eight. Using the props from *Get flowing!* is also fun.

The activities in *Unlock the upper!* create a playful, carefree atmosphere in the room, which promotes a more carefree performance energy. When I use these activities with my students, they often laugh, which helps them release tension in their faces, necks, and entire upper bodies. The next series of activities also use sounding, imagery, and props to help students access Free Flow in their movements.

Unlock the lower! promotes risk-taking during traveling movement phrases. When dancers approach traveling movements with a cautious attitude, they will tighten or grip the muscles around their lower body joints. This restricts the movements of their lower bodies, lessening their ability to travel fully through space. As preparation for the following activities, give your students ample opportunities to perform Free Flowing lower body steps during *barre*: steps such as *petite* and *grand balançoire, balancé*, rebounding *battement piqués, pirouettes*, and so on.

Unlock the lower!

Objective:

Dancers use Free Flow to travel through the space with greater ease.

Haunted House

1   Ask your dancers to exaggerate their Bound Flow during a traveling sequence before they embody Free Flow. This will help them identify how excess Bound Flow affects their movement. Generate an image with your dancers that causes them to be even more cautious

and hesitant in their performance. My students and I often imagine we are patrons in a haunted house. Usually, we create a haunted house "scenario" for the movement sequence, and I play scary music, make loud abrupt sounds (e.g. sudden bangs on a drum), and speak with a "ghost story" inflection as they perform the phrase.

2   Ask the students to perform the movement phrase again using a completely opposite image, one that helps them embody a more Free and abandoned energy.

When do they feel free to "go with the flow" or "be themselves" or "relax and have fun"? Is it on a beach? Is it playing in the leaves on a fall day? Is it when they are around certain people?

After they perform the exercise with the second image in mind, ask them:

What changed when you performed the sequence to this image? How did you feel? Did any movements become easier or harder? What did you notice about your peers' movements as you watched them perform the sequence?

Transitions that flow!

Sounding is an expression of one's breath and is therefore effective to use when dancers hold their breath or approach movement cautiously. For example, in Exercise 10.1 they might sound:

- an unhindered "Whooossshhhh!" during the *chasse croisé en avant* into *relevé croisé attitude derrière;*
- a carefree "Ahhhhhhh!" during the *chassé effacé en avant;*
- a breathy "Whhheeeeeeee & a, Whhhheeeeee & a" during each *balancé á la seconde.*

I recommend they make these sounds together as a whole class. If everyone in the class is sounding "Whooossshhhh!" or "Ahhhhhhh!" at the same time, they will produce louder and more confident sounds.

Don't be surprised if your students initially resist making sounds in class. If the above activities become a regular part of your class, their resistance will likely lessen over time.

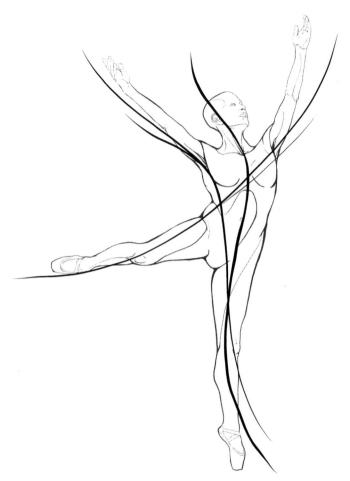

Figure 10.3 Embody an uninhibited, Free Flowing movement quality during class

Ballet dancers need opportunities to perform in-class sequences in an uninhibited manner. So, give them time in class to experience how a new step or
sequence moves and flows Freely through space before you ask them to break
it down or analyze their technique while performing it. They will execute
traveling movements and complex balances with less constraint as they learn
to incorporate Free Flow into their performance. In my experience, this newfound physical ability also improves their overall mental and emotional attitude
in class. Their cautiousness and desire to be perfect lessens, and as this happens,
they begin to take more risks, ultimately improving their overall ability to learn
and develop as ballet technicians and artists.

Notes

1   Hartley, L. (1995). *Wisdom of the Body Moving: An Introduction to Body-Mind Centering*, 2nd edn. Berkeley, CA: North Atlantic Books, p. 201.
2   Hackney, P. (2000). *Making Connections: Total Body Integration Through Bartenieff Fundamentals.* New York: Routledge, p. 51.
3   See also: Laban, R. (2011b). *Mastery of Movement*, 4th edn. Alton, UK: Dance Books. Laban stated: "Flow Effort plays an important part in all movement expression, as through its inward and outward streaming it establishes relationship and communication" (p. 75).

Chapter 11

Varying intensity
Strong and Light Weight

The music begins as a whisper. Soft melodies from flutes and clarinets fill the auditorium, punctuated by light taps on the triangle and delicate plucks from the violins. Dancers skim ethereally across the surface of the stage in a series of pas de bourré couru. Gentle piqué arabesques ripple one after the other, like floating feathers scattering in the space. The music builds in intensity. Soft melodies become forceful as trumpets and trombones join the flutes and clarinets. Pounding drumbeats replace the triangle. Buoyant piqué arabesques transform into exploding leaps. Soft runs now roar across the space with herculean energy.

Floating melodies of a flute. Bellowing cries of the horns. Exploding sounds of the drums. Twinkling taps on a triangle. The changing intensity of the sounds in a musical score creates differing moods and qualities.

Similarly, dancers change their performance intensity to affect the mood and dynamic quality of the choreography. Take, for example, the differences in movement qualities between the White and Black Swan in the classical ballet *Swan Lake*. **Light Weight** characterizes the performance of the White Swan. It dances with a soft and gentle demeanor; the fluttering movements of its arms and the buoyant use of its torso transcend gravity, giving the image of a swan floating on water or flying in the air. Even though the Black Swan also uses Light Weighted gestures, especially in the feather-like movements of its wrists and hands, a **Strong Weight** demeanor is much more characteristic of the Black Swan's personality. It jumps, turns, and lunges with powerful and weighted forcefulness; its disposition is firm and resolute.

"Weight" in the context of Effort does not refer to how much dancers weigh or how strong or weak dancers are, but instead to the quality of how they use their mass while dancing. The same dancer, regardless of the dancer's physical size, might convey a fierce and foreboding onstage personality in one scene and a gentle and demure attitude in the very next scene. As the *Swan Lake* example illustrates, the qualitative or attitudinal use of Weight Effort is important when establishing a character and/or an onstage atmosphere:

Is the movement executed powerfully or delicately?

Does the quality of the choreography require a gentle or commanding use of energy? Is the dancer defying gravity with Lightness or using gravity's pull to power through the space?

Table 11.1 presents a list of synonyms, images, and musical suggestions for teaching Weight Effort. Add to each list as you and your dancers explore Effort.

Table 11.1 Synonyms, imagery, and musical suggestions for Weight Effort

Strong Weight	Light Weight
Synonyms	*Synonyms*
Resolute	Delicate
Powerful	Gently
Firm	Buoyant
Explode	Airy
Push	Sprinkle
Mighty	Billowing
Roaring	Misty
Forceful	Wispy
Herculean	Tip-toe
Vigor	Whisper
Imagery	*Imagery*
Bellowing boom of a bass drum	Soft feathers floating in the air
Thunderous crash of an ocean wave	Billowing chiffon fabric
Sound of thunder	Misty spray from an ocean wave
A mighty growl from a tiger	Helium balloons

Musical suggestions

Album: *The Rodeo Eroded*, Tin Hat Trio
   Light: "Sweep"
   Strong: "Under the Gun"

Album: *Sad Machinery of Spring*, Tin Hat
   Strong: "Dead Season"

Album: *12 Songs*, Jenny Scheinman
   Light: "Satellite"

Album: *The 50 Most Essential Pieces of Classical Music*
   Strong: The Valkyrie: Ride of the Valkyries, Wagner
   Light (mostly): Swan Lake Suite, Op. 20 Scene 9 (moderato), Tchaikovsky
   Light: Nocturne No. 2, Op. 9 in E-Flat Major, Chopin
   Strong: Requiem: Dies Irae, Tuba Mirum, Verdi

Musical variation

Symphony No. 5 in C Minor, Op. 67 "Fate": I. Allegro con Brio, Beethoven
Hungarian Dances: No. 5 in G Minor, Brahams (also excellent Time Effort)

Teachers first: embodying and using Weight Effort

Weight Effort facilitates your body's mobility through space and stability during balances. In order to experience this, Teacher exploration 11.1 focuses on the embodiment of Weight Effort in your torso, specifically in the:

- *Center of levity*—upper torso, including the ribs and shoulder girdle
- *Center of gravity*—lower torso, including the pelvis and hip joints

Teacher exploration 11.1 also explores how Strong and Light Weight travel from the center of your body and outward to the limbs. Notice how this facilitates both the mobility and stability of your body during balletic steps.

Teacher exploration 11.1: Embodying Light and Strong Weight

1 **Explore Light Weight Effort.** Allow your centers of levity and gravity to lift and float upward like helium balloons hovering above the ground with Light buoyancy. Imagine helium filling your pelvis and torso causing your body to transcend gravity's pull. Allow this sensation to travel from your torso to your legs, head, and arms as you embody different balletic movements:
Perhaps a. . . .

> *Wispy gliding tendu*
> *Billowing port de bras*
> *Tiptoeing piqué*
> *Sprinkling pas de bourée couru,*
> *Buoyant relevé sous-sus*

2 **Explore Strong Weight Effort.** Allow your center of gravity to descend causing your hip, knee, and ankle joints to crease and flex slightly. Establish the connection between the ground and your feet. Imagine your body as an immense tree. Your lower body forges deep into the ground through an extensive root system, enlivening your centers of gravity and levity with a powerful and firm intensity. Extending upward from this mighty trunk is a towering display of thick branches. Adopt a commanding posture in the ribs and shoulder girdle and let this energy travel outward to your arms and head. Maintain the strength and power in your upper and lower body as you embody different balletic movements:
Perhaps a. . . .

> *Vigorous balançoîre*
> *Resolute port de bras*
> *Powerful pirouette*
> *Booming pas de bourrée*
> *Roaring grand jeté*

The goal of Teacher exploration 11.1 was to feel how Light and Strong Weight activated your torso and pelvis and enlivened your limbs:

Did you find that one quality was more effective at achieving this goal, or that one quality was easier to feel in different parts of the body? For example, was it easier to embody Light Weight in your upper body and Strong Weight in your lower body?

If so, experiment with the movement explorations again. This time, focus only on enlivening the lower body with Light Weight and the upper body with Strong Weight. *What physical benefits do you experience?*

Next, apply Weight Effort to a recent combination you used in class. Notice how Weight Effort affects your performance of this exercise, and take note of Light or Strong Weighted images or associations that come up for you as you explore the movement.

Teacher exploration 11.2: Exploring Weight Effort in technique class

1   Recall a *barre* or *centre* exercise you used in class recently.
2   Use your own imagery or the imagery and synonyms from Table 11.1 as you rehearse the exercise.
3   Use the following questions to reflect on your experience.

How does Light Weight or Strong Weight enhance your upper body movements?

Imagining your upper body floating upward and outward like glistening mist, for example, may help you achieve a lengthened and lifted posture with greater ease. Similarly, moving your upper body firmly with the resolute power of a lion may help you broaden your torso and arms and adopt a grounded upper body posture.

Take a moment to embody these images.

Weight Effort words, such as "Floating" or "Firmly," and images, such as "glistening mist" and "resolute power of a lion," positively impact your ability to achieve an elongated and expansive upper body posture.

In what other ways did Light and Strong Weight enhance your upper body movements?

How does Light or Strong Weight enhance your lower body movements?
Imagining your lower body as voluminous clouds propelled by delicate puffs of air, for example, may help you achieve greater buoyancy during lower body weight shifts and gestures. This is useful when you need to convey the illusion of defying gravity or when moving lightly and quickly, a quality often required in *petite allegro* sequences. Similarly, imagining the booming sounds of a timpani drum propelling your lower body through space may help you perform jumps, traveling phrases, and balances with greater power, a quality that often appears in grand allegro sequences.
Take a moment to embody these images.
Light and Strong Weight positively impact your ability to shift the lower body through space.
In what other ways did Light and Strong Weight enhance your lower body movements?

Was it ever helpful to embody Strong and Light Weight at the same time during Teacher exploration 11.2? Embodying Light Weight in the upper body simultaneously with Strong Weight in the lower body is quite common in ballet technique. Take a moment to explore a balance or simple movement from your exercise:
Move your upper body with Light Weight, feeling that you are floating upward and outward from the navel, while simultaneously embodying Strong Weight in the lower body, feeling that you are firmly rooting or grounding your lower body into the earth. How do these Weight Effort choices enhance your performance of the exercise?

Cueing and verbal feedback

So far, the *Teachers first* section has focused on experiencing Weight Effort in your own body and identifying how Weight Effort enhances the technique of the upper and lower body. As a teacher, you also spend time in class describing movement and providing verbal feedback to your dancers. Your choice of words and the quality of your voice affect the way your dancers experience Light and Strong Weight during class. Weight Effort words that relate to speaking are particularly useful when describing movement and giving your students verbal feedback:

softly	*whispering*	*gently*	*tenderly*	*faintly*
loudly	*booming*	*firmly*	*powerfully*	*thunderously*

Add to this list of words and use them to do the following:

Enhance the quality of your voice

Do you ever whisper your words to conjure Lightness in an adagio? Or, do you make thunderous sounds with your voice when demonstrating a strongly executed grand battement? If so, you are using your voice to enhance the Weight Effort qualities in your exercises. *Think of your voice as a musical performance.* Change the intensity of your voice to emphasize Weight Effort, similar to how musicians change the loudness or softness of the notes and phrases as they perform a musical score.

Use evocative words and terminology

*   *Expand the names of the balletic steps to include their dynamic quality.* Instead of referring to a balletic step by only its French name—a *balancé*, for example— refer to it by both its dynamic name and French name—a *booming or softly sweeping balancé.* Play with multiple terms this way: a *firm or soft rond de jambe, thunderous or faint sauté,* a *whispering or shouting pas de bourrée,* and so on.
*   *Create lists of Weight Effort words and images, such as those presented in Table 11.1.* Post these lists around the room and give your students the opportunity to add to the lists throughout class. Use the listed words and images as inspiration any time you or your students would benefit from exploring the class phrases more dynamically.

Integrate Effort variety into class exercises

Have you or your students established Weight Effort patterns when performing certain exercises? For example: performing a *center adagio* or *rond de jambe* at *barre* with Light Weight or performing a *grand battement* or *frappé* with Strong Weight. Challenge your movement patterns by performing those movements with the opposite Weight Effort qualities.

Teaching Weight Effort to your students

As with any of the Effort qualities, use Weight Effort in class when it helps you achieve specific artistic and technical goals. Reflect on your own experience for a moment: **What technical and artistic challenges did you experience as you explored Strong and Light Weight?** Based on those challenges:

> *When would you focus on Strong or Light Weight with your students? What technical or artistic goals are you trying to achieve?*

> *How would you explain Strong or Light Weight to your students? What seems important to communicate or emphasize?*

Artistically, the use of Strong and Light Weight may convey a large range of emotional states depending on the mood or context of the choreography or class phrases. Technically, both Light and Strong Weight activate the body's center and enliven the limbs. Light Weight does this with buoyancy and lift, and Strong Weight does it with compression and force. So, either quality is advantageous to access during technique class if your dancers experience difficulty:

- stabilizing the lower body during balances;
- establishing active upper body *port de bras*;
- traveling efficiently during locomotion steps;
- achieving greater rebound during jumps, balances, and weight shifts.

Reference Table 11.2 for suggestions of when to use Strong and Light Weight Effort during technique class. Add to these suggestions as you explore the above questions.

Sensing and feeling Weight Effort! uses imagery, sounding, and evocative words to develop your dancers' knowledge of Weight Effort. Challenge your dancers to embody both Strong and Light Weight during all three activities. This will develop greater technical proficiency. Dancers who prefer using Light Weight during class, for example, will experience new technical challenges as they begin to access Strong Weight. Similarly, inviting the students to make different Weight Effort choices encourages dynamic variation and personal ownership of the material.

Table 11.2 Technical and artistic benefits for Weight Effort

Strong Weight is a practical movement quality to use when teaching students how to:

1. *Ground the lower body and powerfully activate the pelvis and torso.* Strong Weight helps dancers firmly activate the torso and lower body during moments of mobility—a running preparation before a large *grand jeté*—or stability—when balancing or turning on one leg.
2. *Shift their weight and perform direction changes with force and commitment.* Embodying Strong Weight promotes a bounding and driving use of force, which is important when performing lower body movements, such as *tombé, temps lié, pas de basque.* This is useful for dancers who perform direction changes and weight shifts timidly.
3. *Dance with an artistic attitude that conveys a powerful emotional state:* resolute, proud, celebratory, firm, aggressive, boisterous, angry, vigorous, and so on.

Light Weight is a practical movement quality to use when teaching students how to:

1. *Activate the pelvis and torso with lift and delicacy.* Light Weight helps dancers establish greater lift in the torso and arms. This prevents passivity in the spine and arms.
2. *Shift their weight and perform direction changes with buoyancy and lift.* Embodying Light Weight in the lower body promotes "airy" buoyancy and rebound, which is important during fast footwork and *petite allegro.* This is useful for dancers who passively "sink" their weight into the pelvis or dance with excess lower body tension.
3. *Dance with an artistic attitude that conveys a delicate emotional state:* serene, gentle, ethereal, demure, poised, sneaky, delicately commanding, and so on.

+ Artistically, the use of Strong and Light Weight may convey a large range of emotional states depending on the mood or context of the choreography or class phrases.

Figure 11.1 Explore buoyancy and lift in balletic steps

Figure 11.2 Powerfully activate the body's mass in space

Sensing and feeling Weight Effort!

Objective:

Dancers explore how Weight Effort affects their performance in technique class.

Exploration question for all three activities:
How did Light or Strong Weight enhance your technique and performance?

Monotonous no more—Weight Effort

1   Ask your dancers: *Have you ever listened to a monotonous speech where the intensity and tone of the speaker's voice is unchanging?*
2   Instruct them to perform an exercise from class with a monotonous energy as if the steps in the exercise were words in a speech.
3   Instruct the dancers to perform the sequence again by emphasizing some "words" (movements) softly and gently and some powerfully and loudly. Since the dancers are using speech dynamics as a metaphor for movement dynamics, use Weight Effort words that relate to

speech when cueing your dancers. Reference the list of words you created in the *Teachers first* section.

What does Weight sound like?

1   Teach your dancers a *barre* or *centre* exercise with Weight Effort variety. As you teach the exercise, emphasize the Weight Effort changes with your voice.

2   Ask your dancers to change the intensity of their voices as they verbally review the exercise. For example, the entire class says:

> *"tombé pas de bourée, pirouette and land."*
> [softly whispering] [firmly shouting]

3   Instruct them to perform the exercise simultaneously with their dynamic sounding.

4   Instruct them to perform the exercise without the dynamic sounding, but still emphasizing the Weight Effort changes.

Same exercise, different Weight

1   Choose a well-rehearsed exercise from class.

2   Post the list of Weight Effort words you created in the *Teachers first* section in the dance studio.

3   Ask the students to choose 2–3 words from the Strong Weight list.

4   Ask them to apply the words to their performance of the exercise. Choice is important here. Even though they will all be working with the concept of Strong Weight, a student using the word *Firmly* will embody Strong Weight differently than a student using the word *Booming*.

5   Repeat steps 2–4 with the same exercise, but this time, instruct them to choose 2–3 words from the Light Weight list.

Using Weight Effort to develop artistry

Weight Effort is a practical tool for teaching dancers how to develop onstage characters, personalities, or attitudes. The overall "character" or attitude of a movement changes as the Weight Effort changes. For example, in Act II of *Swan Lake*, Prince Siegfried embodies a Strong Weighted personality; his performance is characterized by commanding and confident solo variations and pantomime sequences with the Black Swan and courtesans. In Act III his use of Weight Effort shifts as he dances with the dying White Swan. His touch softens, his gaze is gentle, and his overall demeanor is tender and softhearted.

This type of theatricality is also important in contemporary ballet choreography. Many current choreographers challenge dancers to develop characters or personalities in rehearsals, or to portray different moods through their dancing. The technique class is an ideal setting to develop these artistic skills. Not only does it promote an artistic attitude in class, but it also teaches dancers how to imbue meaning and expression into highly technical movement.

The following activity, *Dance the classics!* presents an expressive approach for embodying Strong and Light Weight. This activity uses classical ballet variations from the 19th and early 20th centuries as inspiration for your technique exercises. Use this activity to:

• promote imagination and expressive play;
• provide opportunities for dancers to practice different artistic qualities; and
• strengthen your dancers' aesthetic and historical understanding of different ballets.

Using dynamically rich classical variations as an inspiration for your technique exercises is also a great method for improving technique. Even though the attitudinal experience of Light and Strong Weight is different, embodying either quality engages the physical mass of the body. For example, your dancers will embody greater power when performing a Strong Weight in-class exercise inspired by the bold and confident Black Swan, or the unfaltering Moor from *Petroushka*, or the many fiery and commanding dances from *Don Quixote*. Embodying these expressive qualities—boldness, power, confidence, unfaltering, stalwart—is especially useful for dancers who:

• dance "on the surface" of the floor;
• lose the form and tone of their arms during complex movements;
• experience difficulty stabilizing their lower body during balances or pushing off of the ground during jumps and *relevé*.

Dance the classics!

Objective:

Dancers embody a range of qualities along the Weight Effort continuum. Dancers practice approaching technique exercises with an artistic attitude.

Step 1: Choose a variation

Choose a Light or Strong Weighted variation from a ballet your dancers are familiar with, such as *The Nutcracker* or *Sleeping Beauty*, or one they are less familiar with, such as Michel Fokine's *Petroushka* or *Firebird* or Jules Perrot's *Pas de Quatre*. You will not teach the variation in its entirety. Instead, you will use it as inspiration to create select exercises at *barre* and *centre*.

Note: It does not matter if the variation is for a male or female dancer. Dancers of all genders and body types benefit when they learn how to embody both Light and Strong Weight in a variety of steps and phrases.

Step 2: Identify the artistic attitude of the variation and generate evocative language

a   Identify the overall artistic attitude of the variation. Is it primarily Light or Strong Weighted? Or, does the Weight Effort change—beginning softly and end boldly, for example?

b   Create a list of descriptive words, phrases, and images as you watch the variation on your own. Use this list while you teach the class phrases and coach your dancers. For example, when watching a Light Weighted variation, perhaps you are reminded of feathers floating in the air or light reflecting off of misty air crystals. Or, perhaps you use verbal phrases, such as "*delicate effervescence*" or "*lofty buoyancy*" when teaching the exercises to your students. Or, you might choose to write down actual images from the variation: snow falling during the Dance of the Snow Queen in the Nutcracker, for example.

Step 3: Create class exercises that reference the steps, phrases, and use of Weight Effort in the variation

a   Identify key phrases and/or steps from the variation and include them in 2–3 *barre* exercises and 2–3 *centre* exercises. I like to choose steps or phrases that will challenge my dancers technically. I often integrate entire movement phrases (i.e. an 8–16 count phrase) from the variation in the *centre* exercises. Then, I choose singular steps or smaller phrases from the *centre* exercises to integrate into my *barre* exercises. This ensures that the students will be physically prepared for the *centre* combinations.

b   Clarify the Weight Effort qualities for the *barre* and *centre* exercises you created.

Note: Keep the other exercises in class simple in terms of sequencing, so that the dancers don't get overwhelmed learning a lot of complex sequences. Plus, you can still ask them to highlight the Weight Effort quality in these simpler exercises. For example, if working with a Strong Weighted variation, ask the dancers to embody a commanding attitude during *grand battement en croix*.

Step 4: Contextualize the variation for your dancers (optional)

Before you teach your variation-inspired exercises in class, give the dancers information that helps them understand the variation. You do not need to provide them with a verbal synopsis of the entire ballet, but do communicate:

- relevant background information for the ballet (i.e. year it was performed, original choreographer, musical composer);
- the general artistic theme or storyline of the ballet;
- the artistic intent of the variation.

Show the variation in class. Ask the dancers: *how does the movement make you feel? What is the attitude or personality of the movement? Is it firm or gentle? Commanding or ethereal? Thundering or tranquil? Powerful or delicate? Do any images or descriptive words come to mind when you perform the class phrases?* Generate a list of words and images as a class.

Step 5: Teach, practice and perform!

Class 1: Begin teaching the variation-inspired *barre* and *centre* exercises. Note: the activities in Step 4 will take 20–30 minutes, so you may choose to complete Step 4 on a different day.

Classes 2–4: Continue learning and rehearsing the exercises. Challenge the dancers to embody the variation-inspired exercises with the intended Weight Effort qualities. Also incorporate the Weight Effort qualities from the variation in other exercises that were not directly inspired by the exercise.

Classes 5 and 6: Give the dancers the option of making their own Weight Effort choices in the variation-inspired exercises. Perhaps they embody the opposite Weight Effort quality. Or, perhaps they choose other moments in the exercises to play with Weight Effort in their own way and with their own words and images.

When they make different choices, ask them: *How did the expressive quality of the movement change when the Weight Effort quality changed? Did those changes invoke different feeling-tones or characters?*

Dance the classics! is a great activity for teaching dancers about ballets from the 19th and 20th centuries, and those ballets, in particular, provide ample material for exploring Strong and Light Weight. But, it is equally as fun for dancers to explore the contemporary choreography from the 21st century and late 20th century. As a contemporary choreographer, I use phrases from ballets I have created, particularly those pieces that clearly use Weight Effort. In these pieces, all of the dancers perform both Light and Strong Weighted movements regardless of their gender or body type. In a contemporary environment, it is important for dancers of all genders, sizes, and abilities to experience Effort diversity.

Do you choreograph contemporary ballets? And if so, have you created choreography that utilizes Strong or Light Weighted movement phrases? If so, look to your own work for inspiration when designing your classes around Weight Effort.

I also study the choreography of other contemporary artists and use their work as inspiration for my classes. In these cases, I am careful that I do not copy exactly their movement or phrases. Instead, I use qualities or themes in their choreography as inspiration for my classes. For example, if the choreography utilizes Strong Weighted angular upper and lower body movements, I create *barre* and *centre* exercises that incorporate Strong Weighted angular movement in a variety of ways. Additionally, when contemporary choreographers set pieces on the dancers in my classes, I often ask them if I can incorporate phrases from their ballets into my classes.

Drawing on both classical and contemporary ballets during class gives dancers the opportunity to embody different balletic styles. As teachers, it gives us the opportunity to broaden our movement palettes and create exercises that we might not have created otherwise. This challenges everyone in the classroom, both technically and artistically.

Chapter 12

Rhythmical nuance

Sudden and Sustained Time

The music in the background catches my attention. Its volume has steadily increased. At the top of the crescendo, the musicians prolong the last note of the phrase, causing me to linger in anticipation for the next series of notes. As the melody continues, the musicians accent some notes with urgency, creating a percussive staccato rhythm. Their rhythmical play intensifies as they improvise with the musical phrasing in unpredictable ways. The interplay between acceleration and deceleration is exciting. I leave my chair and begin to dance to their syncopated rhythms; lingering notes suspend my whole body in space, and bursts of speed dart from limb to limb.

Dancers, like musicians, layer their movements with sharp unexpected accents and lingering suspensions. They, too, alternate between acceleration and deceleration, staccato and legato. Reflect on your own teaching practices:

Have you ever instructed your students to perform the glissade before a grand jeté en avant quickly so they have more time to suspend the grand jeté in the air?

Or, perhaps, you have asked your students to perform a fast chassé in order to elongate a jeté entrelacé (tours jeté)?

If so, you are teaching your dancers to enhance their performance through the use of **Sudden** and **Sustained Time**. "Time" in the context of L/BMA Effort does not refer to the dancer's quantitative use of time—how many minutes have gone by or how many beats to a measure—but instead to the dancer's qualitative sense of time. Does the dancer perform the movement with lingering suspension or with brisk immediacy? Does the choreography require an indulgent or urgent atmosphere?

The use of a specific Time Effort quality affects the artistic tone of the movement. The Bluebird solo in Act III of *Sleeping Beauty*, for example, is notorious for its skittering *pas de bourées*, brisk *batterie*, and whipping *piqué* turns. Even though the Bluebird moves at a fast tempo, it is the performer's inner attitude of immediacy that creates an exciting onstage atmosphere. The Grand Pas de Deux in this same act is filled with elongated balances *en pointe*, suspenseful *promenades*, and lingering moments of embrace; the couple prolongs intimate moments for the audience, creating an indulgent on stage atmosphere. In contemporary choreography, artists, such as William Forsythe, create complex movement phrases that alternate seamlessly between Sudden and Sustained Time. This syncopated use of time contributes to an unpredictable, exciting, and rhythmically sophisticated choreographic style.[1]

Table 12.1 presents a list of synonyms, images, and musical suggestions for teaching Time Effort. Add to each list as you and your dancers explore Effort.

Table 12.1 Synonyms, imagery, and musical suggestions for Time Effort

Sudden Time	Sustained Time
Synonyms	*Synonyms*
Urgently	Elongate (*allongé*)
Crisp	Lingered
Instantaneously	Gradual
Staccato	Legato
Burst	Prolong
Dart	Drawing out
Briskly	Suspended
Swiftly	Leisurely
Imagery	*Imagery*
Instantaneous pop of a firecracker	Dripping of thick honey
Sudden upsweep of fall leaves in a brisk breeze	Elongating a rubber band before it's shot
A hummingbird's ravenous flight	An air current suspends the soaring eagle

Musical suggestions

Album: *Hush*, Bobby McFerrin and Yo-Yo Ma
   Sudden: Rimsky-Korsakov, "Flight of the Bumblebee"
   Sustained: Bach, "Orchestral Suite #3 in D, BWV 1068—Air"

Album: *Essential Vivaldi*, Christopher Hogwood
   Sudden: Concerto in G "alla rustica," RV 151—I Presto

Album: *Two Foot Yard*, Carla Kihlstedt
   Sustained: "When Will Tomorrow End?," "Far and Wee," and "Tough Guy"

Music with timing variation

Most Tangos or Mazurkas: The syncopated rhythms encourage timing play

Album: *The 50 Most Essential Pieces of Classical Music*
   "Hungarian Dances: No. 5 in G Minor"

Album: *The Inevitable*, Squirrel Nut Zippers
   "You're Drivin' Me Crazy," "Danny Diamond," and "Lover's Lane"

Album: *All Time Greatest Hits*, Louis Armstrong
   "Skokiaan", Mack the Knife," and "It Takes Two to Tango"

Teachers first: embodying and using time effort

Sustained and Sudden Time Efforts permeate the rhythms found in ballet technique classes. For example, a *battement frappé devant* is often phrased with a
Sudden burst of the leg downward and forward in space as the foot strikes the
floor. The leg is then Sustained in the *devant* position until it urgently travels in
and out of *sur le cou de pied*. This way of performing a *battement frappé* does not
follow an even rhythm.

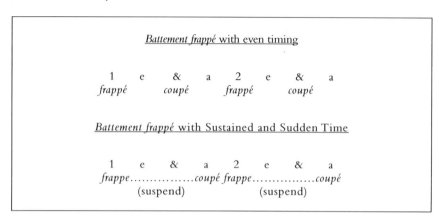

Ballet teachers often ask dancers to prolong their movements with legato-
like suspensions or attack their movements with urgent, staccato-like accents, as
the above example illustrates. As a way to practice this in your body, first learn
the following *barre* exercise (Exercise 12.1). Do not focus on counts or meter;
simply learn the actions.

Exercise 12.1: *Battement tendu* at the *barre*

1   Begin in *fifth position*, right leg *devant* and left hand on the *barre*.
2   *Battement tendu devant* with the right leg three times. Finish in *pointe
    tendu devant*.
3   *Temps lié en avant* to *pointe tendu derrière* with the left leg.
4   *Battement tendu derrière* with the left leg three times, ending in *fifth
    position*, left leg *derrière*.
5   *Battement tendu changé á la seconde* with the right leg four times.
6   *Relevé retiré devant* bringing the right leg to *retiré*.
7   *Tombé* on the right, *coupé* the left, *pas de bourée en tournant* to the left end-
    ing in *fifth position plié* ready to start the combination on the other side.

Teacher exploration 12.1: Embodying Sudden and Sustained Time

1   **Rehearse the *battement tendu* exercise focusing on Sudden Time**.

    For example: Sharply and swiftly accent the outward movement of your right leg during each *battement tendu devant*. Like the "pop!" of a firecracker, instantaneously move your leg from *fifth position* to *tendu devant*.

    Explore Sudden Time in five additional movements: during the *temps lié en avant*, or the *pas de bourée*, for example.

2   **Rehearse the exercise focusing on Sustained Time**.

    For example: Prolong the movement of your leg backward into each *tendu derrière* like the elongated pull of an elastic band.

    Explore Sustained Time in five additional movements: during the ascent of the leg from *fifth position* to *retiré*, or the descent into *plié* during the *temps lié en avant*, for example.

3   **Rehearse the exercise focusing on both Sudden and Sustained Time**.

    For example: Quickly accent the movement of your leg from *fifth position* to *battement tendu devant*. Follow this by a prolonged closure of the leg back into the *fifth position*. Reverse this phrasing during the next *tendu*, drawing out the outward reach of the leg followed by a brisk return to *fifth position*.

    Where else can you play with a Sudden to Sustained movement phrasing?

4   **Apply the above three explorations to other steps and exercises**.

    For example:

    •   Perform a *battement développé* with Sudden Time and then Sustained Time. Or, perform a *balancé* with a Sustained first step followed immediately by two Suddenly phrased steps. *How do the movements change technically?*
    •   Incorporate swift movements in a *centre adagio* and sustained movements in a *petite allegro*. *How do these timing choices affect the expressive quality of the exercises?*

5   Reflect: *How did Time Effort affect your technical and artistic embodiment of the balletic vocabulary?*

Similar to your explorations with Weight Effort, when or how you focus on Time Effort in technique class depends on the artistic and technical goals you are working on with your students. There are a number of ways to incorporate Time Effort into your technique classes.

Create technique exercises that vary in Time Effort

- *Design your exercises to music with timing variation or syncopated rhythms*, such as tangos or mazurkas. In a *grand battement* at *barre*, for example, this might encourage you to accent the movements into and out of *fifth position* with immediacy, or prolong the descent of the leg from the top of the *grand battement*, or draw out balances on *relevé* a split second longer, adding a little suspense to the movement.
- *Use Time Effort inspired characters or artistic attitudes as inspirations for your exercises*: sprightly court jesters, leisurely lions, or feelings of excitement, indulgence, and so on. Return to *Dance the classics!* in the previous chapter. Identify classical or contemporary ballet variations that highlight Time Effort and use those as inspiration for your class exercises.
- *Experiment with Time Effort during the transition steps in your exercises*: steps such as *pas de bourée*, *glissé*, *temps lié*, *pas de couru*, *tombé coupé*, *plié*, and so on. Focusing on transition steps in this way enhances the musicality and rhythm of the entire exercise, and teaches students to pay attention to the technical nuances of these steps, in general.

Generate evocative words and terminology with your students

- *Expand the names of the balletic steps to include their dynamic quality*: a *leisurely* or *quick soutenu*, an *urgent* or *lingering degagé*, a *crisp* or *prolonged rond de jambe*. Encourage dancers to use this terminology when they give feedback to each other.
- *Create lists of Time Effort words and images with your students and post them around the room*. Add to the lists as you practice Time Effort in class. Embody select words from the lists as you and your students perform and rehearse *barre* and *centre* exercises.

Emphasize Time Effort with your voice

Generate a series of sounds that invoke Sustained or Sudden Time and speak the balletic vocabulary with different rhythms and inflection. Sometimes, in the effort to provide students with clear tempos and meters, it is easy to use a monotone voice when presenting new exercises in class. If this seems familiar to you, practice speaking with different Time emphases during your second or third demonstrations of a new exercise (i.e. speeding up or drawing out your words as you describe the movement). This provides your students with needed qualitative information for the exercises. Teacher exploration 12.2 presents lists of words and sounds to get you started. *Add your own words and sounds to these lists.*

Teacher exploration 12.2: Using Time Effort in your verbal cueing

1   **Create a list of Time Effort sounds and words.**

   Example 1: Pop! Pow! Snap! Tap! Whip! Burst! Prick!

   These one-syllable words evoke Sudden Time. They are good to use for quickly executed balletic steps or specific movements of the body, such as the whip of the head during turns, the bounce of the leg *battement piqué*, the brush of the leg into a *grand jeté*, and so on. *Generate a list of other steps that would benefit from this type of verbal cueing.*

   Example 2: A trilled sound, such as "d'd'd'd'd'ding!" or "skit't't't't'ter!"

   A series of quickly executed sounds are appropriate for consecutive movements that build in urgency, such as a *pas de bourée couru* that ends in a *sous-sus*, or a series of *pas de bourée en tournant* performed consecutively. *Generate a list of other steps that would benefit from this type of verbal cueing.*

   Example 3: "Biiiilloooooooow . . ." or "Elooooonnnngate . . ." or "Aaaahhhhhh"

   Sustained words or sounds, such as these, are effective when accompanied by changes in the inflection of your voice. For example, the "Aaaaahhhhh" might rise in inflection throughout the word, like an *arabesque* where the leg and arms slowly ascend in space and suspend at the end. Reversing the inflection for "Aaaaahhhhh" might encourage the opposite action—an *arabesque* where the leg and arms prolong their descent to a *tombé*. Words like "Elooooonnnngate" or "Biiilllloooow" may rise in inflection during the middle of the word, yet again changing where the suspension occurs. When you change the inflection and timing of your voice, you encourage students to Sustain their movements in different places: at the beginning, middle, or end.

2   **Practice speaking balletic words with different Time Effort dynamics.**

   Example 1, Sustained emphasis: "Tennnnnduuuuuuuu 3& 4&"
   Sustain............

> **Example 2, Sudden emphasis: "Degage! hold Pique!pique! close!"**
>   1   3   &   4
>
> 3   **Practice cueing with and without Time Effort.** Before class begins, practice describing an exercise from your class out loud. Describe the combination using a monotonous voice; speak every word with the same rhythm and do not vary the tone or melody of your voice. Then, describe the combination again, using the Sudden and Sustained Time words and sounds listed in this exploration and in Table 12.1. Also draw from the Time Effort lists you generated with your students.

Teaching Time Effort to your students

In my experience, upper-level dancers often phrase their movements evenly, emphasizing each step with the same timing and attack. Often, however, this is not the type of movement phrasing required of them in most rehearsals and performances. Dance researcher Paulette Coté-Laurence describes rhythm as pertaining "to the timing of sounds and movements whereas musicality refers to sensitivity to music as a whole, which includes not only rhythm but also melody, harmony and tone colour."[2] Both rhythm and musicality are important in ballet training. Ballet dancers must know how "to move to the beat ... to identify the accent, differentiate between different meters, recognize various rhythmic patterns made up of different durations, and maintain a tempo"[3] and to "perform phrases of movement to phrases of music."[4] **Time Effort is therefore an effective tool to use when teaching dancers how to perform more musically, rhythmically, and variedly.**

Reflect on your own experience for a moment: **What technical and artistic challenges did you experience as you explored Sudden and Sustained Time?** Based on those challenges:

When would you focus on Sustained and Sudden Time with your students? What technical or artistic goals are you trying to achieve?

How would you explain Sustained and Sudden Time to your students? What seems important to communicate or emphasize?

Sudden Time teaches dancers how to accent movements with swiftness and immediacy and how to accelerate a movement after an *allongé* position. Sudden Time is therefore effective to access when dancers need to perform movements quickly and urgently and attack movements with immediate confidence. Sustained time teaches dancers how to prolong and suspend movements and how to decelerate movements after a series of quickly performed steps. Sustained Time is therefore effective to access when dancers need to perform with a lingering attitude and draw movements out with elongated aplomb.

Table 12.2 provides suggestions of when to use Sudden and Sustained Time in ballet technique class. Add to these lists as you explore Time Effort in your classes.

As you plan your classes, choose one of the technical and artistic benefits in Table 12.2 and use it as an organizing movement concept for technique class. For example, if you want to teach your students how to "perform with a quick and urgent attitude":

•   Choreograph *barre* and *centre* exercises that are typically performed slowly with Sudden Time instead—exercises such as *rond de jambe à terre* or *developpé à quatrieme*.

Table 12.2 Technical and artistic benefits for Time Effort

Sudden Time is a practical movement quality to use when teaching students how to:
1. *Perform with a quick and urgent attitude*: moving briskly and swiftly in a *petite allegro*, for example.
2. *Attack movements with immediate confidence*, such as, using Sudden Time during the preparatory movements prior to a balance or turn.
3. *Accelerate after performing slower, elongated movements*, such as performing a quick *pas de bourée* after an *allongé arabesque*.
4. *Dance with an artistic attitude that conveys an urgent emotional state or mood*: excited, happy, panicked, bustling, frantic, nervous, terror, sprightly, and so on.[+]

Sustained Time is a practical movement quality to use when teaching students how to:
1. *Perform with a lingering attitude*, such as indulging in the moments of suspension and *allongé* scattered throughout an *adagio*.
2. *Accent movements with elongated aplomb*, such as when a dancer performs an *allongé arabesque* at the end of a *double grand attitude pirouette* or when a dancer lingers and suspends the end of a balance during *barre* or *centre* work.
3. *Decelerate after performing quick movements*, for example, the dancer decelerates and suspends a final *piqué arabesque* after moving across the floor with a series of quick *chassés* or *grand jetés*.
4. *Dance with an artistic attitude that conveys a drawn-out emotional state*: luxuriating, sorrowful, confident, shock, sneaky, indulgent, solemn, leisurely, and so on.[+]

[+] Artistically, the use of Sudden or Sustained Time may convey a large range of emotional states depending on the mood or context of the choreography or class phrases.

- Include quickly accented movements into all of your class exercises, similar to the way you initially experimented with Sudden Time in the *battement tendu* at *barre* exercise.

When first teaching Time Effort to your students, I suggest starting with an activity similar to Teacher exploration 12.1. Teaching each element in isolation helps dancers identify how Sudden or Sustained Time affects their technique differently. I also recommend playing music in class that supports Sudden and Sustained musical phrasing. Table 12.1 provides a number of musical suggestions; also sift through your musical library for selections to use in class. Sometimes, however, I turn the music off during class. This gives the dancers the opportunity to experiment with Sustained and Sudden Time in silence as they perform select *barre* and *centre* exercises. While this is initially uncomfortable for them, they eventually enjoy experimenting with their own movement phrasing independent of the music.

Dancing rhythmically and musically! presents other ideas for introducing Time Effort to your students. Collectively, these activities challenge students to embody diverse rhythmical patterns and experiment with different Time Effort choices. Alternating between Sudden and Sustained accents during a basic exercise teaches students how to dance "in the moment" and it develops their musical sensibilities.

Dancing rhythmically and musically!

Objective:

Dancers learn to perform their movements with greater timing and rhythmical variation.

Monotonous no more: Time Effort

1   Ask your dancers: *Have you ever listened to a monotonous speech where every word is spoken evenly?*
2   Instruct them to perform an exercise from class with a monotonous rhythm as if the steps in the exercise were evenly phrased words in a speech.
3   Instruct them to perform the sequence again by emphasizing some "words" (movements) with sudden bursts of insight and some with prolonged contemplation.

Time the tune!

Create an exercise to familiar rhymes or songs and ask the students to sing the melodies and rhythms of the song out loud before their performance of the balletic sequence. Nursery rhymes, Broadway tunes, and popular music are great places to look for inspiration; the songs you choose should include clear timing variation. Balletic steps are musical by nature; you will be surprised how easy it is to find steps that parallel the melodies of the songs or rhymes you use. Here's an example of short center floor combination to "Do-Re-Mi" from the *Sound of Music*. This example includes both Sudden and Sustained Time variations.

Lyrics:	Doe	a deer	a fe—male	deer
Counts:	1	a 2	a 3 &	4
Steps:	*elongated piqué arabesque*	*brisk plié relevé*	*drawn out arabesque*	*plié into scurrying pas de bourée*	*brisk plié into a suspended sous-sus*

Lyrics:	Ray	a drop	of	gol——den	sun
Counts:	5	a 6	e &	a	7
Steps:	*glissé arabesque*	*coupé sauté devant pas de bourée effacé en avant, tombé coupé*		*piqué balance into a suspended écharté derrière*

Experimenting with Time Effort in this way during class makes learning ballet technique fun, and it will add timing variation and rhythmical nuance to your in-class exercises.

Clapping, stomping, sounding!

Ask your dancers to clap, stomp, and/or sound out the rhythms of the in-class exercises. This will help them identify where the accelerations, decelerations, and Sudden or Sustained accents are in the sequences. For example, a *tombé pas de bourée en avant* may be phrased with a Sustained *tombé* followed by three Suddenly phrased steps in the *pas de bourée*. Stomping with a pause for the slow *tombé* and clapping quickly three times for the *pas de bourée* will teach your dancers how to rhythmically organize their movements. Exclaiming out loud, "Sloooooowwww, pa! pa! pa!" will have a similar effect.

Dancers also deepen their knowledge of Time Effort when they have opportunities to generate their own rhythms during class and improvise with the timing of the class phrases. *Choose the time!* presents three activities for developing your dancers' performance and improvisational skills with Time Effort. If you recall from Chapter 2, improvisation is a great tool for assessing your dancers' knowledge of movement/technique concepts. If your dancers physically and cognitively understand Time Effort, they will be able to comfortably improvise with Sustained and Sudden Time during class.

Choose the time!

Objective:

Dancers learn how to make rhythmical and musical choices, and to improvise with Time Effort.

Student-led clapping, stomping, sounding!

Option #1

1   *Ask one student to clap/stomp/sound a Time Effort-inspired rhythm.* Continue this process until you have a series of rhythms to work with:

Example:

Student 1—*Clap*.............. *Clap, Clap, Clap*
              (Sustain)   (Suddenly phrased triplet)
Student 2—*Clap, Clap, Clap. Clap*............
              (Sudden triplet)   (Sustain)
Student 3—*Whooshhhhhhh   Stomp/Stomp.   Whooshhhhhhh   Stomp/Stomp.*
     (Sustain)   (Sudden)   (Sustain)   (Sudden)

2   *Create a movement phrase that complements each rhythm.* Play with one step in different ways—working with a series of *tendus* to different rhythms—or link different steps together—working with *plié, tendu,* and *pas de bourée,* for example. If you decide to link different steps together, experiment with repeating the same movement phrase to different rhythms (a good approach if your students generate complex rhythms), or creating a new movement phrase for each rhythm (a more challenging approach).

You should create the movement phrases when first introducing this activity to your students. Once your students grasp the intent of the exercise, challenge them to create the movement phrases.

Option #2

Reverse the above activity. Create the movement phrases first, and then determine the rhythms. Play with more than one rhythm for each movement phrase, so that the students experience different rhythms for the same series of steps.

Timely improvisations!

Musical improvisation

1   *Choose a centre exercise to explore in class.* It will be difficult for your students to improvise with Time Effort if they are uncertain of the steps or sequencing in the exercise. So, rehearse the exercise with your dancers in 2–3 classes before attempting this activity.
2   *Choose musical accompaniment:* live music, recorded music, or silence.

If working with live musicians: ask them to improvise with *legato, staccato, accelerando,* and *decelerando* as the dancers perform the exercise. The dancers should physically respond to the improvised music as they perform the exercise.

If working with recorded music: Use music that alternates between Sustained and Sudden Time. Surprise the dancers with different pieces of music and ask them to immediately perform the exercise based on what they hear in the music.

If working in silence: Cue the dancers to follow their own instincts as they perform the exercise, alternating between Sudden and Sustained Time in their own way.

Free improvisation

Ask the dancers to freely improvise with both Sudden and Sustained Time in a variety of movements as a transition from *barre* to *centre.* Provide the option of using both balletic and non-balletic steps in their improvisation.

Music suggestions: See "Music with timing variation" in Table 12.1.

Structured improvisation

Ask the dancers to perform an exercise, such as an *adagio,* with different timing choices each time the exercise is repeated in class that day; this will teach them how to move beyond personal movement preferences.

Playing time!

This activity is more complex. So, use it in class once your students have demonstrated the ability to embody and improvise with Time Effort. I recommend first applying this activity to simple exercises—exercises with repetitive movements and easy sequencing. Begin with a simple *battement tendu en croix* at *barre*:

> Four *battement tendu devant* (counts 1–4)
> Four *à la seconde* (counts 5–8)
> Four *derrière* (counts 1–4)
> Four *à la seconde* (counts 5–8)

There are two rules in this activity:

1   Avoid performing the *battement tendu* evenly, which means the students cannot perform one *battement tendu* per one count of music.
2   Start the new direction at the beginning of each meter, which means they must begin *à la second* on count five, *derrière* on count one, and so on.

Based on these rules, if a student Sustains the first *battement tendu devant*, taking two counts to perform it, then s/he would have to perform the remaining three *tendus* with Sudden Time during the last two counts in order to sync up with the musical timing again. If your students want a real challenge, they can perform three *tendus* in one count, or one *tendu* in three counts, maintaining the movement of the leg in space during the entire three counts. There are many possibilities!

Musical suggestions: If your students experience difficulty with this approach, use music with syncopated timing, such as a tango or a mazurka. This will give them a clear timing structure to play with. As your students become more familiar with this approach, use music without rhythmic variability. This will push them to listen to their own phrasing instincts.

There are many ways to explore Time Effort during class. As you improvise with and explore Time Effort in your own way, your students will be more likely to do the same. So, have fun with Time Effort in class and add to the activities presented in this chapter!

Notes

1 Reference the online ballets of the following contemporary choreographers: William Forsythe (*Forsythe Company*); Crystal Pite (*Kidd Pivot*); Alonzo King's (*Lines Ballet*); and Jiří Kylián, Sol León, and Paul Lightfoot (*Nederlands Dans Theater*).
2 Coté-Laurence, P. (2000). The Role of Rhythm in Ballet Training. *Research in Dance Education*, 1(2): 178.
3 Ibid., p. 175.
4 Ibid., p. 177.

Chapter 13

Attentive movement
Direct and Indirect Space

Even when dancing in studio spaces that were quite small, I remember my teachers telling me to:

Imagine your audience in front of you.
Keep the energy flowing past your fingertips toward your audience.

And, when rehearsing both contemporary and classical ballets, I remember my teachers asking questions, such as:

What are you trying to communicate to your audience?
Where are you directing your attention?
How does your focus communicate what you're feeling?

In a dance style that emphasizes line, form, and an outward radiation of energy, questions and statements such as these are common.

Figure 13.1 Where are you directing your attention?

Ballet is an outwardly expressive art form, and as such, ballet dancers are taught to use their face, eyes, and limbs communicatively. **Space Effort** is a useful tool for teaching dancers how to effectively channel their energy and attention in space. Sometimes the dancer's awareness must be pinpointed, or **Direct**, and sometimes it must be all encompassing, or **Indirect**. For example, during a curtain call the dancers typically begin their bows with outstretched arms and lifted gazes as they Indirectly scan the vast audience before them. They then present a Direct gesture of their arms and focus of their eyes toward the conductor for appreciation.

The word "space" in Space Effort can be misleading. "Space" in the context of Effort does not refer to locomotive pathways through space, Kinesphere, or even to a dancer's locale within a space. Instead, it pertains to the quality of how dancers use their attention as they dance: does the dancer convey a single-focused or multi-focused use of energy? Does the choreography require an expansive or channeled use of attention among the dancers?

In the "Mad Scene" from the Romantic Ballet *Giselle*, Giselle's emotions are conveyed, in part, through the use of Direct and Indirect Space. She searches frantically and Indirectly among the crowd for a sword and then Directly grabs the sword and pushes it toward her heart. At other times, she gazes remorsefully and Directly into space at fading memories, and often she darts Directly across the stage toward her mother for a yearning embrace. There are also many instances when Giselle is devoid of Space Effort, when her awareness of her surroundings disappears completely. The contrast between these moments and those previously described creates a highly charged and emotional scene of desperation, shock, longing, and anguish.

Table 13.1 presents a list of synonyms, images, and musical suggestions for teaching Space Effort. Add to each list as you and your dancers explore Effort.

Table 13.1 Synonyms, imagery, and musical suggestions for Space Effort

Direct Space	Indirect Space
Synonyms	Synonyms
Channeled attention	Expansive attention
Single-focused	Multi-focused
Honing in	Taking it all in
Piercing	Enveloping
Laser-like	Octopus-like
Linear Focus	Circuitous/widespread focus
Located awareness	Overlapping awareness
Pinpointed	Scanning

(Continued)

Table 13.1 (Continued)

Direct Space	Indirect Space
Imagery	*Imagery*
Attentively listening to a speaker talking	Tour guide gesturing to the vast landscape
Aiming an arrow at a bulls eye	Looking for someone in a large crowd
Bottle rocket rising in the air	Bubbles rising in the air
Gazing at the moon at night	Gazing at the vastness of the Milky Way galaxy

Musical suggestions

Album: *Two Foot Yard*, Carla Kihlstedt
  Indirect: World of Made

Album: *The Sad Machinery of Spring*, Tin Hat
  Direct: Janissary Band
  Indirect: Dionysus

Album: *The 50 Most Essential Pieces of Classical Music*
  Direct: Suite No. 1, Op. 46: IV. In the hall of the mountain king, Gynt
  Indirect: Concerto for Two Violins, Strings and B.C. in D Minor, BWV 1043: I. Vivace, Bach
  Direct: Concerto No. 1 for Mandolin, Strings and B.C. in C Major, RV 425: I. Allegro, Vivaldi

Teachers first: embodying and using Space Effort

Awakening the senses of the face, skin, and body is a great way to embody Space Effort. The sensory system is designed to take in information from the environment, whether that is the internal environment of the body or the external environment beyond the body. Simply watch how infants or toddlers move to witness this in action. What they see, taste, hear, touch, smell, and/or feel in their bodies motivates them to move toward and away from stimuli around them. This desire to explore and interact with their world impacts their physical development; they begin to strengthen the muscles needed for locomotion and the bodily coordination needed for more complex actions in space.

Obviously you are not an infant anymore, but two important lessons from those years remain with you as an adult:

1   You use your sensory system to explore and receive information from your environment.
2   Your curiosities and desires cause you to move your whole body toward and away from stimuli in your environment.

Notice how your awareness in space motivates you to move in Teacher exploration 13.1.

Teacher exploration 13.1: Coordinating the senses with the movements of the body

1   Stand in a comfortable position. Turn your head to the right and look at something behind you. Do not allow the rest of your body to facilitate the movement; only rotate the head and neck. Once you reach a maximum range of motion, return to the opening position.

2   Repeat this action again. This time when you reach the maximum range of motion in your head and neck, allow the rest of your body to follow the movement so that you eventually face the object. Notice how your body naturally follows the curiosity of your eyes.

3   Repeat this process with different sensory modalities: turning toward something you hear or smell or want to taste. Don't forget about moving toward something you want to touch. Using touch is a great way to practice Space Effort in other parts of the body, besides the head and senses of the face. For example, locate something in your environment that is just beyond your reach. Reach toward the object with your fingers. Notice how this causes your entire arm to move through your Kinesphere toward the object, and subsequently how the reach of your arm causes you to step toward the object and move through space.

4   Repeat this activity, reaching with your arms, legs, and senses of the face toward objects that "grab" your attention.

Note: The above explorations require you to use pinpointed focus (Direct Space Effort) when moving toward various objects in your environment. It would, of course, also be possible to use Indirect Space Effort by dividing your focus between multiple objects. In this way, your movement in space would take on a multi-focused, circuitous quality. *Try it! What happens when you reach with multiple parts of your body toward multiple objects all at once?*

The above movement exploration required you to do the following:

1   Notice your environment, a task your sensory system is designed to accomplish.

2   Initiate movement toward something in your environment.

3   Follow through with the initiation so that the whole body participated in the action.

So, how does this relate to the movements performed in a ballet technique class? In order to answer this question, create a *centre floor port de bras* exercise. Use the criteria shown in Exercise 13.1 to get you started.

Exercise 13.1: *Centre floor port de bras*

Include the following elements:

- *Port de bras* **with right and left symmetry.** Moving both arms from *bras bas*, to *first position*, to *fifth position* is an example of symmetry.
- *Port de bras* **with right and left asymmetry.** Using traditional *croisé* or *effacé* or *first arabesque port de bras* are examples of asymmetry.
- **Stable lower body movements.** Maintaining *fifth position*, for example, while the upper body moves through the *port de bras*.
- **Mobile lower and upper body movements.** Performing a *battement tendu devant* in coordination with *croisé port de bras* is one example.
- **Direction changes.** The *port de bras* may move the body facing from *croisé* right to *effacé* left or *en face*, and so on.

Teacher exploration 13.2 uses imagery and props in order to invoke your use of Space Effort as you perform the *centre floor port de bras* you created. The intent of this exercise is to awaken the senses of your face and body.

Teacher exploration 13.2: Embodying Direct and Indirect Space

Preparation

- Hold an object in each hand: markers, tennis balls, or scarves, for example.
- Begin in the opening position of your *port de bras* exercise.
- Before you begin moving, imagine:

The entire room filled with your favorite smell . . . or, listening to your favorite piece of music playing through surround sound speakers . . . or, standing on stage and expanding the attention of your face and body to the vast audience before you.

Indirect your focus to take in those imagined scents or sounds or sights surrounding your body.

Begin the port de bras

1   **Use Direct Space Effort during your first performance.** Focus on the object in your right or left hand with pinpointed precision during the entire exercise. Use any (or all) senses of the face to follow the object in space: ears, eyes, nose, or mouth. Allow the movements of your head to naturally influence the movements of your spine. Repeat to the other side.

Example: In my *port de bras*, my eyes and nose attended to my right marker as it moved upward in *fifth position*, sideward in *second*, forward and upward in *arabesque*, and so on.

2   **Use Indirect Space Effort during your second performance.** Repeat Step 1, but this time attempt to focus on both objects in your hands simultaneously as you move your arms in space. Maintain this multi-focused use of your attention throughout the *entire* exercise.

3   **Alternate between Direct and Indirect Space Effort in your third performance.** Repeat Steps 1 and 2, but this time alternate between Direct and Indirect Space. At times, channel your awareness to one object, and other times overlap your awareness to take in both objects at the same time.

Using the senses of your face to convey an awareness of your surroundings coordinates the movements of your head, limbs, and torso, similar to the movements of the infant described earlier. *Practice Step Three again keeping the following question in mind:* **How does your use of Space Effort coordinate the movements of your whole body?** For example: my spine arced and lengthened in a slight *cambré* as I Directed my attention upward and backward; focusing rightward caused *épaulment* positioning in my torso; Indirecting my attention between both objects as my arms opened to *second position* caused my torso and feet to Widen.

Figure 13.2 Explore Direct and Indirect Space during *battement tendu à la seconde*

What did you notice happening in your body?

Listed below are additional ways to deepen your knowledge of Space Effort when demonstrating movement, creating class exercises, and cueing your dancers. Add to this list as you explore Space Effort.

Warm up Space Effort in your whole body before class

Warm up your Space Effort as you prepare for your technique classes.

Teacher exploration 13.3: Space Effort warm up

1   Imagine you have "eyes" on different parts of your body. Imagine this in simple places first, such as the tips of your fingers or toes, or on your elbows.

2   As you perform your own warm-up ritual or practice an exercise you plan to use in class, allow the "eyes" on those parts of your body to actively attend to the space around you. Do this one at a time: try the fingertips first, then the toes, and finally the elbows. What do those parts "see" as they move through space?

3   Eventually imagine "eyes" on more complex body parts, such as the top of your head, the bony projections of your vertebrae, the insides of your knees, the bottoms of your feet or shoulder blades. What do you experience in your body when you imagine "eyes" in these places?

Note: I used "eyes" as the image, but you can also imagine "ears" or "noses" or "mouths."

The above exploration is an extension of the activities in Chapter 8. In that chapter, you explored spatial directions and pathways in your Kinesphere with different parts of the body. Revisit some of those explorations from the perspective of Space Effort. *What do you discover as you consciously integrate Direct and Indirect Space with the Chapter 8 activities?*

Create a "bank" of Space Effort images and activities to use in class

•   **Create imagery for the hands and feet.** Similar to Teacher exploration 13.3, this helps students be attentive with parts of their bodies other than the face and head: *"Notice your toes splashing in a pool of water during each* *battement piqué,"* or *"Touch your favorite color of velvet with your fingers and toes during rond de jambe."*

- **Use sound.** Walk around the room as your students stand in *centre* and say: *"When you hear me clap my hands, direct your head and the energy of your body toward the sound."* This scenario is similar to Teacher exploration 13.1.
- **Ask dancers to face a partner during *barre* or *centre* work.** *"Touch your partner's fingers with your fingers as you move toward them in space in a temps lié en avant with arabesque arms, for example."* Or, *"Reach toward your partner's toes with your toes as you développé devant."* Partner work is explored in greater detail later in the chapter.

Incorporate Space Effort in your exercises and demonstrations

- **Attend to the space around you as you demonstrate exercises.** Look around the room, free up your head and neck, notice the sounds in the room, and express your whole body in space with an attentive spirit.
- **Communicate what you see, hear, and feel in your body when demonstrating exercises.** For example: *"Direct your attention to the clock on the wall as you piqué arabesque, then scan the space around you as you promenade en dehors in attitude."* Cueing, such as this, will remind them to also notice their surroundings and project their awareness outwardly when dancing.

Figure 13.3 Explore Direct and Indirect Space during *croisé attitude derrière*

- **Notice how you use Space Effort in your class exercises.** What parts of the body attend to space in any given exercise? Is it only the eyes or do other parts of the body also have "eyes"? Does an exercise have a theme of Directing or Indirecting?

Teaching Space Effort to your dancers

Any movement in ballet can be performed with either Direct or Indirect Space. Determining which Effort quality to use is therefore dependent on the technical or artistic goals of the class exercises. Both Direct and Indirect Space Effort require dancers to be actively aware of their surroundings. Space Effort is therefore a good tool to use when teaching dancers how to perform more communicatively with the whole body. Based on your experiences embodying Space Effort in the previous section:

When would you focus on Direct and Indirect Space with your students? What technical or artistic goals are you trying to achieve?

How would you explain Sustained and Sudden Time to your students? What seems important to communicate or emphasize?

Table 13.2 provides suggestions of when to use Direct and Indirect Space in ballet technique class. Add to these lists as you explore Space Effort in your classes.

Similar to your experiences in the *Teachers first* section, I suggest using activities that engage the movements of the head and the senses of the face when first teaching Space Effort to your dancers. Space Effort is also easy to focus on during *centre* exercises because the external environment continuously shifts: dancers stand in different places in the room, face different directions during exercises, travel through the space, and watch their peers perform.

During *barre*, however, dancers tend to stand in the same spot for extended periods of time. This causes some dancers to "tune out." When this happens, they may demonstrate some (or all) of the following behaviors:

- Blank, "daydream-like" stares into space.
- Inward or narrow use of focus, as if the energy stops at the skin.

Table 13.2 Technical and artistic benefits for Space Effort

Direct Space is a practical movement quality to emphasize when teaching students how to:
1. *Channel the body's energy*, such as when dancers execute a *piqué first arabesque* by sending all of their attention and energy in the direction of the forward extending arm.
2. *Move with located awareness.* Many steps in ballet require this energy.
3. *Dance with an artistic attitude that conveys a laser-like or single-focused emotional state*, such as concentrating, fixated, investigating, engaged, desperate, eager, and so on.[+]

Indirect Space is a practical movement quality to use when teaching students how to:
1. *Send the body's energy to multiple locales*, such as when a dancer executes a *piqué first arabesque* by scanning the audience with the shoulders, head, and eyes, while simultaneously extending the arms and legs forward and backward in space.
2. *Move with overlapping awareness.* In a compound step, such as *contretemps*, one side of the body gathers inward as the other side opens outward. This is often accompanied by a circuitous "scanning" of the upper body and head.
3. *Dance with an artistic attitude that conveys an all-encompassing or multi-focused emotional state*, such as shifty, exploring, sneaky, distracted, worried, anticipation, enthusiastic, impatient, and so on.[+]

[+] Artistically, the use of Direct and Indirect Space may convey a large range of emotional states depending on the mood or context of the choreography or class phrases.

- Heads and eyes are fixed straight ahead.
- Inattentive or unintentional placement of the limbs in space.

These are not all negative in all contexts. Asking the dancers to close their eyes or focus inwards, for example, is a good approach for developing kinesthetic awareness. When, however, the *barre* exercises benefit from an outward use of focus, as they often do, the above behaviors will not support their movements. A change in the environmental stimuli is therefore an effective way to positively change these behaviors. There are many ways teachers do this—changing the musical selections, standing in different places when demonstrating exercises, using touch when giving corrections, and incorporating a conscious use of Space Effort during *barre*.

Barre exercises are intended to improve the dancers' technique, warm up their bodies, and prepare them for both the artistic and technical demands of centre work and on stage performance. Since communicating to an audience and moving proficiently with other dancers is essential in ballet performance, dancers must have opportunities to develop those qualities during *barre*. *Attending at barre!* explores this in four simple activities.

Attending at *barre!*

Objective:

Dancers perform communicatively and attentively at barre.

Musical *barre!*

Ask the dancers to stand in different places throughout *barre*. Each time they perform a *barre* exercise in a new spot, remind them to notice the people around them and to Direct and Indirect their limbs to the new environmental stimuli.

Change directions!

Create *barre* exercises that include direction changes, and ask them to consciously "spot" (Direct Space) each new facing in space. This is also a great way to develop their spotting skills during *pirouette, promenade,* and *fouetté* (see also the class activities in Chapter 8. While not addressed at the time, these activities were also exploring Direct and Indirect use of one's attention).

Dance with props!

Ask them to hold objects in their hands and to follow those objects with their eyes, as you did during the *port de bras* exercise. Also revisit the class activities that used props in Chapters 7 and 8 from the perspective of Space Effort.

Face a partner!

Ask the dancers to face a partner and instruct them to:

Use Direct Space Effort as you reach your arms and legs toward or away from your partner; can you touch their fingertips or toes?

Notice how your torsos move toward and away from each other during balançoire and chassé en avant/arrière.

Instruct the dancers to stand with their back body surfaces facing each other. Cue them to:

Rotate your head until you can see your partner behind you.
Reach your legs derrière toward your partner.
Reach for your partner's hands as you cambré derrière.

This develops performance energy through the back surfaces of the body and engages spinal rotation and *épaulment* at *barre*. Also revisit the *Dancing with others!* activities in Chapter 4 from the perspective of Space Effort.

The above activities promote a more attentive use of body during *barre* and teach dancers how to project their energy into space. *Face a partner!* is one of my favorite activities to use in class because it reminds dancers to project their movements toward someone tangible, to lift their focus and attend to different stimuli with their limbs, and it often causes them to smile or laugh, which Frees up their Flow Effort. *Face a partner!* also teaches dancers to concentrate on their own movements simultaneously with the movements of the partners, a necessary skill in ensemble performances.

Many dancers keep their heads and eyes "locked" in the same direction when traveling across the floor and facing the mirror. This not only eliminates the *épaulment* positioning of the body but it also contributes to a more tense upper body posture. *Seeking and searching!* addresses this common technical issue by promoting the use of spinal rotation, *épaulment*, and an expansive use of the Kinesphere. Range of motion in the upper body increases as the dancers learn to Direct and Indirect the head and eyes to different environmental stimuli. Additionally, the body's equilibrium is challenged as the dancers learn to send their focus to places other than straight ahead.

Seeking and searching!

Objective:

Dancers use the senses of the face more attentively and intentionally.

Look around!

1   Create a simple *barre* or *centre* exercise. For example, I created a *grand battement* in *centre*:

   Four *grand battement devant*, four *à la seconde*, four *derrière* *Plié relevé retiré* balance

2   Choreograph the focus of the face and head in different directions during each set of four *grand battement*. For example, in the above *grand battement*: ask the dancers to channel their attention diagonally upwards during the *battement devant*, away from the gesturing leg during *à la seconde*, and down and forward during *derrière*.

3   Choreograph the focus of the face and head in different directions during each *grand battement*: for example, using Direct Space Effort, look diagonally upwards during the first *battement devant*, down during the second, to the left during the third, and behind and to the right of the body during the fourth.

4   Instruct the dancers to choreograph their own head/face movements for the exercise.

In the round!

In the round! #1

1   Begin your ballet class in a circle with the dancers facing the center of the circle. I begin every ballet class I teach in a circle. The dancers come together as a community, experience a spatial formation other than a line, and warm-up their Space Effort.

2   Conduct the first three exercises of class in this formation: the opening warm-up, *demi* and *grand plié*, and the first *battement tendu*, for example.

   •   Instruct the dancers to sometimes *Indirect* their attention throughout these exercises by scanning their attention to the group as a whole, similar to scanning the audience when performing onstage.

   •   Instruct them to sometimes *Direct* their attention by channeling their limbs (arms, legs, and head) to someone across the circle or to the people on either side of them (attending to people alongside the circle also promotes Spatial Intent and efficient placement of the arms and legs in *à la seconde* positions).

In the round! #2

This activity teachers dancers how to relay their attention to multiple audiences, a skill needed in live performance.

1   Create a *centre port de bras* exercise.
2   Split the dancers into groups of four. One dancer performs while the other three stand in a semicircle surrounding the performer: one to the performer's right, one to the left, and one directly behind the performer.
3   The performers Direct and Indirect their eyes, head, and arms to the other dancers while performing the *port de bras* exercise.

Variation: Complete this activity in pairs as opposed to quartets; the dancers who are observing slowly change their locations around the dancers who are moving.

If short on time: Ask the four dancers to perform at the same time by standing in a circle with their backs facing the circle. Other spatial formations will also work: far away from each other, in an arc-like line, a line with each dancer facing different directions, and so on. Regardless of the formation, their challenge is to attend to each other as they perform the *port de bras*.

The ability to attend to space with different parts of the body, other than the face, is also important in ballet technique. Dancers might use their feet, arms, the back surfaces of the torso, or even the sides of their ribs to communicate shifts in external awareness. When dancers practice moving with different foci and expressing their movements with different surfaces of the body, they strengthen their kinesthetic awareness and artistic variability. *Focusing here, there, and everywhere!* teaches dancers to use their bodies communicatively with parts of the body other than the head and eyes.

Focusing here, there, and everywhere!

Objective:

Dancers practice attending to space with the whole body.

Activity 1: "Eyes on the body"

This is one of my favorite activities to use in class. As the dancers imagine "eyes" on different parts of their bodies, they learn how to use those parts more communicatively in space, which enhances their movement clarity and artistic intentions.

Preparation: Bring a pack of stickers to class.

1   Invite the dancers to put the stickers on different parts of their bodies. Similar to the activities in Chapter 8, the dancers may choose to place the stickers on their distal, mid-limb, proximal, or core regions of the body (reference *Painting the space!* in Chapter 8).
2   As they perform the *barre* or *centre* exercises, ask them to imagine that the stickers represent their eyes: *How can they "see" and be curious with those parts of their body as they dance?*

Examples:

- "Seeing" with the insides of the thighs and heels engages outward rotation of the hips, which is useful during *grand rond de jamb*, *pas de cheval*, and *pirouettes* in *retiré*.
- "Seeing" with the *barre* arm keeps the elbow or shoulder or hand active and attentive along the *barre*.
- "Seeing" with the top of the head or with the bony projections of each vertebra enlivens the spine. They notice when the spine twists during *épaulment*, arcs during *cambré*, and ripples upward when returning from a *grand port de corps*.

Note: Similar to Teacher exploration 13.3, you might ask them to imagine ears, noses, or mouths instead of eyes. Also revisit *Body connections!* in Chapter 7 from the perspective of Space Effort.

Where's my audience?

1   Split the dancers into two groups during a *centre* floor exercise. One group acts as the audience and stands along the "front" wall in the dance studio. The other group performs the *centre* combination facing away from the audience so the audience only views the back surfaces of their bodies.
2   The performers project their energy and attention to the audience with the backs of their arms, legs, and torsos.
3   During the next class, repeat this activity but change the relationship between the dancers and the audience—what if the audience only views the right or left surfaces of their bodies? Or, provide the dancers with imagined audience scenarios—what if the audience was

above or below them? *How do the dancers enhance the movements with those body surfaces?*

4   Reflect:

What did you notice or feel as the audience member?

What did you notice or feel as the performer? Did your movement change? Did you experience any technical or artistic benefits?

Front, back, side, and side

1   Teach your dancers an across the floor sequence, such as a *traveling waltz* or *grand allegro*.

2   After they are comfortable with the sequencing of the exercise (approx. 1–2 classes), ask them to use Light, sweeping touches on the front surfaces of their bodies starting at the feet and moving upward until they reach the face and the top of the head. This awakens the sensory receptors of the skin, heightening the awareness of those surfaces of the body.

3   Ask the dancers to perform the across the floor exercise, imagining their favorite color emanating in space from the front surfaces of their bodies.

4   Repeat steps 2–3, but explore other surfaces: the back, then the right, and finally the left surfaces. Finally, ask the dancers to perform the sequence one last time imagining *all* surfaces of their body emanating their favorite color.

Note: I suggest taking three classes to complete step 4—front/back surfaces in one class; right/left surfaces in another class; all surfaces in the last class.

5   Reflect: the dancers will likely find different ways to accomplish and interpret this activity. Allow for different interpretations when answering these questions:

What differences did you notice between the back and front surfaces when "expressing" the movement? What about the right versus the left?

What did the movement feel like when you used your whole body to attend to space? Did you find that you still preferred one surface to the other? Did you alternate between surfaces?

As you learn to improvise with and explore Space Effort, your students will be more likely to do the same. So, have fun with Space Effort in class and add to the many activities presented in this chapter!

Chapter 14

Playing with the Effort palette

This chapter explores ways in which teachers challenge dancers to experiment with the entire Effort palette creatively and artistically during the technique class. **Why is this important?** In order to answer that question, consider the following statement from Chapter 10: "As your students learn to navigate through the vast landscape of Effort qualities, they will expand their expressive range and strengthen their ability to make conscious choices about their performance energy when executing balletic sequences and choreography."

Chapters 10–13 focused on the first part of the above statement: learning about Effort and expanding the students' expressive range as technicians and artists. This chapter therefore focuses on the second part of the above statement: strengthening the students' ability to make conscious choices about their use of dynamics, or in other words to learn how to "play" with Effort in the technique classroom.

For a performing artist, such as a ballet dancer, artistry involves making conscious choices about how a movement is performed, whether that involves making those choices autonomously or analyzing the choices made by the choreographer or teacher. Regardless, in order for ballet dancers to develop as creative practitioners, they need opportunities to experiment with artistic choices during the ballet technique class. **Effort, in particular, is an ideal tool for teaching dancers how to make varied and nuanced artistic choices.** *Why is that?*

As the previous chapters demonstrated, L/BMA Effort is a broad and multifaceted framework for exploring movement dynamics, and as such, using it to teach dynamics in the classroom facilitates a dancer's ability to make a wide variety of dynamic choices when performing class phrases. Even when the dancers are performing the same exercise with the same steps during a technique class, challenge them to make individual choices about the quality of their performance energy. This promotes individual uniqueness and artistry, which is important in codified techniques, such as ballet.

Teachers first: play with Effort

Your students will be more likely to dance with dynamic variety when you also "play" with dynamics in your exercises and verbal cueing.

Create Effortful personal warm-ups

Warming up your energy is just as important as you warming up your muscles. A dynamically rich warm-up will help prepare your voice and body for class. It will also invigorate your sensory system, neuromuscular connections, and breath support.

Embrace a playful and experimental attitude when planning classes

As you prepare your classes, continually ask yourself, "What if I performed this step or movement phrase with a different Effort life?" Then, try it with a different dynamic quality. You may be surprised by the new technical and artistic challenges you discover in your own body.

Use Effort clearly in your demonstrations

Part III provided numerous examples of how to use your voice and body dynamically to convey the energetic quality of the class exercises:

- Create a "bank" of evocative imagery and words when giving critical feedback to your dancers.
- Practice speaking and sounding your class demonstrations in multiple ways.
- Support your Effort choices with Effortful music.

Create simple exercises for students to "animate"

Playing with Effort need not be complex for you or your students. Even a simple exercise, such as *four battement tendu* in each direction *en croix*, becomes a fun and dynamically rich exercise when dancers animate it with their own Effort choices. Create a series of simple *barre* and *centre* exercises like this throughout class, and observe the different Effort choices your dancers make.

Create dynamically varied lesson plans

Did your students have an opportunity to experience Sudden and Sustained Time in different exercises? Or, Strong and Light Weight? Or, Direct and Indirect Space? Or, Free and Bound Flow? Did they have opportunities to perform a similar movement in more than one way? Once with Sudden Time and once with Sustained Time, for example? Even when Effort is not the primary focus in your class, designing dynamically rich lesson plans is important to your students' overall technical and artistic development.

Teaching your students how to play with Effort

Playing with Effort during class teaches students how to discern differences in movement qualities and it develops their improvisation and creative problem-solving skills. These skills are important to develop as they work with choreographers and perform different roles in ballet productions. Provide time for students to share their Effort choices with a peer or with the class as a whole. This is especially important for students who experience difficulty generating their own sounds, images, and words. Sometimes this difficulty arises from a fear of looking "stupid" or of being wrong or uncreative. Listening to a peer's ideas reaffirms the value of personal interpretation. This, in turn, helps students become more skilled and comfortable when generating their own ideas during class.

Table 14.1 How to play with Effort

Task for students	Pedagogical benefits
• *Embody a classmate's Effort imagery and sounds* For example: a *rond de jambe à terre en dehors* feels different when imagining the leg circling in a pot of honey versus the leg as a marker painting an arc on the ground	The students learn there are different ways to think about and perform the same step
• *Generate evocative Effort images and words* You may be surprised by the images and words the dancers use to describe their physical experiences!	You gain insight into how the students think about and physically interpret the Effort concepts
• *Create and experiment with different sounds* How does a double *pirouette en dehors* feel different when it's performed with a sudden "Zzziiippp!" versus an elongated "whooooeeeeeeee," for example?	Your students learn how their Effort choices impact their technical execution and the artistic quality of the movement
• *Experiment with different Efforts* Students animate an exercise with different Effort choices, and learn to make different Effort choices from class to class.	Your students learn to challenge their habitual movement patterns by imbuing the balletic steps with different Efforts
• *Generate the choreography for the class* Students can participate in the creation of class exercises by generating the Effort-life for the movement on their own or together	Your students practice the skills needed for making dances and develop greater ownership of the class concepts

All of the in-class activities presented in this chapter develop the skills needed for making intelligent artistic choices in class. This process is not always easy and some of your students will find this type of experimentation and autonomy uncomfortable at first. The students will progress at their own rate and it may take many classes before the students effectively embody the Effort qualities, let alone experiment with making their own Effort choices. There are a few ways to increase your dancers' degree of comfort with the approaches presented in this chapter:

1   *Provide examples of how you played with Effort before asking the students to do it.* If you demonstrate how to play with one movement in multiple ways, your students will be more likely to generate their own ideas.
2   *Ask for individual contributions and then invite the class to experiment with that person's idea.* This is similar to the previous example except a student provides the examples.
3   *Pair a dancer who enjoys Effort experimentation with a dancer who finds this type of experimentation uncomfortable.* The students become role models for each other.
4   *Provide positive feedback.* Let your dancers know when their Effort choices positively impacted their technical or artistic performance! Then, ask other students in the class to embody a dancer's Effort choices and invite them to share how those choices impacted their movements.

The activities in *Choose to be dynamic!* challenge dancers to employ creative and critical thinking processes in order to make, analyze, and follow through with dynamic effort choices. Your dancers will perform the movement with greater ownership and integrity when they make their own dynamic decisions. These activities are therefore helpful to use in class when your dancers are performing with low energy or lack of specificity.

The Effort quality (or qualities) your students choose to explore will change both the technical demands and feeling-tone of the movement. The reflective questions listed at the beginning of *Choose to be dynamic!* push them to identify these differences. Provide time in class for students to address these questions; they can share their responses with the whole class or, if you're short on time, with a partner.

Choose to be dynamic!

Objective:

Dancers develop their artistic sensibilities as they explore making different Effort choices during class.

Exploration questions for all activities:

How did the exercise change as you played with different dynamic qualities?
What did you learn about artistic choice and movement expression?
How did your choices affect your technique?

Play with single Effort qualities!

1   Ask your students to incorporate a particular Effort quality in three to five places during an exercise.
2   The next time they perform the exercise ask them to perform the opposite movement quality in those same three to five places. For example, they might choose to play with Light Weight during their first performance of a *centre adagio* and Strong Weight during their next performance.

Play with combined Effort qualities!

Ask your more advanced students to perform a combined Effort configuration in three to five places during an exercise. For example, a student might play with Strong Weight and Direct Space during a *battement degagé*, or Light Weight, Free Flow, and Sudden Time in *petite allegro*.

Play with dynamic rhythm!

Challenge students to alternate between opposite Effort qualities in the same exercise. For example, they might alternate between Quick and Sustained moments in *battement frappé*, or Light and Strong moments in *adagio*, Free and Bound moments in a traveling waltz, Indirect and Direct moments in a *centre port de bras*. Using musical accompaniment that encourages this type of movement phrasing will help the dancers experiment with these choices.

The next series of activities—*Playing with effort preferences!*—challenges students to identify their movement capacities, challenges, and preferences. When students have the opportunity to explore their stylistic patterns and preferences, they become better skilled at making movement choices that challenge those preferences. For example, a student might learn to ask:

- *"Am I more likely to embody fast, quick movement verses slow, sustained movement? If so, what technical skills would sustained movement help me achieve?"*

- *"Do I prefer balletic characters that are Strong and powerful versus Light and gentle? If so, what artistic skills would Light Weight help me develop?"*

There are, of course, many questions to explore. Facilitate this inquiry process by generating questions, such as these, in class.

In *Playing with effort preferences!*, your students' Effort choices will vary from one dancer to the next. I therefore instruct the dancers in my classes to "create their own timing and counts for the exercise as they play with Effort." The dancers begin the exercise at the same time, but their individual Effort choices cause them to finish the exercise at different times. In order to support their movement choices, sometimes they perform the exercises in silence and other times I play music with dynamic variety. When live musicians play for my class, I instruct the accompanists to improvise or vary the tempo of the music as the dancers perform the exercise.

Playing with Effort preferences!

Objective:

Dancers deepen their body knowledge, and therefore their technical and artistic abilities.

Exploration questions for all activities:

What dynamic choices did you make and why?
What artistic goals were you working toward?
What technical goals were you working toward?

Honoring movement preferences

Give your students opportunities to make Effort choices that feel good! In this activity, it is important that the students: 1) verbally and physically identify the Effort quality they like, and 2) why they like it. During a *centre adagio*, for example, some dancers might Quickly and Freely phrase an *en dedans promenade* in *first arabesque* because they enjoy performing it with momentum, whereas others perform it with Sustainment and Bound Flow because they enjoy the feeling of elongation and control.

Challenging movement preferences

This is a great activity if your dancers have personal movement goals they are working toward. In this activity, it is important for dancers to: 1) verbally and physically identify the Effort quality that is difficult, and 2) the technical or artistic goals that quality helps them achieve.

During a *centre adagio*, for example, dancers might perform a *grand developpé* with Sustained Time and Direct Space if they need to increase muscular strength and practice stabilizing long balances, while some students might perform the same movement with Sudden Time and Strong Weight if they need to work on initiating one-legged balances quickly and confidently.

It is important for you, as the teacher, to contextualize how the Effort qualities address specific technical or artistic goals. Over time, dancers will become better skilled at identifying (and feeling) this on their own. Tables 10.2, 11.2, 12.2, and 13.2 from the previous chapters outline the technical and artistic goals each Effort quality addresses.

Use the information from these tables with your students when you use this activity in class (*Creative Ballet Learning* includes similar tables).

Play with a partner's preferences

At any point during the above activities, ask the dancers to teach their Effort choices to a peer. When they teach their peer their dynamic choices, they have to use clear verbal cuing and physical demonstrations. Likewise, when your dancers learn a peer's Effort choices, they experience yet another way of performing the movement. For this reason, I enjoy pairing peers together who make different dynamic choices. When your dancers work together encourage them to ask each other the following questions:

- *Why did you choose to perform it this way?*
- *What imagery or words do you think of when you perform the movement with this quality?*
- *How does this quality challenge or improve your technique?*

Observing the Effort choices your students make during class is a great assessment tool. Ask yourself the following questions as you observe your students during class:

Do the students demonstrate a physical and intellectual understanding of Effort?

Is their dynamic range increasing over time?

How do their Effort choices affect their technique and performance?

If your students demonstrate difficulty using Effort in their own way during an exercise or describing their Effort choices to a partner, provide more time for them to experiment with Effort in a prescribed way during class. If, however, they make clear Effort choices during class, use that as an opportunity to observe how their choices affect their technique and performance. This will help you plan future classes that challenge the students appropriately. It will also help you provide the students with individualized feedback, which will positively impact their artistic potential and self-understanding.

In my experience inviting Effort play into the ballet technique classroom promotes an energetic, collaborative, and engaged classroom culture. Students learn quickly that there are multiple ways to embody the balletic vocabulary. When this happens, they begin to take more risks when generating and talking about their Effort choices in class.

Enjoy playing with Effort!

Glossary

Barthenieff Fundamentals (BF): a body training practice developed by Irmgard Barthenieff that focuses on total body coordination, mind–body integration, and personal expression. While not the primary focus, BF concepts are explored indirectly throughout this book through investigations in conscious breathing, core-to-limb relationships, limb-to-limb relationships, upper and lower body relationships, and spinal connectivity. Reference *Making Connections* (2000) by Peggy Hackney for further information about BF and the Patterns of Total Body Connectivity. (Introduction, Chapter 2, Parts II and III)

Body awareness: developing sensory awareness of individual movement patterns and fundamental movement concepts. (Chapter 2)

Body category in L/BMA: dancers focus on alignment, whole body coordination, body part articulation, mobilizing and stabilizing forces in the body, and body phrasing. (Chapter 5 and Parts II and III)

Body Half Connectivity: the fifth of six Patterns of Total Body Connectivity in the Barthenieff Fundamentals. In this book, dancers explore how one side of the body is actively stable while the other side of the body is actively moving. (Indirectly explored in Chapters 7 and 8)

Body knowledge: developing one's physical and expressive skills and making purposeful decisions about one's movements. (Chapter 2)

Bound Flow Effort: contained or controlled use of one's Flow Effort. (Chapters 9 and 10)

Breath Connectivity: the first of six Patterns of Total Body Connectivity in the Barthenieff Fundamentals. Breath Connectivity involves both cellular and lung respiration. Breath initiates three-dimensional shape changes in the torso during the process of inhalation and exhalation. Using one's breath rhythmically, expressively, and directionally in dance technique training supports movement phrasing and the flow of the body's form and energy in space. (Chapters 6 and 10)

Core-Distal Connectivity: the second of six Patterns of Total Body Connectivity in the Barthenieff Fundamentals. In this book, dancers explore the connection between the core and each of the six limbs (head, tail, arms, and legs), and the connection from one limb to another limb via the core. Expressively, Core-Distal Connectivity follows rhythms of moving outward from the core to the distal edges of the body and moving inward from the distal edges to the core. (Indirectly explored in Chapters 2, 7, 8, and 10)

Countertensions: oppositional spatial tensions that support dynamic, three-dimensional stability and balance. (Chapter 7)

Cross-Lateral Connectivity: the sixth of six Patterns of Total Body Connectivity in the Bartenieff Fundamentals. In this book, dancers explore lines of connection in the body between the one arm and the opposite leg via the core. (Indirectly explored in Chapters 7 and 8)

Direct Space Effort: pinpointed, single-focused, or channeled use of one's Space Effort. (Chapters 9 and 13)

Distal skeletal joints: hands/wrists, feet/ankles, and head. (Chapter 7)

Effort category in L/BMA: Dancers analyze the overall energy and dynamic quality of movement through investigations in Flow, Weight, Time, and Space Efforts. (Chapter 5 and Part III)

***Elancer* as a movement concept:** identifying how the body darts, bursts, and whips through space. (Chapter 1)

***Entendre* as a movement concept:** investing in the elongation of the torso and limbs, and identifying movements that stretch and lengthen. (Chapter 1)

Flow Effort: the quality of a dancer's ongoing fluidity when moving. Is the dancer's continuous Flow controlled (Bound Flow) or outpouring (Free Flow)? (Chapters 9 and 10)

Free Flow Effort: outpouring use of one's Flow Effort. (Chapters 9 and 10)

Function and Expression: analyzing movement from both functional and expressive perspectives is a Foundational Principle in L/BMA. (Chapter 5)

***Glisser* as a movement concept:** investing in a gliding use of the upper and lower body, and identifying movements that slide. (Chapter 1)

Head-Tail Connectivity: the third of six Patterns of Total Body Connectivity in the Bartenieff Fundamentals. In this book, dancers explore three-dimensional stability and mobility of the spine, the vertical axis of the torso, and the curiosity of the senses of the face. (Indirectly explored in Chapters 2, 7, 8, and 13)

Indirect Space Effort: all-encompassing or multi-focused use of one's Space Effort. (Chapters 9 and 13)

Inner and Outer: analyzing how movement is shaped by one's inner experiences (sensing, feeling, and thinking sensibilities) and by one's interactions with the outer world (with other people and the surrounding environment) is a Foundational Principle in L/BMA. (Chapter 5)

Intent: Making conscious movement choices about how to perform or think about balletic movement. (Chapter 2)

Kinesphere: the space around your body that you can reach with your limbs. (Chapter 8)

Kinesphere Size: the size of the Kinesphere changes depending on the size of one's movements—small-reach, mid-reach, and large-reach. (Chapter 8)

Kinesphere Zones: spatial regions around the body—up, down, right, left, forward, backward—and combinations of those six regions—e.g., forward up, back down right. (Chapter 8)

Laban/Bartenieff Movement Analysis (L/BMA): a comprehensive framework for observing and analyzing the functional and expressive qualities of human movement. Human movement is analyzed via four movement categories: Body, Effort, Shape, and Space. This book uses movement concepts from these four categories prescriptively to enhance a dancer's self-understanding, skill development, and expressive capacity. (Introduction, Chapter 5)

Light Weight Effort: engaging one's mass delicately or gently, as if transcending gravity's pull. (Chapters 9 and 11)

Mid-limbs skeletal joints: elbows and knees. (Chapter 7)

Movement concepts: overarching movement principles that are applied to different steps and exercises and support the development of expressive and technical balletic skills. (Chapter 1)

Parts and Whole: analyzing movement through a study of its parts and a study of how the parts relate to the whole is a Foundational Principle in L/BMA. (Chapter 5)

Personal expression: dancing with feeling and emotion, and reflecting on the expressive content of movement. (Chapter 2)

***Plier* as a movement concept:** investing in bending and yielding movement qualities, and identifying how the body folds and creases during balletic steps. (Chapter 1)

Proximal skeletal joints: shoulder girdle (shoulders/scapulae/clavicles) and hips joints. (Chapter 7)

***Relever* as a movement concept:** investing in an expansive use of the body, and identifying steps that soar, grow, and ascend into space. (Chapter 1)

***Sauter* as a movement concept:** investing in the springing nature of balletic steps, and identifying how the body bounces and rebounds. (Chapter 1)

Shape category in L/BMA: Dancers analyze the form of the body, how the form of the body changes from one movement to the next, and how external and internal stimuli motivate Shape change. (Chapter 5 and Part II)

Shape Flow Support: Growing and Shrinking of the body's three-dimensional inner volume: Lengthening and Shortening, Widening and Narrowing, Bulging and Hollowing. In this book, Shape Flow Support is explored in relationship to the three-dimensional shape changes that occur in the torso (Chapter 6):

- **Lengthening and Shortening:** Growing and Shrinking of the torso upward and downward, both Lengthening toward the head or tail and Shortening from the head or tail toward the torso center.

- **Widening and Narrowing:** Growing and Shrinking of the torso sideward, both away from and toward the midline.
- **Bulging and Hollowing:** Growing and Shrinking of the front and back surfaces of the torso forward and backward.

Shape Qualities: describes where the shape change is going in space. Shape Qualities focus on the process of shape change—the forming process. Is the dancer's movement Rising or Sinking, Spreading or Enclosing, Advancing or Retreating (or some combination of those six Shape Qualities)? (Chapter 6)

- **Rising and Sinking:** shape change in the body that moves upward and downward.
- **Spreading and Enclosing:** shape change in the body that Opens and Closes sideward, both away from and toward the midline of the body.
- **Advancing and Retreating:** shape change in the body that moves forward and backward.

Space category in L/BMA: Dancers explore their Kinespheres, investigate spatial pulls and pathways, use counter-pulls in space to stabilize the body, and analyze the one-, two-, and three-dimensional quality of the movement. (Chapter 5 and Part II)

Space Effort: the quality of a dancer's use of attention when moving. Does the dancer move with Direct or Indirect Space? (Chapters 9 and 13)

Spatial Intent: conscious decisions dancers make about their use of space. (Chapter 7)

Strong Weight Effort: engaging one's mass powerfully or forcefully. (Chapters 9 and 11)

Subject-Centered Classroom: a teaching-learning model proposed by Palmer Parker that places the subject of study in the center of the educational learning environment. This is in contrast to the Teacher-Centered Classroom, which places the teacher in the center, or the Student-Centered Classroom, which places the students in the center. This book uses the subject-centered model to create a collaborative and interactive technique classroom environment among students and teachers. (Introduction)

Sudden Time Effort: urgent, quick, or accelerating use of Time. (Chapters 9 and 12)

Sustained Time Effort: lingering, drawn out, or decelerating use of Time. (Chapters 9 and 12)

Teaching "tools": the teaching methods, techniques, and activities dance educators use to teach ballet technique. (Chapter 3)

Time Effort: the quality of a dancer's intuitive sense of time. Do they move with Sudden or Sustained Time. (Chapters 9 and 12)?

Torso Skeletal Joints: pelvis, spine, and ribs. (Chapter 7)

***Tourner* as a movement concept:** identifying movements that turn and spin, and exploring how the body rotates and spirals. (Chapter 1)

Traceforms: the spatial pathways traced by the body in the Kinesphere. (Chapter 8)

Upper-Lower Connectivity: the fourth of the six Patterns of Total Body Connectivity in the Bartenieff Fundamentals. In this book, dancers explore the functional and expressive use of the upper and lower body via Traceforms and Weight Effort. (Chapters 8 and 11)

Weight Effort: the quality of how dancers engage their mass in relationship to gravity while moving. Do they move with Strong or Light Weight? (Chapters 9 and 11)

Bibliography

Alexias, G. and Dimitropoulou, E. (2011). The Body as a Tool: Professional Classical Ballet Dancers' Embodiment. *Research in Dance Education*, 12(2): 87–104.

Alterowitz, G. (2014). Toward a Feminist Ballet Pedagogy: Teaching Strategies for Ballet Technique Classes in the Twenty-First Century. *Journal of Dance Education*, 14(1): 8–17.

Anttila, E. (2007). Mind the Body Unearthing the Affiliation Between the Conscious Body and the Reflective Mind. In L. Rouhiainen (ed.), *Ways of Knowing in Dance and Art*. Helsinki: Theatre Academy, p. 96.

Bailin, S., Case, R., Coombs, J.R., and Daniels, L.B. (1999). Common Misconceptions of Critical Thinking. *Journal of Curriculum Studies*, 31(3): 285–302.

Bartenieff, I. (1980, 2002). *Body Movement: Coping with the Environment*. New York: Routledge.

Biasutti, M. (2013). Improvisation in Dance Education: Teacher Views. *Research in Dance Education*, 14(2): 120–140.

Bradley, K. (2009). *Rudolf Laban*. Oxford: Routledge.

Bresnahan, A. (2014). Improvisational Artistry in Live Dance Performance as Embodied and Extended Agency. *Dance Research Journal*, 46(1): 84–94.

Burnidge, A. (2012). Somatics in the Dance Studio: Embodying Feminist/ Democratic Pedagogy. *Journal of Dance Education*, 12(2): 37–47.

Carter, C.L. (2000). Improvisation in Dance. *The Journal of Aesthetics and Art Criticism*, 58(2): 181–190.

Cohen, B.B. (2012). *Sensing, Feeling, and Action: The Experiential Anatomy of Body-Mind Centering*, 3rd edn. Toronto, Canada: Contact Edition Publishers.

Coté-Laurence, P. (2000). The Role of Rhythm in Ballet Training. *Research in Dance Education*, 1(2): 173–191.

Csikszentmihalyi, M. (1996). *Creativity: Flow and the Psychology of Discovery and Invention*. New York: Harper Collins.

Dempster, E. (1995). Women Writing the Body: Let's Watch a Little How She Dances. In Goellner, E.W. and Murphy, J.S. (eds), *Bodies of the Text: Dance as Theory, Literature as Dance*. Princeton, NJ: Rutgers University Press, pp. 21–38.

Dixon, E. (2005). The Mind/Body Connection and the Practice of Classical Ballet. *Research in Dance Education*, 6(1/2): 75–96.

Dyer, B. (2010). The Perils, Privileges and Pleasures of Seeking Right from Wrong: Reflecting Upon Student Perspectives of Social Processes, Value Systems, Agency and the Becoming of Identity in the Dance Technique Classroom. *Research in Dance Education*, 11(2): 109–129.

Erkert, J. (2003). *Harnessing the Wind: The Art of Teaching Modern Dance*. Champaign, IL: Human Kinetics.

Euichang C. and Na-ye, K. (2015). Whole Ballet Education: Exploring Direct and Indirect Teaching Methods. *Research in Dance Education*, 16(2): 142–160.

Evans, B. (2008). Dance Education: Aliveness in the Present: Cultivating Openness to Continual (and Positive) Change. Keynote Address given at the *Invention-In Conference*. Brockport, NY: SUNY College of Brockport.

Foster, R. (2010). *Ballet Pedagogy: The Art of Teaching*. Gainesville, FL: University Press of Florida.

Fraleigh, S. (1987). *Dance and the Lived Body*. Pittsburgh, PA: University of Pittsburgh Press.

Franklin, E. (1996a). *Dance Imagery for Technique and Performance*. Champaign, IL: Human Kinetics.

Franklin, E. (1996b). *Dynamic Alignment through Imagery*. Champaign, IL: Human Kinetics.

Franklin, E. (2012). *Dynamic Alignment through Imagery*, 2nd ed. Champaign, IL: Human Kinetics.

Franklin, E. (2013). *Dance Imagery for Technique and Performance*, 2nd ed. Champaign, IL: Human Kinetics.

Gilbert, A.G. (1992). *Creative Dance for all Ages*. Reston, VA: The American Alliance for Health, Physical education, Recreation and Dance.

Green, J. (2001). Socially Constructed Bodies in American Dance Classrooms. *Research in Dance Education*, 2(2): 155–173.

Grieg, V. (1994). *Inside Ballet Technique: Separating Anatomical Fact from Fiction in the Ballet Class*. Pennington, NJ: Princeton Book Publishers.

Groff, E. (1990). Laban Movement Analysis: A Historical, Philosophical and Theoretical Perspective. Unpublished Masters Thesis, Connecticut College, New London, CT, USA.

Hackney, P. (2000). *Making Connections: Total Body Integration Through Bartenieff Fundamentals*. New York: Routledge.

Hämäläinen, S. (2007). The Meaning of Bodily Knowledge in a Creative Dance-Making Process. In L. Rouhiainen (ed.), *Ways of Knowing in Dance and Art*. Helsinki: Theatre Academy, pp. 56–78.

Hanna, J.L. (1999). *Partnering Dance and Education: Intelligent Moves for Changing Times*. Champaign, IL: Human Kinetics.

Hanna, J.L. (2015). *Dancing to Learn: The Brain's Cognition, Emotion, and Movement*. Lanham, MD: Rowman & Littlefield.

Hannaford, C. (1995). *Smart Moves: Why Learning is not all in your Head*. Arlington, VA: Great Ocean Publishers.

Hartley, L. (1995). *Wisdom of the Body Moving: An Introduction to Body-Mind Centering*, 2nd edn. Berkeley, CA: North Atlantic Books

Heckler, R.S. (1993). *The Anatomy of Change: East/West Approaches to Body/Mind Therapy*. Berkeley, CA: North Atlantic Books

Henley, M. (2014). Sensation, Perception, and Choice in the Dance Classroom. *Journal of Dance Education*, 14(3): 95–100.

Jackson, J. (2005). My Dance and the Ideal Body: Looking at Ballet Practice from the Inside Out. *Research in Dance Education*, 6(1–2): 25–40.

John-Steiner, V. (2000). *Creative Collaboration*. New York: Oxford University Press.

Johnson, L. (2011a). More than Skin Deep: The Enduring Practice of Ballet in Universities. *Theatre, Dance and Performance Training*, 2(2): 181–197.

Johnson, L. (2011b). Teaching Ballet in Universities: How to Engage Contemporary Dancers. *Dance Teacher Magazine*, 33(9): 96–98.

Johnston, D. (2006). Private Speech in Ballet. *Research in Dance Education*, 7(1): 3–14.

Kauppila, H. (2007). Becoming an Active Agent in Dance and Through Dancing: A Teacher's Approach. In L. Rouhiainen (ed.), *Ways of Knowing in Dance and Art*. Helsinki: Theatre Academy, pp. 133–143.

Laban, R. (1975). *Modern Educational Dance*, 3rd edn (L. Ullman, ed.). London: Macdonald & Evans.

Laban, R. (1984). *A Vision of Dynamic Space* (L. Ullman, ed.). London: Laban Archives in Association with Falmer Press.

Laban, R. (2011a). *Choreutics*, 4th edn (L. Ullman, ed.). Alton, UK: Dance Books.

Laban, R. (2011b). *Mastery of Movement*, 4th edn. Alton, UK: Dance Books.

Lakes, R. (2005). The Messages behind the Methods: The Authoritarian Pedagogical Legacy. *Arts Education Policy Review*, 106(5): 3–18.

McCutchen, B.P. (2006). *Teaching Dance as Art in Education*. Champaign, IL: Human Kinetics.

Mainwaring, L.M. and Krasnow, D.H. (2010). Teaching the Dance Class: Strategies to Enhance Skill Acquisition, Mastery and Positive Self-Image. *Journal of Dance Education*, 10(1): 14–21.

Moore, C.L. (2009). *The Harmonic Structure of Movement, Music, and Dance According to Rudolf Laban*. Lewiston, NY: The Edwin Mellen Press.

Moore, C.L. (2014). *Meaning in Motion: Introducing Laban Movement Analysis*. Denver, CO: MoveScape Center.

Moore, C.L. and Yamanoto, K. (2011). *Beyond Words: Movement Observation and Analysis*, 2nd ed. New York: Routledge.

Morris, G. (2003). Problems with Ballet: Steps, Style, and Training. *Research in Dance Education*, 4(1): 17–30.

Morris, G. (2008). Artistry or Mere Technique? The Value of the Ballet Competition. *Research in Dance Education*, 9(1): 39–54.

Musil, P.S. (2001). Chaos Theory and Dance Technique. *Journal of Dance Education*, 1(4): 148–153.

Palmer. P. (2010). *The Courage to Teach: Exploring the Inner Landscape of a Teacher's Life*. 2nd edn. San Francisco, CA: John Wiley & Sons.

Paskevska, A. (1992). *Both Sides of the Mirror: The Science and Art of Ballet*, 2nd edn. Pennington, NJ: Princeton Book Company.

Paskevska, A. (2005). *Ballet Beyond Tradition*. New York: Routledge.

Parviainen, J. (1998). *Bodies Moving and Moved: A Phenomenological Analysis of the Dancing Subject and the Cognitive and Ethical Values of Dance Art*. Tampere, Finland: Tampere University Press.

Preston-Dunlop, V. (1998). *Rudolf Laban: An Extraordinary Life*. Alton, UK: Dance Books.

Preston-Dunlop, V. and Sawyers, L. (eds) (2010). *The Dynamic Body in Space: Exploring and Developing Rudolf Laban's Ideas for the 21st Century*. Alton, UK: Dance Books.

Radford, M. (2004). Emotion and Creativity. *Journal of Aesthetic Education*, 38(1): 53–64.

Råman, T. (2009). Collaborative Learning in the Dance Technique Class. *Research in Dance Education*, 10(1): 75–87.

Rouhiainen, L. (ed.) (2007). *Ways of Knowing in Dance and Art*. Helsinki: Theatre Academy.

Rouhiainen, L. (2008). Somatic Dance as a Means of Cultivating Ethically Embodied Subjects. *Research in Dance Education*, 9(3): 241–256.

Salosaari, P. (2001). *Multiple Embodiment in Classical Ballet: Educating the Dancer as an Agent of Change in the Cultural Evolution of Ballet*. Helsinki: Theatre Academy.

Sawyer, K. (2007). *Group Genius: The Creative Power of Collaboration*. New York: Basic Books.

Spohna, C. and Prettyman, S.S. (2012). Moving is Like Making Out: Developing Female University Dancers' Ballet Technique and Expression Through the Use of Metaphor. *Research in Dance Education*, 13(1): 47–65.

Stinson, S. (2004) Lessons from Dance Education. In L. Bresler (ed.), *Knowing Bodies, Moving Minds: Towards Embodied Teaching and Learning*. Dordrecht: Kluwer Academic, pp. 153–167.

Sweigard, L.E. (1974). *Human Movement Potential*. New York: Harper & Row.

Ullman, L. (1959). The Value I see in Laban's Ideas. *The New Era in Home and School*, 40(5): 94–98.

Watson, D.E., Nordin-Bates, S.N., and Chappell, K.A. (2012). Facilitating and nurturing creativity in pre-vocational dancers: Findings from the UK Centres for Advanced Training. *Research in Dance Education*, 13(2): 153–173.

Warburton, E.C. (2008). Beyond Steps: The Need for Pedagogical Knowledge in Dance. *Journal of Dance Education*, 8(1): 7–12.

Whittier, C. (2006). Laban Movement Analysis to Classical Ballet Pedagogy. *Journal of Dance Education*, 6(4): 124–132.

Whittier, C. (2010). Classical Ballet Pedagogy. In V. Preston-Dunlop, and L. Sawyers (eds), *The Dynamic Body in Space: Exploring and Developing Rudolf Laban's Ideas for the 21st Century*. Alton, UK: Dance Books, pp. 235–246.

Whittier, C. (2013). Transforming Tradition: The Integration of Laban Movement Analysis and Classical Ballet. In *NOFOD/SDHS Conference Proceedings*. Oak Creek, WI: Society of Dance History Scholars, pp. 399–405.

Index